Travel the Globe

Travel the Globe
Multicultural Story Times

Desiree Webber, Dee Ann Corn, Elaine Harrod, Donna Norvell, Sandy Shropshire

Illustrated by

Sandy Shropshire

1998
LIBRARIES UNLIMITED, INC.
Englewood, Colorado

To my guys, Steve and Clay. D.W.
To Greg, Stephanie, and my parents. D.C.
In memory of my mother, Evalyn McDaniel. E.H.
To the kids in my life:
Shereen, Rick, Shay, Tony, Darren, Bryce, Brandon, and Kelsey. D.N.
For all those who share the magic of books and literature. S.S.

Libraries Unlimited, Inc.
P.O. Box 6633
Englewood, CO 80155-6633
1-800-237-6124
www.lu.com

Production Editor: Kay Mariea
Copy Editor: Jason Cook
Proofreader: Suzanne Hawkins Burke
Indexer: Linda Running Bentley
Design and Layout: Pamela J. Getchell

Library of Congress Cataloging-in-Publication Data

Travel the globe : multicultural story times / Desiree Webber . . . [et
al.].
    xxvii, 245 p. 22x28 cm.
    Includes bibliographical references and index.
    ISBN 1-56308-501-1
    1. Multicultural education--Activity programs--United States.
 2. Children's libraries--Activity programs--United States.
 3. Ethnology--Study and teaching (Early childhood)--United States.
 4. International education--United States. 5. Storytelling--United
States. 6. Children's stories. I. Webber, Desiree, 1956-   .
LC1099.3.T73   1998
370.117--dc21   97-44225
                                                         CIP

Contents

List of Illustrations

Acknowledgments

For those works that are not acknowledged here, the authors have searched for a known author without success.

"Baby Rattlesnake." From *Baby Rattlesnake*, told by Te Ata, adapted by Lynn Moroney, illustrated by Veg Reisberg (San Francisco: Children's Book Press, 1989). Reprinted by permission of the publisher.

"Billy Beg and the Bull." A retelling based on two variants, found in *Best Stories to Tell to Children* by Sara Cone Bryant (Boston and New York: Houghton Mifflin, 1912); and *In Chimney Corners: Merry Tales of Irish Folk Lore* by Seumas MacManus (Garden City, NY: Doubleday, Page, 1924).

"The Coyote Scolds His Tail." From *Picture Tales from Mexico* by Dan Storm, illustrated by Mark Storm (Houston TX: Gulf Publishing, 1995). Reprinted by permission of the illustrator.

"The Dragon Who Ate the Sun." Based upon information found in *Moon Lore* by Rev. Timothy Harley, F.R.A.S. (London: Swan Sonnenschein, Le Bas & Lowrey, 1885).

"Hello Song." Words and music adapted from "Hello Song" in *Mother Goose Time: Library Programs for Babies and Their Caregivers* by Jane Marino and Dorothy F. Houlihan (New York: H. W. Wilson, 1992). Adapted by permission of the publisher.

"How Jerboa Tricked Lion." A retelling of "How the Cunning Jerboa Killed the Strong Lion" in *Hausa Superstitions and Customs: An Introduction to the Folk-Lore and the Folk* by Major A.J.N. Tremearne (London: John Bale, Sons & Danielsson, 1913).

"How the Brazilian Beetle Won the Race." A retelling of "How the Brazilian Beetles Got Their Gorgeous Coats" in *Fairy Tales from Brazil* by Elsie Spicer Eells (n.p.: Dodd, Mead, 1917).

"How the Tiger Got His Stripes." A synthesis of four variants, found in *Vietnamese Legends*, adapted from the Vietnamese by George F. Schultz (Rutland, VT: Charles E. Tuttle, 1965); *Once in Vietnam: The Bridge of Reunion, and Other Stories* by Trân Van Diên and Lê Tinh Thông, illustrated by Kim Bang (Lincolnwood, IL: National Textbook, 1983); and *Fairy Tales from Vietnam* by Dorothy Lewis Robertson, illustrated by W. T. Mars (New York: Dodd, Mead, 1968); and *Asian-Pacific Folktales and Legends* edited by Jeanette Faurot (New York: Simon & Schuster, 1995).

"Lionbruno." A retelling from *Italian Popular Tales* by Thomas Frederick Crane, A.M. (Boston and New York: Houghton Mifflin, 1885).

"Mummy Hunt." From *Raising the Roof: Children's Stories and Activities on Houses* by Jan Irving and Robin Currie (Englewood, CO: Teacher Ideas Press, 1991). Reprinted by permission of the authors.

"My Hands." Action rhyme reprinted from *Ring a Ring o' Roses*. Reprinted by permission of the publisher, Flint Public Library, 1026 E. Kearley St., Flint, MI 48502 (810) 232-7111, 1977.

"The Pearl Thief." A retelling of "No Pearls E'er Placed in His Care" in *Tales and Poems of South India* by Edward Jewitt Robinson (London: T. Woolmer, 1885).

"The Thirsty Frog." A retelling of two variants, found in *The Land of the Kangaroo: Adventures of Two Youths in a Journey Through the Great Island Continent* by Thomas W. Knox, illustrated by H. Burgess (Boston: W. A. Wilde, 1896); and *Aboriginal Mythology* by Mudrooroo Nyoongah (London: Thorsons, 1994).

"A Tower for the King." A retelling based on two recorded versions: "Tower to the Moon" from *Folk Tales of Latin America*, adapted by Shirlee P. Newman (Indianapolis, IN: Bobbs-Merrill, 1962); and "El Rey Derrumbao" (The King's Tower) from *Folk-Lore from the Dominican Republic*, by Manuel J. Andrade, translated by Julia Contreras (New York: American Folk-Lore Society, G. E. Stechert, 1930).

"What Is an Elephant?" A retelling of "Blind Religion" in *Tales and Poems of South India* by Edward Jewitt Robinson (London: T. Woolmer, 1885).

Introduction

Many of us love to travel. We feel exhilarated and adventurous at the thought of going somewhere new—especially to a foreign land. We look at our world with a new pair of eyes.

However, the next best thing to traveling through the interior of Australia, for example, is to become an armchair explorer. Children can also experience the thrill of encountering and learning about other cultures through stories, objects such as toys and clothing, songs, pictures, foods, and crafts.

This book is designed for those working with preschool through third-grade children. The authors have worked with children in public library and classroom settings. This book came about as we developed our own in-house booklets and notes of planned storyhours for various countries around the world. *Travel the Globe: Multicultural Story Times* was written to assist librarians, media specialists, teachers, parents, and caregivers who are interested in sharing the uniqueness and wonder of our global neighbors.

Each chapter focuses on one country, and each follows a similar format throughout so that needed information can be found easily. At the beginning of each chapter are two suggested story time outlines, one for preschoolers and one for children in kindergarten through third grade. This is followed by a song for opening each story time, the "Hello Song," and an action rhyme for closing the story time, "My Hands." The song and action rhyme not only set the mood and provide closure, respectively, but they also introduce words (*hello*, *goodbye*, and *thank you*) from the major language for each country.

In addition to the "Hello Song" is the song "Travel 'Round the Globe." The story time presenter can also use this latter song to open the storyhour. The original lyrics and sheet music for both songs follows the introduction.

Next is an annotated bibliography of suggested books to read aloud, followed by a story using either flannel board characters, puppets, audience participation, or some type of visual device or action; patterns and instructions for the visual presentations are provided. A section with fingerplays, songs, action rhymes, and games and an annotated listing of videos and filmstrips follow. The last part of the chapter contains crafts, also with patterns and instructions. For most categories of presentation (flannel board stories; puppet plays; fingerplays, songs, action rhymes, and games; and crafts), an annotated list of sources follows the sample presentations.

All the crafts use low-cost supplies and are simple to prepare and execute. At least two craft projects are included in each chapter, one of which is designed for preschoolers (with suggestions for additional simplification), and one of which is designed for children in kindergarten through third grade.

The authors of *Travel the Globe* have parents and volunteers help preschoolers with their crafts when conducting a story time. Consider asking the parents who bring their children to a story time to assist you, or recruit senior or teen volunteers. If volunteers are not available, simplify the steps involved when using the crafts with three- and four-year-olds.

In the absence of an authentic, age-appropriate craft, a literature-related craft is provided. For example, in the chapter on Greece, " 'The Fox and the Grapes' Stick Puppet Theater" is suggested as a craft project. The storyteller might introduce the craft by telling or reading fables by Aesop (a Greek who lived about 620–560 B.C.), and stating that the Greeks have a long history of developing and enjoying theater.

In regards to the annotated bibliography of suggested books to read aloud, the listing contains both currently published titles and out-of-print titles. These bibliographies are not meant to be comprehensive. These are titles of merit enjoyed by children in this age group. Children ages 3 to 8 have a wide range of abilities and attention spans. Therefore, we have noted which titles may be better suited for children ages 5 and older by stating "Recommended for school-age children." This notation is to serve as a guide only. If a title is not available at a library or media center, pursue it through interlibrary loan.

It is not our intent that all books, presentations, media, and activities listed in each chapter be used in a single story time. The purpose is to provide a selection from which the librarian, media specialist, or teacher may choose. For example, a media specialist might share a few of the suggested books and presentations, and then give the teacher a packet of follow-up activities (crafts, songs, media) for the classroom. The public librarian might pick and choose from the suggested story time outlines to create a 30- to 45-minute story time.

To further enhance the learning process, create an atmosphere for traveling the globe. A sample passport designed for this book follows the introduction. As a story time for a new country begins, have children stamp their passports with a decorative rubber stamp. If possible, play music (audiocassettes are suggested in most chapters) to set a mood. Bring clothing, toys, travel posters, and other items from that country to decorate the room. Make available items for children to touch or handle. Young children need as much concrete experience as possible to learn something new. One suggestion is to visit stores and restaurants that feature or might have items from the countries you will be "visiting." For example, visit a Greek restaurant or store and tell them what you are planning. Ask if they have music and other items from Greece that you could borrow for the day. Many people are eager to share their culture with children.

Whenever possible, show children what the people and places currently look like. Folktales and other traditional stories may portray lifestyles, clothing, and attitudes that are no longer typical in the modern world. A bibliography of current series titles published on various countries is provided at the back of the book.

If a series of story times is conducted, you may want to conclude your travels by returning to the United States. The final chapter, "Let's Visit the United States—Native Americans," is organized in the same format as other chapters, with books, presentations, media, and activities related to or from various Native American tribes in the United States.

It is the sincere wish of the authors that you find this material useful and enjoyable. Our sole purpose in the development of this book has been to share teaching and learning methods that might expand the awareness of children living in our diversified world.

The authors have striven to present information as fairly as possible. We have the greatest respect for all cultures and ethnicities. Consequently, we ask that those who use this resource do so with compassion and consideration for all peoples, beliefs, and customs. Good traveling to all of you!

Passport Directions

The authors have used the Reading Passport in story time sessions to help the children make believe that they are presenting their personal travel document at a check station to begin their journey to another country. As the Passport Agent, welcome the children with the appropriate greeting from the country they will be visiting as you stamp their passport. Encourage them to respond back to you with this greeting. In the same way that wearing a colorful shawl or playing ethnic music will influence the children, using a shamrock stamp for Ireland or a kangaroo sticker for Australia, when added to the passport, will produce an immediate connection with a country. Another connection can be easily made by pointing out the country's flag on the border of their Reading Passport. Refer to pages xxii–xxiv for the passport, as well as a list of flags represented on the passport border.

To create your own Reading Passports, photocopy the cover onto 8½-by-11 inch colored paper, then copy the inside of the passport onto the reverse side of the cover. If enlarging capabilities are available on your copier, you may want to enlarge front and back 30 percent so that images and words are as large as possible.

Fold the passports in half like a book. Use a calligraphy pen or colorful marker to add the children's names on the blank line of the certificate, which is on the back cover. Write the names of the countries you will visit on the inside of the passport. Print the country's name in small letters at the bottom of each rectangle so that there will be room for the stamp or sticker.

If your program is a weekly library session for preschoolers, the passports can be easily distributed by laying them name side up on a table outside the story time room. Accompanying adults can help their young children find their own passport prior to the program. If traveling the globe is part of a classroom study unit, the passports can be readily passed out to the students at their desks.

A final note: The program presenter can add his or her name on the Travel Agent line at the end of the final session. In this way, the children can be recognized individually as you sign your name with an official flourish, shake hands, and present them their Reading Passports as a memento of their world travels.

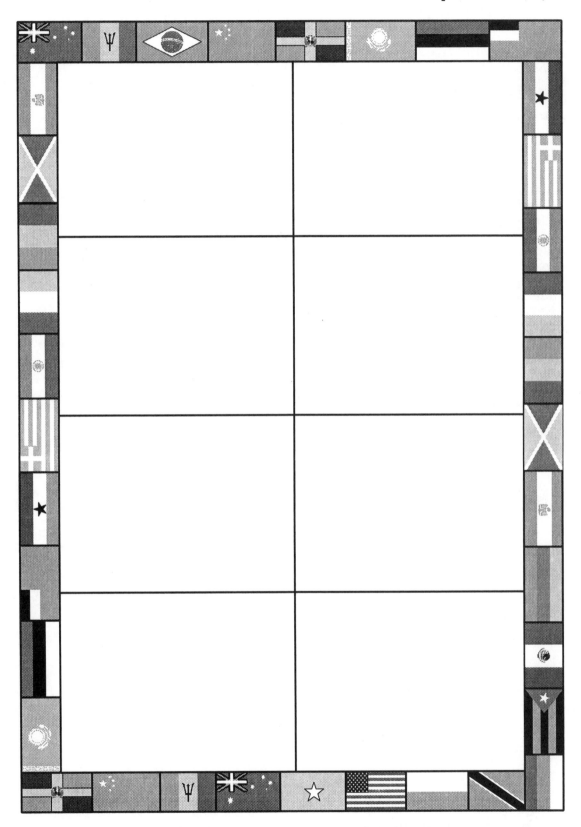

Flags Represented on Passport Border

Begin with the Australian flag in the upper left corner and proceed clockwise around the border.

Australia
Barbados*
Brazil
China
Dominican Republic*
Egypt
Estonia**
Georgia**
Ghana
Greece
India
Ireland
Italy
Jamaica*
Kazakhstan**
Lithuania**
Mexico
Puerto Rico*
Russia**
Trinidad and Tobago*
Ukraine**
United States
Vietnam

*representing the Caribbean Islands
**representing the Commonwealth of Independent States (formerly Soviet Union)

Music

Travel 'Round the Globe
words and music by Sandy Shropshire

Travel 'round the globe with us.
We'll learn of other lands.
And we'll see the sights and share a laugh.
We'll smile and hold some hands.

We'll learn of other children's ways:
Their language and their name.
And then we'll understand how we
Are very much the same.

We'll cross the seas and deserts,
And we'll climb the mountains high.
We'll play a game and sing a song,
And then we'll say "good-bye."

Travel 'round the globe with us.
How awesome the world looks!
And we'll never have to leave our seats.
We're traveling with books!

Travel 'Round the Globe

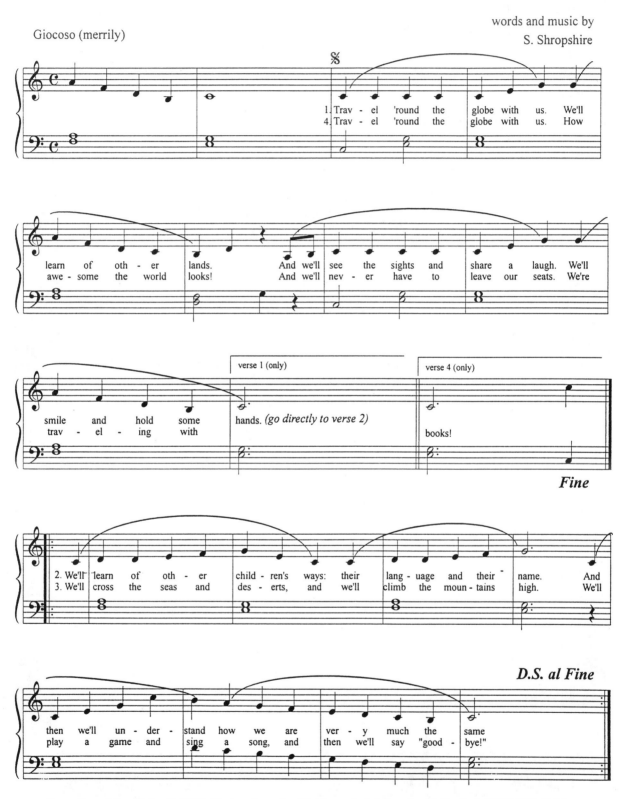

Hello Song

words and music
adapted by S. Shropshire

Giocoso (merrily)

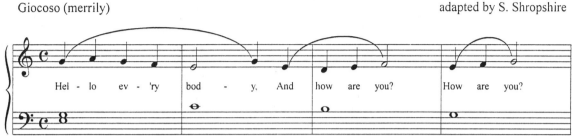

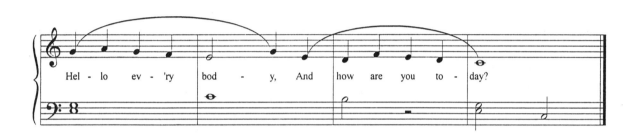

Hello Song
words and music adapted by Sandy Shropshire

Hello ev'rybody,
And how are you? How are you?
Hello ev'rybody,
And how are you today?

My Hands
(Suit actions to words)

My hands say thank you.
With a clap, clap, clap.
My feet say thank you.
With a tap, tap, tap.
Clap! Clap! Clap!
Tap! Tap! Tap!
Turn myself around and bow.
Thank you.

Let's Visit

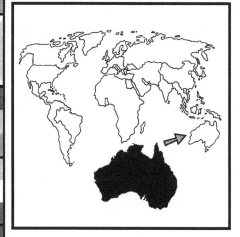

Australia

Sample Story Times

Story Time for Preschool

Song: "Hello Song"

Book: *Snap!* by Marcia Vaughan

Fingerplay: "Five Baby Emus"

Oral Story: "The Sing-Song of Old Man Kangaroo" from *Just So Stories* by Rudyard Kipling

Flannel Board Presentation: "The Thirsty Frog"

Book: *Flood Fish* by Robyn Eversole

Video: *Three Legends of Australian Aboriginals* by Andrew Leku Bunua and Miriam-Rose Wilson

Craft: "Sponge Painting the Animals of Australia"

Action Rhyme: "My Hands"

Story Time for Kindergarten Through Third Grade

Song: "Hello Song"

Book: *Bossyboots* by David Cox

Song: "Kookaburra" from *Mel Bay's Action Songs for Children* by Pamela Cooper Bye

Oral Story: "Oodgeroo" in *Dreamtime: Aboriginal Stories* by Oodgeroo

Flannel Board Presentation: "The Thirsty Frog"

Book: *Enora and the Black Crane* by Arone Raymond Meeks

Video: *The Rainbow Serpent* by Dick Roughsey

Craft: "Platypus Puppet" in *Pocketful of Puppets: Never Pick a Python for a Pet* by Tamara Hunt

Action Rhyme: "My Hands"

Begin the story time with the "Hello Song." Then sing the song again, substituting the word *hello* with the Australian greeting *g'day mates*. (See p. xxvii for "Hello Song" music.)

Hello Song

Hello ev'rybody,
And how are you? How are you?
Hello ev'rybody,
And how are you today?

G'day mates,
And how are you? How are you?
G'day mates,
And how are you today?

End the story time with the "My Hands" action rhyme, substituting the words *thank you* with the Australian word *ta*, and *goodbye* with *ta ta*. Have children stand up and follow the actions in the rhyme.

My Hands

My hands say ta. *(hold up hands)*
With a clap, clap, clap. *(clap hands)*
My feet say ta. *(point to feet)*
With a tap, tap, tap. *(stamp or tap feet)*
Clap! Clap! Clap! *(clap hands)*
Tap! Tap! Tap! *(stamp or tap feet)*
Turn myself around and bow. *(turn and bow)*
Ta ta. *(wave goodbye)*

Books to Read Aloud

Baker, Jeannie. *Where the Forest Meets the Sea.* New York: Greenwillow Books, 1987. (28 pages)
Father and son travel by boat to a remote island. They spend the day enjoying the beauty and history of the island.

Cobb, Vicki. *This Place Is Lonely.* Illustrated by Barbara Lavallee. New York: Walker, 1991. (30 pages)
Australia can be a lonely place. Discover the Australian lifestyle, including education, transportation, and work.

Cox, David. *Bossyboots.* New York: Crown, 1985. (26 pages)
Abigail is a bossy stagecoach passenger who saves the day when she is bossy during a bad situation.

Eversole, Robyn. *Flood Fish.* Illustrated by Sheldon Greenberg. New York: Crown, 1995. (32 pages)
Finke River is as dry as a bone. Then the rains come, and so do the fish.

Maddern, Eric. *Rainbow Bird: An Aboriginal Folktale from Northern Australia.* Illustrated by Adrienne Kennaway. Boston: Little, Brown, 1993. (24 pages)
A crocodile is the first animal to have fire, but Rainbow Bird finds a way for all the animals to have fire.

Meeks, Arone Raymond. *Enora and the Black Crane: An Aboriginal Story.* New York: Scholastic, 1991. (30 pages)
Enora's life changes forever when he follows a flickering splash of color deep into the rain forest.

Roughsey, Dick. *The Rainbow Serpent.* Milwaukee, WI: Gareth Stevens, 1975. (32 pages)
The mythological Aboriginal story of Goorialla, a giant serpent who forms the rivers and mountains as he travels across the land.

Vaughan, Marcia. *Snap!* Illustrated by Sascha Hutchinson. New York: Scholastic, 1994. (30 pages)
Joey the Kangaroo and his friends must work together to escape the jaws of Slytooth the Crocodile after playing a game of Snap.

Storytelling

Flannel Board Presentation

"The Thirsty Frog." This story is a retelling of an Aboriginal myth about a large, greedy frog named Tiddalick. Some believe that the myth of Tiddalick originated from a type of frog called a Water-Holding Frog (Cyclorananovaholandia) found in Australia. This frog gorges itself with as much water as it can hold and then burrows into the sand, where it can stay for long periods of time waiting for rain. Desert dwelling Aborigines have a history of digging for these frogs as a source of water during droughts.

See figures 1.1–1.8 for patterns. Trace the patterns on felt, or photocopy and color them. If photocopying, glue small pieces of felt to the backs of the paper figures so they will hold to the flannel board. For a tree, use figures 2.5 and 2.12 from the chapter "Let's Visit Brazil." Before beginning the story, place the tree on the flannel board and place the koala in the tree. Place other figures on the flannel board as they are introduced in the story.

The Thirsty Frog
retold by Elaine Harrod

Long ago in Australia, there lived a Frog. He lived deep in the sand, where he had burrowed after drinking so much water he could not even hop. After many days and many nights had passed, he began to feel very thirsty. So he began to dig his way back to the surface of the earth. *(place the small Frog on the flannel board)*

When the Frog came out of the ground, the other animals were frightened, for they did not know what the Frog wanted. They soon knew why the Frog had come out. He began to drink from the river. The animals watched as he drank and drank. He drank until the river was gone! Then he drank all the rivers dry! Then he drank all the streams and lakes dry! The animals were very concerned.

"Oh, no!" the animals cried. "The Frog is even drinking the ocean!" The Frog grew large with water. *(replace the small Frog with the large Frog; place the Platypus on the flannel board)*

The Platypus begged, "Please don't drink all the water in the sea!" But the Frog continued to drink from the ocean, paying no attention to the Platypus. As he drank more and more from the ocean, *(place the Sea Turtle on the flannel board)* a Sea Turtle pleaded, "Frog, if you drink all the water in the sea, my friends and I will have no home." But the Frog had gone so long without water that he did not even hear the pleas of the Sea Turtle.

The animals began gathering around the Frog to beg him not to drink all the water. *(place the Dingo on the flannel board)* The Dingo howled, "Please stop! We will share with yooooooo, but you don't need all the water! We will die if yooooooo do not return the water!" But the Frog said nothing. He sat with his mouth tightly closed. He had now drunk every drop of water in the world!

The animals talked to one another, trying to decide what to do. How could they get the water back that the Frog had drunk? *(place the Kookaburra on the flannel board)* The Kookaburra said she had an idea: "What if I make my Kookaburra sound? Everyone knows that it sounds like a laugh." All the animals thought this was a great idea, for if they could make the Frog laugh, his mouth would open, and all the water would spill back onto the earth. The Kookaburra began, "Ka-ha-ha-ha, ka-ha-ha-ha, ka-ha-ha-ha."

"What is all the noise about?" *(place the Kangaroo on the flannel board)* All the noise had awakened the sleeping Kangaroo. The animals explained what had happened. The Kangaroo offered to do a funny hopping dance to try to make the Frog laugh. The Kangaroo hopped higher and higher, trying her best to be funny. Before she realized what had happened, she had hopped so high that she landed in a tree and found herself sitting next to a Koala Bear. *(place the Kangaroo in the tree, beside the Koala)*

When the Frog saw this, he could not help but grin, and the grin turned into a smile, and the smile turned into a great, roaring laughter. Just as the other animals had hoped, the water spilled out of his mouth and back onto the earth. *(replace the large Frog with the small Frog)*

As for the Kangaroo, the animals had to stand on each others' backs to help her out of the tree. *(following the narrative, place the animals, one on top of another, beneath the Kangaroo)* The Dingo stood on the Sea Turtle's back, and then the Platypus stood on the Dingo's back. The Kookaburra stood on the Platypus's back, and then the Frog stood on the Kookaburra's back *(take the Kangaroo out of the tree)* and helped the Kangaroo out of the tree.

On this most unusual day, the Frog became great friends with the other animals. With these newfound friendships, he promised his new friends that he would never again drink all the water!

Flannel Board Presentation

Fox, Mem. *Possum Magic*. Illustrated by Julie Vivas. Nashville, TN, Abingdon Press, 1983. (32 pages)
   This story introduces the reader to Australian food. A baby possum named Hush eats many kinds of food to become visible again after Grandma Poss uses magic to make him invisible. He even eats a vegemite sandwich.

Vaughan, Marcia K. *Wombat Stew*. Illustrated by Pamela Lofts. Morristown, NJ: Silver Burdett, 1984. (32 pages)
   A dingo tries to make wombat stew, but the other animals try to help the wombat.

Make felt figures to represent the characters from *Wombat Stew*, and create a flannel board story. Individual restaurant-serving packets of vegemite (a very salty yeast extract that many people like to spread on bread or crackers) for children to taste can be ordered from the Australian Catalogue Company, 7605 Welborn St., Suite 112, Raleigh, NC 27615. (919) 878-8266; fax (919) 878-0553.

Audience Participation

Following the picture book *Wombat Stew*, develop a participatory version of this story. Use half-sheets of posterboard to create likenesses of each character in the story: a dingo, a wombat, a platypus, an emu, a lizard, an echidna, and a koala. Draw each animal and cut out the eye holes. Using a hole punch, punch two holes at opposite ends of the top of the posterboard. Cut a piece of yarn long enough to make the animal (posterboard) hang around the child's neck. It needs to be long enough for the child to comfortably hold the animal in front of him or her, below their face. Tie the ends of the yarn, one in each hole.

Make a picture of each ingredient that the characters in the story add to the stew. Using black posterboard, cut out a kettle shape; tape the kettle shape to a bucket to create a stew pot. Invite seven children to help tell the story. As the child's character adds an ingredient to the stew, have the child put the picture of that ingredient into the bucket.

Eating Wombat Stew

Have children make their own "Wombat Stew Trail Mix." Supply a large pot for mixing the stew, and ask each child to bring to class one of the ingredients listed on page 10. Invite children to help tell the story. As characters add ingredients to the stew, have children put their ingredients into the pot.

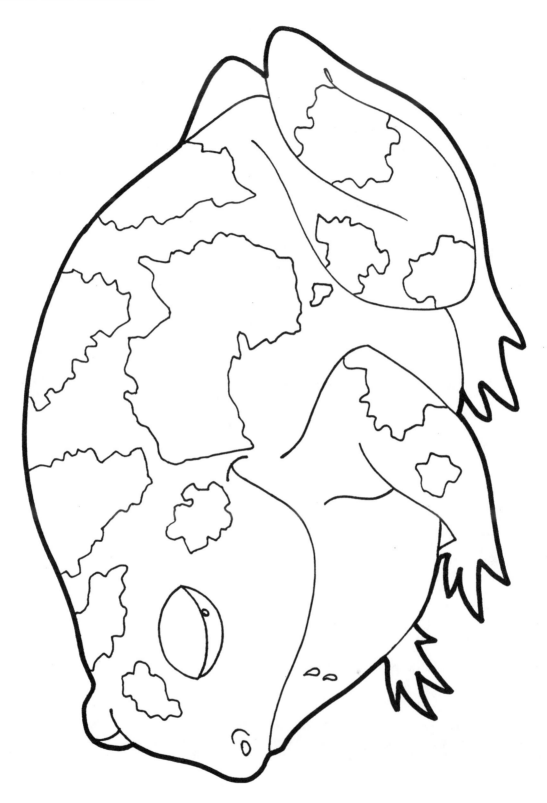

Fig. 1.1. Thirsty Frog.

Fig. 1.2. Kookaburra. Fig. 1.3. Koala. Fig. 1.4. Platypus.

From *Travel the Globe.* © 1998. Desiree Lorraine Webber, et al. Libraries Unlimited. (800) 237-6124.

Fig. 1.5. Kangaroo. Fig. 1.6. Sea Turtle.

From *Travel the Globe*. © 1998. Desiree Lorraine Webber, et al. Libraries Unlimited. (800) 237-6124.

Fig. 1.7. Small Frog. Fig. 1.8. Dingo.

Wombat Stew Trail Mix

1. Mud (Chocolate chips)
2. Feathers (Chinese noodles or sesame sticks)
3. 100 flies (Raisins)
4. Slugs and bugs (Dried apricots, apple chips, or coconut flakes)
5. Gum nuts (Walnuts, pecans, or peanuts)

Sources for Oral Stories

Kipling, Rudyard. "The Sing-Song of Old Man Kangaroo." In *Just So Stories: For Little Children*. New York: Weathervane Books, 1978. (page 67)
   The humorous tale of Yellow Dog Dingo and how he changes Old Man Kangaroo forever.

Oodgeroo. "Oodgeroo" (Paperbark Tree). In *Dreamtime: Aboriginal Stories*. Illustrated by Bronwyn Bancroft. New York: Lothrop, Lee & Shepard, 1972. (pages 80–81)
   An autobiographical account of the author's journey into dreamtime, the Aboriginal time of creation in the mythology of Australian natives.

Fingerplays, Songs, Action Rhymes, and Games

"Five Baby Emus." For this fingerplay, begin with five emu puppets, one on each finger; bend down a finger each time an emu exits the poem. The storyteller will wear the finger puppets. The children will hold up five fingers and follow along. To make finger puppets, photocopy figures 1.9 and 1.10 on white tagboard or construction paper. Use markers to color the emus. Laminate and cut out the emus and finger attachments. Tape together the three flaps of each finger attachment. This will fit over the tip of each finger like a thimble. Tape an emu to each finger attachment.

Five Baby Emus
by Elaine Harrod

Five baby emus, wishing they could soar. *(five emus)*
One went to try and that left four. *(remove a puppet)*
Four baby emus hungry as can be. *(four emus)*
One went to eat and that left three. *(remove a puppet)*
Three baby emus go off to the zoo. *(three emus)*
Only one ran away and that left two. *(remove a puppet)*
Two baby emus were looking for some fun. *(two emus)*
One found a playmate and that left one. *(remove a puppet)*
One baby emu playing in the sun. *(one emu)*
Then all were gone and that left none. *(remove last puppet)*

Sources for Fingerplays, Songs, Action Rhymes, and Games

Beall, Pamela Conn, and Susan Hagen Nipp, with Nancy Spence Klein. "Kookaburra." In *Wee Sing Around the World*. Los Angeles: Price Stern Sloan, 1994. Book with audiocassette. Words and music for children's songs from around the world.

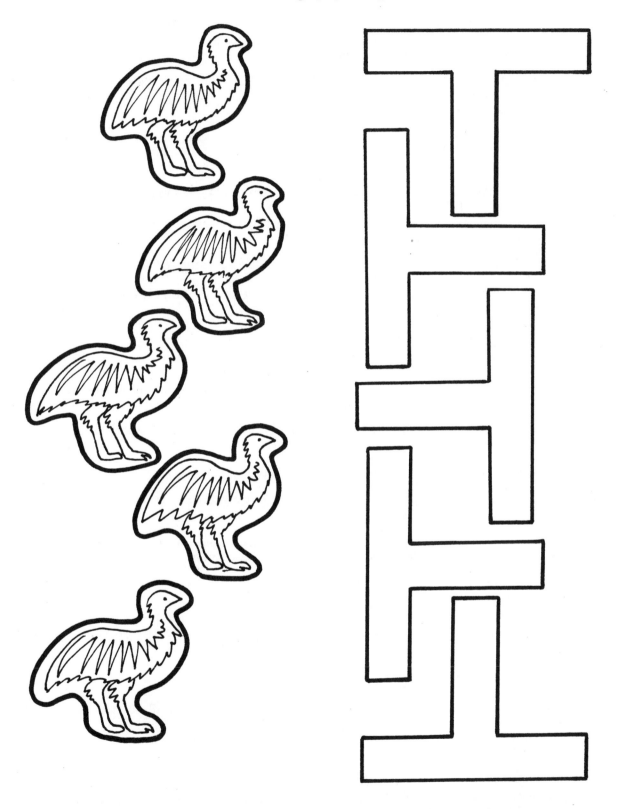

Fig. 1.9. Emu Finger Puppets. Fig. 1.10. Finger Puppet Attachments.

Bye, Pamela Cooper. "The Crawdad Song" and "Kookaburra." In *Mel Bay's Action Songs for Children.* Pacific, MO: Mel Bay, 1992. (pages 3 and 5)
> The lyrics and music for two Australian songs.

Dunn, Clancy. *20 Aussie Animal Songs.* Mona Vale, Sydney: Fo'c'sle Records/Hughes Leisure Group, 1993. Audiocassette.
> A collection of humorous Australian animal songs.

Maza, Bob. *Music and Dreamtime Stories of My People: Australian Aboriginal Music and Legends.* Northbridge NWS: Twintrack Productions, [n.d.]. Compact disc.
> Native music of Australia, from its Aboriginal people. Some oral stories are also included.

Paterson, A. B. *Waltzing Matilda.* Illustrated by Desmond Digby. New York: Holt, Rinehart and Winston, 1972. (32 pages)
> A picture book of the poem that is considered by most Australians to be the "national anthem."

Stewart, Georgiana. "Waltzing Matilda." In *Multicultural Rhythm Stick Fun.* Long Branch, NJ: Kimbo Educational, 1992. Audiocassette.
> The music for "Waltzing Matilda" is played while instructions are given for children to keep time by tapping rhythm sticks (or clapping).

Media Choices

Show a video or filmstrip as a transition between storytelling activities and crafts. This gives children an opportunity to rest quietly for a few minutes.

Bunua, Andrew Leku, and Miriam-Rose Wilson. *Three Legends of Australian Aboriginals.* 10 min. Chatsworth, CA: AIMS Media, 1992. Videocassette.
> Three Aboriginal stories about Australian animals: "How the Kangaroo Got His Tail," "The Thirsty Sand Frog," and "How the Animals Were Divided."

Kent, Jack. *Joey Runs Away.* 8 min. Weston, CT: Weston Woods, 1993. Videocassette.
> Joey runs away because he does not want to clean his pouch.

Roughsey, Dick. *The Rainbow Serpent.* 11 min. Weston, CT: Weston Woods, 1993. Videocassette.
> A mythological Aboriginal snake creates the lakes, rivers, and mountains.

Crafts and Other Activities

Choose a craft suited for the age level of the group and the time allotted for the story time.

Sponge Painting

Ryden, Hope. *Joey: The Story of a Baby Kangaroo.* New York: Tambourine Books, 1994. (37 pages)
> In this book of full-color photographs, a baby kangaroo observes other animals in his environment as he grows up.

There are many interesting animals in Australia. Some of these animals cannot be found anywhere else in the world, except in zoos. *Joey: The Story of a Baby Kangaroo* is an engaging book to share before beginning this sponge painting project.

Supplies

Sponge sheets	Paintbrush
Scissors	Cookie sheets
Pen	Colored markers and crayons
Tempera paint	White construction paper

Photocopy figures 1.11–1.14 and cut out the patterns. Lay the patterns on the sponge sheets and trace the shapes with a pen. The teacher then uses sharp scissors to cut out several sponges of each animal shape (one for each color so colors won't become mixed). Wet the sponge shapes (they will expand). Prepare the tempera paint and pour a small amount of each color onto a cookie sheet. Spread the paint using a paintbrush. Have children dip the sponge animals into the paint and press them onto the construction paper. After the paint is dry, have children use crayons and markers to design a background for their Australian scene.

Cave Painting

Some of the most impressive cave paintings in Australia are found in the Northern Territory. Some of these paintings are estimated to be more than 5,000 years old. Many Aborigines still create art using techniques developed long ago. Several of the illustrators of the books listed in this chapter are Aborigines; show some of their art to children before beginning this activity.

Supplies

Butcher paper	Tape
Colored markers, crayons, or chalk	

Share with children the following two books which show traditional Aboriginal art: *Dreamtime: Aboriginal Stories* by Oodgeroo (see "Sources for Oral Stories"), and *Enora and the Black Crane* by Arone Raymond Meeks (see "Books to Read Aloud"). Hang a long piece of butcher paper on the wall and have children make their own Aboriginal cave paintings.

Sources for Craft Ideas and Activities

Chupela, Dolores. *Ready, Set, Go! Children's Programming for Bookmobiles and Other Small Spaces.* Fort Atkinson, WI: Alleyside Press, 1994. (page 29)
   Includes patterns for a mother and baby kangaroo. The baby fits inside the pouch of the mother.

Everix, Nancy. *Ethnic Celebrations Around the World: Festivals, Holidays, and Celebrations.* Carthage, IL: Good Apple, 1991. (pages 13–14)
   This craft book includes a pattern for a fairy penguin. Fairy penguins are found near Melbourne on Phillip Island.

Hunt, Tamara. *Pocketful of Puppets: Never Pick a Python for a Pet, and Other Poems.* Illustrated by Nancy Renfro. Austin, TX: Nancy Renfro Studios, 1984. (pages 27–34)
   This craft book includes puppet patterns for a lizard, a joey, and a platypus.

Milord, Susan. *Tales Alive! Ten Multicultural Folktales with Activities.* Illustrated by Michael A. Donato. Charlotte, VT: Williamson, 1995. (pages 100–101)
   Aborigines have painted on many natural surfaces, including bark and rocks. *Tales Alive!* contains information about bark painting. Instructions are also given for a bark painting craft.

Fig. 1.11. Kangaroo (top left). Fig. 1.12. Goanna Lizard (top right). Fig. 1.13. Platypus (bottom left). Fig. 1.14. Australian Opossum (bottom right).

Let's Visit

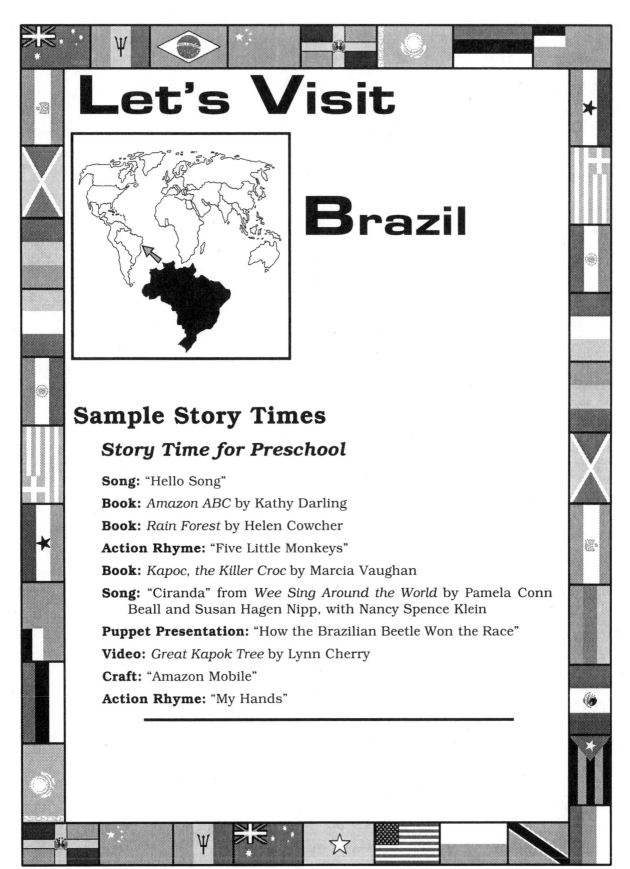

Brazil

Sample Story Times

Story Time for Preschool

Song: "Hello Song"

Book: *Amazon ABC* by Kathy Darling

Book: *Rain Forest* by Helen Cowcher

Action Rhyme: "Five Little Monkeys"

Book: *Kapoc, the Killer Croc* by Marcia Vaughan

Song: "Ciranda" from *Wee Sing Around the World* by Pamela Conn Beall and Susan Hagen Nipp, with Nancy Spence Klein

Puppet Presentation: "How the Brazilian Beetle Won the Race"

Video: *Great Kapok Tree* by Lynn Cherry

Craft: "Amazon Mobile"

Action Rhyme: "My Hands"

Story Time for Kindergarten Through Third Grade

Song: "Hello Song"

Book: *Amazon Boy* by Ted Lewin

Book: *How Night Came from the Sea: A Story from Brazil* by Mary-Joan Gerson

Game: "Kapok Tree Guessing Game"

Book: *The Great Kapok Tree* by Lynn Cherry

Song: "Tico Tico" from *Multicultural Rhythm Stick Fun* by Georgiana Stewart

Puppet Presentation: "How the Brazilian Beetle Won the Race"

Video: *The Beginning of the Armadillos* by Rudyard Kipling

Craft: "Carnival Mask"

Song: "Brazilian Carnival" from *Children of the World: Multicultural Rhythmic Activities* by Georgiana Stewart

Action Rhyme: "My Hands"

Begin the story time with the "Hello Song." Then sing the song again, substituting the word *hello* with the Portuguese greeting Olá [oh-LAH]. (Portuguese is the primary language spoken in Brazil; see p. xxvii for "Hello Song" music.)

Hello Song

Hello ev'rybody,
And how are you? How are you?
Hello ev'rybody,
And how are you today?

oh-LAH ev'rybody,
And how are you? How are you?
oh-LAH ev'rybody,
And how are you today?

End the story time with the "My Hands" action rhyme, substituting the words *thank you* with the Portuguese word *obrigado* [oh-bre-GAH-doh], and *goodbye* with *adeus* [a-DAY-oosh]. Have children stand up and follow the actions in the rhyme.

My Hands

My hands say oh-bre-GAH-doh. *(hold up hands)*
With a clap, clap, clap. *(clap hands)*
My feet say oh-bre-GAH-doh. *(point to feet)*
With a tap, tap, tap. *(stamp or tap feet)*
Clap! Clap! Clap! *(clap hands)*
Tap! Tap! Tap! *(stamp or tap feet)*
Turn myself around and bow. *(turn and bow)*
a-DAY-oosh. *(wave goodbye)*

Books to Read Aloud

Cherry, Lynne. *The Great Kapok Tree: A Tale of the Amazon Rain Forest*. San Diego, CA: Harcourt Brace Jovanovich, 1990. (32 pages)
A man walks into the Amazon rain forest and begins to chop down a Kapok tree that is a home to many animals. When the man falls asleep, each animal whispers in his ear a reason not to chop down the tree.

Cobb, Vicki. *This Place Is Wet*. Illustrated by Barbara Lavallee. New York: Walker, 1989. (32 pages)
A nonfiction story about the people, animals, land, and climate of the city of Manaus, located in northern Brazil. Recommended for school-age children.

Cowcher, Helen. *Rain Forest*. New York: Farrar, Straus & Giroux, 1988. (32 pages)
This simple picture book depicts a few of the animals that live in the rain forest and their concern that man is destroying their home.

Darling, Kathy. *Amazon ABC*. Photographs by Tara Darling. New York: Lothrop, Lee & Shepard, 1996. (32 pages)
A beautifully photographed alphabet book showing for each letter an animal from the Amazon.

Gerson, Mary-Joan. *How Night Came from the Sea: A Story from Brazil*. Pictures by Carla Golembe. Boston: Little, Brown, 1994. (32 pages)
The daughter of the African sea goddess Lemanja marries a man who lives in the land of daylight. Lemanja's daughter begins to miss the night from her mother's kingdom. The sea goddess gives the gift of night to the land so the people of Brazil are able to rest.

Haskins, Jim, and Kathleen Benson. *Count Your Way Through Brazil*. Illustrated by Liz Brenner Dodson. Minneapolis, MN: Carolrhoda Books, 1996. (24 pages)
Children will learn the history and culture of Brazil while learning to count to 10 in Portuguese.

Jordan, Martin, and Tanis Jordan. *Amazon Alphabet*. New York: Kingfisher Books, 1996. (40 pages)
This picture book depicts animals from the Amazon, representing each letter of the alphabet.

———. *Jungle Days, Jungle Nights*. New York: Kingfisher Books, 1993. (33 pages)
A nonfiction account of life in the Amazon, describing the various plants and animals active during the day and at night. Recommended for school-age children.

Lewin, Ted. *Amazon Boy*. New York: Macmillan, 1993. (32 pages)
For a birthday gift, Paulo is allowed to travel down the Amazon River with his father to Belem, a port city. He sees the gifts that the Amazon gives them.

———. *When the Rivers Go Home*. New York: Macmillan, 1992. (32 pages)
A picture book about the Pantanal Marsh in Brazil. As the waters recede during the dry season, the animals must search for food.

Troughton, Joanna. *How Night Came: A Folk Tale from the Amazon*. New York: Bedrick/Blackie, 1986. (25 pages)
A popular version of how night came to the land, from the Tupi, a native culture of Brazil: The Great Snake beneath the waters keeps night a prisoner until his daughter asks him to release night to the land so she may sleep.

Vaughan, Marcia. *Kapoc, the Killer Croc.* Pictures by Eugenie Fernandes. Morristown, NJ: Silver Burdett, 1995. (32 pages)
Kapoc, the crocodile, challenges Sloth to a race down the Amazon River.

Storytelling

Puppet Presentation

"How the Brazilian Beetle Won the Race." This puppet play is based on a Brazilian folktale that has been passed down from generation to generation. The agouti in the story is a large rodent of Brazil that can run quickly. See figures 2.1–2.3 for patterns. Trace the patterns on thick, brown posterboard, or photocopy them on brown paper and glue to posterboard. If possible, use two colors of brown, to differentiate between the two stick puppets. Cut carefully outside the heavy black lines; for the beetle's legs, it is best to cut well outside the lines to avoid cutting them too thin. Hot glue (or tape) a paint stick, available at paint supply stores for mixing paint, to the back of each puppet. Lamination can add brightness, and it makes the puppets more durable.

To add the wings to the beetle, make holes where indicated (on wings and body) with an object no larger than an ice pick. Attach the front of wings to the body using brass fasteners. Bend an 18-inch piece of thick florist wire (or any thick, pliable wire) to form a V. Working from the back of the puppet, attach the ends of the wire to the side holes in the wings (see fig. 2.4). Use pliers to crimp the ends if necessary. Adjust the wire so that when holding the puppet by the stick with one hand and moving the V of the wire with the other hand, the wings open and close over the body of the beetle.

Hold both puppets while telling the story. To create a surprise, do not spread the beetle's wings until the end. After the story, share with the group a picture of a Brazilian beetle that shows its myriad of brilliant colors.

How the Brazilian Beetle Won the Race
retold by Dee Ann Corn

Various beetles from Brazil today are wonderfully colorful insects. In fact, people often make jewelry, such as earrings, necklaces, and pins, from these beetles because they are so beautiful. But some say that the beetle has not always been so beautifully colored. It is said that these beetles were once a dull, brown color. This is the story of how the beetle became so colorful.

There was once a little brown beetle crawling along, enjoying a lovely day. *(raise beetle puppet)* All of a sudden, a large, brown Brazilian rat known as an agouti stopped the beetle in his path and began teasing him. *(raise agouti puppet)*

"Look at the little, slow beetle crawling down the road," said the agouti. "You are so slow it doesn't even look like you are moving at all. Watch how fast I can run." With that, the agouti took off down the road as fast as he could, then turned around and came back. The little brown beetle continued along at his own slow, steady pace down the path.

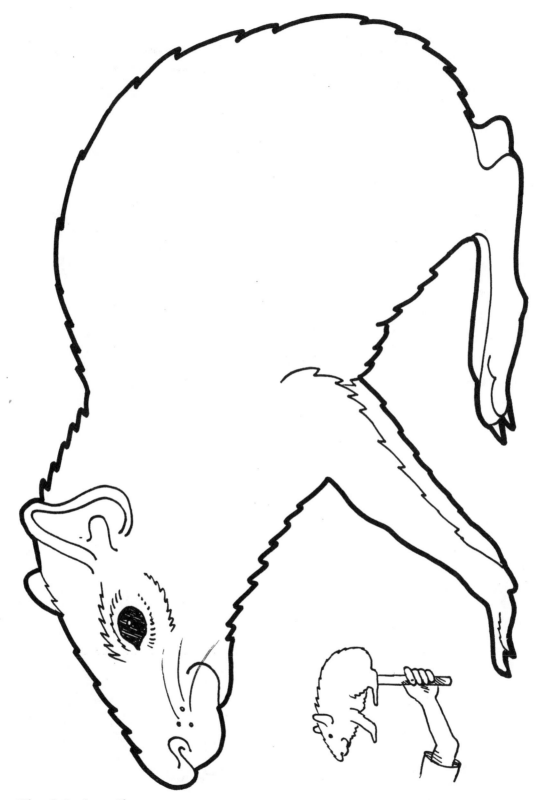

Fig. 2.1. Agouti.

Fig. 2.2. Beetle.

From *Travel the Globe.* © 1998. Desiree Lorraine Webber, et al. Libraries Unlimited. (800) 237-6124.

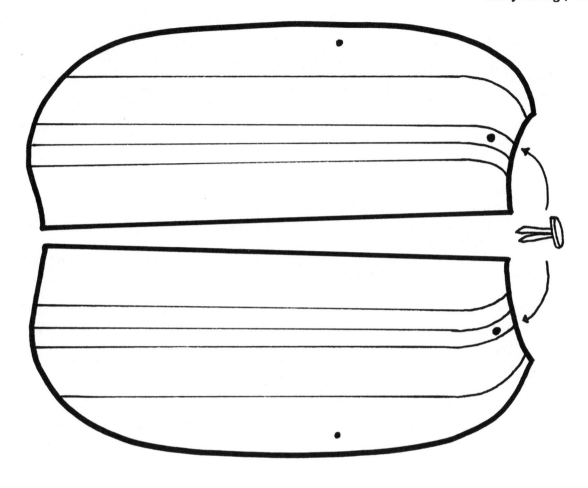

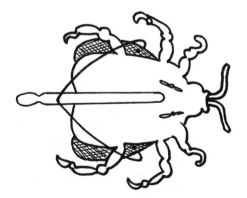

Fig. 2.3. Beetle Wings. Fig. 2.4. Beetle Puppet Example (back view).

From *Travel the Globe.* © 1998. Desiree Lorraine Webber, et al. Libraries Unlimited. (800) 237-6124.

"I bet you wish you could be like me and run like the wind!" exclaimed the agouti with a large grin. The agouti was extremely proud of himself for his quickness.

The little brown beetle just shyly nodded and smiled, not wanting to draw any more attention to himself. His parents had always taught him never to brag about the things he could do. "You do run like the wind. You should be very proud," the little brown beetle whispered timidly, then continued on his way.

Just then, a beautiful parrot flew down and landed on a tree limb above the little brown beetle and the agouti. "Excuse me, but I was listening to both of you and wondered if you would like to see who truly is the fastest. How would you like to have a race?" asked the beautiful parrot. "I will even give the champion a prize for winning."

The agouti perked up his ears when he heard the word *prize.* "Prize? What kind of prize would I win, I mean, would *the champion* win?" The agouti was very confident that he would win the race.

The parrot began to think of prizes that both the little brown beetle and the agouti would like. "I know," said the parrot, "I will give the winner a beautifully colored coat of his choice."

The agouti jumped up and yelled, "I want a coat like the jaguar who lives in the rain forest!" The jaguar was admired throughout the land as being beautiful, graceful, and strong.

The little brown beetle shyly said to the parrot, "I would like to be the color of the gold and green feathers in your tail."

The agouti laughed loudly. He laughed so hard he rolled over in the road. "Why are you even thinking about a prize? You know I'm the fastest runner!"

The parrot mapped out a trail for the two to follow. Then he said, "On your mark. Get set. Go!" And the parrot flew to the finish line to meet the winner.

The agouti took off down the road in a hurry. After a little while, he began to get tired. "Why am I in such a hurry? There is no way the beetle could run faster than me and win the race," bragged the agouti. He began to walk rather than run, but as he was walking, he began to think it would probably be best if he were to finish the race quickly—then he could truly rest. So off he ran again, as fast as he could go.

As agouti came upon the finish line, he saw something that made his eyes become as big as mangoes: Sitting right beside the beautiful parrot, with the green and gold feathers, was the little brown beetle. The agouti's mouth dropped open with surprise.

"I don't believe what I am seeing. How did you ever beat me?" asked the agouti in amazement as he came to the finish line. "I never saw you run past me."

The little brown beetle spread his wings out to the side and replied, "The parrot didn't say we had to *run* the race." *(spread the beetle's wings)*

The agouti was shocked by what he saw. "I didn't know you had wings!" he exclaimed.

"Proud agouti, you should never judge someone by what's on the outside," said the parrot. Then the parrot gave the little brown beetle his prize—a beautiful coat of gold and green. "Congratulations, little beetle, on winning the race," said the parrot. "No longer will you be the color brown."

To this day, however, the agouti still remains the same brown color he always was.

Puppet Presentation

Cherry, Lynne. *The Great Kapok Tree: A Tale of the Amazon Rain Forest.* San Diego, CA: Harcourt Brace Jovanovich, 1990. (32 pages)

Following the picture book, *The Great Kapok Tree*, develop a puppet presentation version of the story. Use posterboard to create likenesses of each character in the story: a man, a boa constrictor, a bee, a monkey, a toucan, a tree frog, a jaguar, a tree porcupine, an anteater, a three-toed sloth, and a child. Attach each character to a craft stick (paint sticks, available at paint supply stores, are sturdier than craft sticks). The storyteller may hold the puppets or have children from the group hold them.

Sources for Oral Stories

Brusca, María Cristina, and Tona Wilson. *When Jaguars Ate the Moon, and Other Stories About Animals and Plants of the Americas.* New York: Henry Holt, 1995. (42 pages)
A collection of tales, six of which are retellings of stories from native cultures in Brazil. Each story is one page in length.

DeSpain, Pleasant. "The First Lesson." In *Thirty-Three Multicultural Tales to Tell.* Illustrated by Joe Shlichta. Little Rock, AR: August House, 1993. (pages 111–12)
A tale from Brazil about a hunter who wants to learn how to become wise.

Fingerplays, Songs, Action Rhymes, and Games

"Kapok Tree Guessing Game." Play this game to introduce the book The Great Kapok Tree *by Lynne Cherry (see "Books to Read Aloud"). Use figures 2.5–2.12 to make flannel board figures for the game. Trace the tree patterns (half-patterns) on folded felt and cut along the solid, curved lines in the tree to make flaps. Because of the detail, you may want to photocopy the patterns of the animals and color them. Glue small pieces of felt to the backs of the paper figures so they will hold to the flannel board.*

Kapok Tree Guessing Game
by Dee Ann Corn and Sandy Shropshire

To play this guessing game, the storyteller hides the animals behind the flaps. The animals in the game include a butterfly, a monkey, a toucan, a jaguar, a tree frog, and a boa constrictor. The object of the game is for the children to guess where the monkey is hiding. During the game, have children say this verse:

> Little monkey we want to see,
> Are you in the Kapok tree?

Repeat this verse as the storyteller lifts each flap, one after each repetition, until the monkey is found.

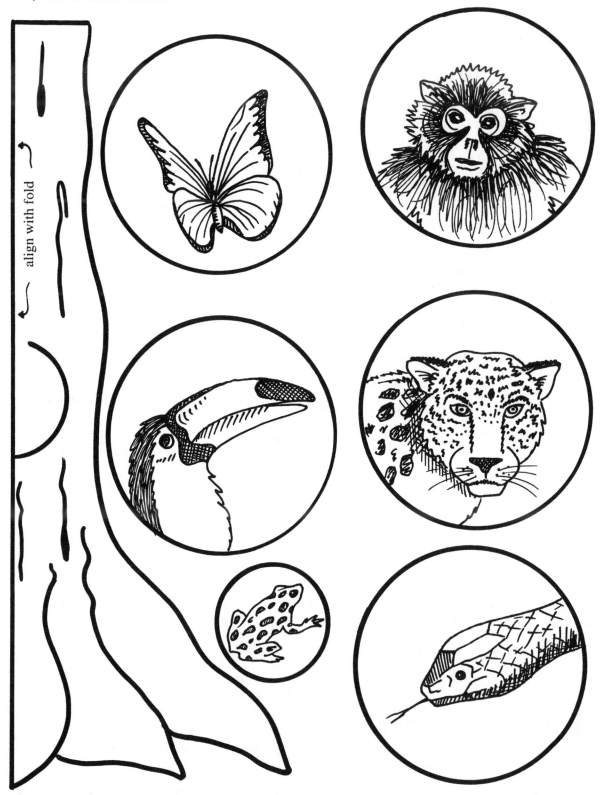

align with fold

**Fig. 2.5. Kapok Tree Trunk.   Fig. 2.6. Butterfly.   Fig. 2.7. Monkey.   Fig. 2.8. Toucan.
Fig. 2.9. Jaguar.   Fig. 2.10. Tree Frog.   Fig. 2.11. Boa Snake.**

align with fold

Fig. 2.12. Kapok Treetop.

From *Travel the Globe*. © 1998. Desiree Lorraine Webber, et al. Libraries Unlimited. (800) 237-6124.

"Five Little Monkeys." In this action rhyme, substitute the Portuguese numbers 1 through 5:

1	um	[OONG]
2	dois	[DOH-eez]
3	três	[TRAY-ees]
4	quatro	[KWAH-troo]
5	cinco	[SEEN-koo]

Five Little Monkeys
(author unknown)

Five (cinco) little monkeys, sitting in the tree. *(show five fingers)*

[chorus]
Teasing Mr. Crocodile,
"You can't catch me, you can't catch me!" *(shake index finger)*
Along comes Mr. Crocodile, quiet as can be. *(with palms together,*
slowly stretch out arms to represent the crocodile)
SNAP! *(clap hands)*

Four (quatro) little monkeys, sitting in the tree. *(show four fingers)*
[chorus]
Three (três) little monkeys, sitting in the tree. *(show three fingers)*
[chorus]
Two (dois) little monkeys, sitting in the tree. *(show two fingers)*
[chorus]
One (um) little monkey, sitting in the tree. *(show one finger)*
[chorus]
No more monkeys, sitting in the tree. *(shake head back and forth)*

Sources for Fingerplays, Songs, Action Rhymes, and Games

Beall, Pamela Conn, and Susan Hagen Nipp, with Nancy Spence Klein. "Ciranda" (Circle Game). In *Wee Sing Around the World.* Los Angeles: Price Stern Sloan, 1994. Book with audiocassette.
A circle game sung in both Portuguese and English.

Stewart, Georgiana. "Brazilian Carnival." In *Children of the World: Multicultural Rhythmic Activities.* Long Branch, NJ: Kimbo Educational, 1991. Audiocassette.
A circle game played to a samba rhythm.

———. "Tico Tico." In *Multicultural Rhythm Stick Fun.* Long Branch, NJ: Kimbo Educational, 1992. Audiocassette.
While listening to a samba rhythm, children use rhythm sticks (or clap their hands) to tap and count the numbers 1 to 12 on a clock.

Media Choices

Show a video or filmstrip as a transition between storytelling activities and crafts. This gives children an opportunity to rest quietly for a few minutes.

Cherry, Lynne. *The Great Kapok Tree*. 10 min. DeSoto, TX: SRA/McGraw-Hill, 1996. Videocassette.
   A man begins to cut down a Kapok tree in the Amazon forest, but the animals try to change his mind.

Kipling, Rudyard. *The Beginning of the Armadillos*. 11 min. Raleigh, NC: Charles Clark, 1984. Videocassette.
   A hedgehog and a tortoise, who live on the banks of the Amazon River, transform themselves into armadillos to trick a jaguar who wants to eat them.

Crafts and Other Activities

Choose a craft suited for the age level of the group and the time allotted for the story time.

Amazon Mobile

The Amazon region is home to many unique, beautiful plants and animals. Have children create a mobile representing Amazon flora and fauna.

Supplies

Crayons or colored markers
Wire hanger
Paper
Glue stick
Yarn
Scissors
Hole punch

Fig. 2.13. Mobile Example.

Photocopy figures 2.14–2.18. Make two copies of each figure for each child, if desired, to make two-sided mobile ornaments. Color the figures before cutting (cut along the thick, outside lines only). Color suggestions: poison dart frog—red and black, or yellow and black, on a green leaf; bromeliad—red flower with green leaves; blue morpho butterfly—blue wings with black edges; howler monkey—reddish brown; macaw—a mixture of yellow, red, green, and blue. If making two-sided figures, use a glue stick to attach matching pieces back-to-back (white liquid glue can cause wrinkling on lightweight paper unless used sparingly). Punch holes where indicated. Tie pieces of yarn with loose knots to the paper figures and tight knots to the hanger (use various lengths of yarn so the figures will hang at various lengths). Trim the ends of the yarn pieces at the knots.

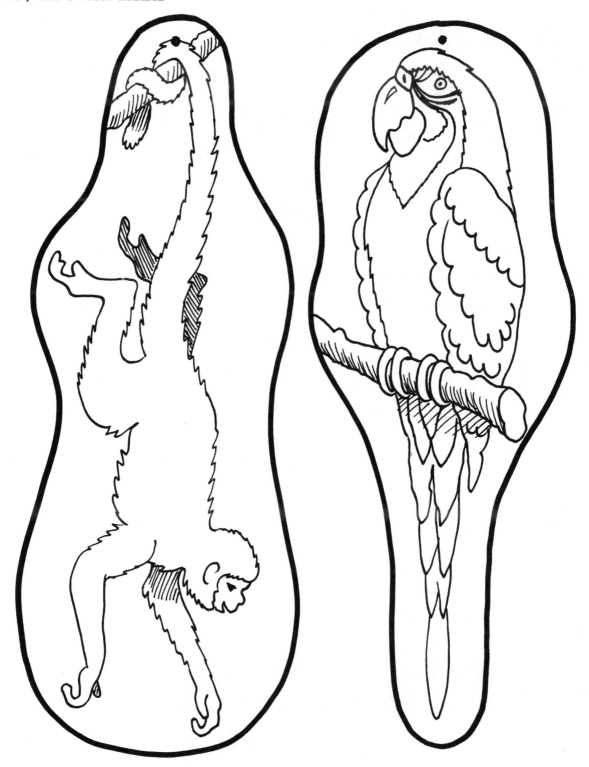

Fig. 2.14. Howler Monkey. Fig. 2.15. Macaw.

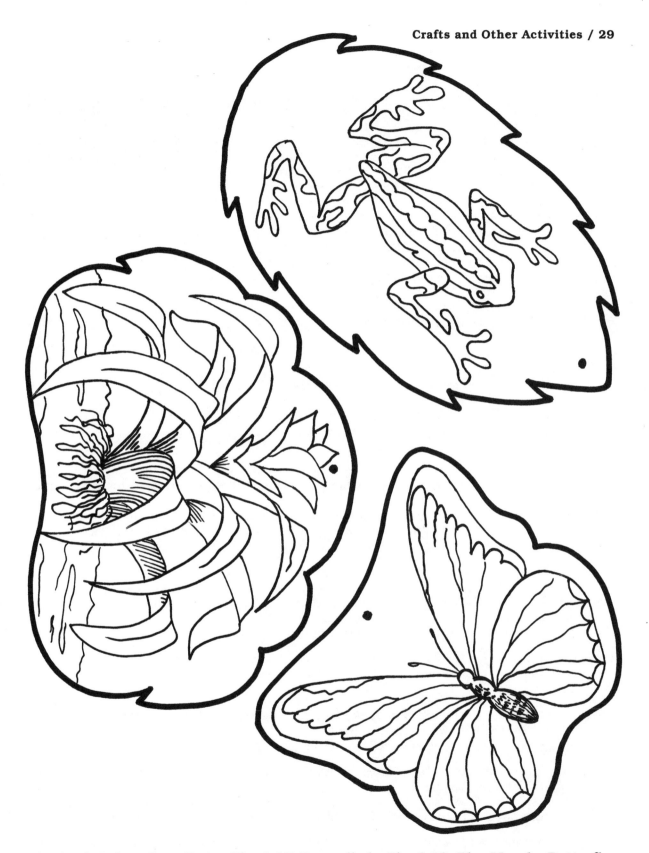

Fig. 2.16. Poison Dart Frog.   Fig. 2.17. Bromeliad.   Fig. 2.18. Blue Morpho Butterfly.

Carnival Mask

Brazilian people enjoy celebrating holidays. One of the most famous holidays they celebrate is Carnival, which is celebrated during the four days before Lent. People dress in colorful costumes and masks and dance to samba music in the streets. Brazil has what are known as "samba schools." These schools parade down the streets, dancing to the music. Members in each school have the same costumes and do the same dance. The schools are judged and awarded prizes.

In this craft project, children create masks similar to those worn for Carnival. After they have completed their masks, play Carnival-style music and have a Brazilian Carnival parade! Play the song "Brazilian Carnival" from *Children of the World: Multicultural Rhythmic Activities* by Georgiana Stewart (see "Sources for Fingerplays, Songs, Action Rhymes, and Games").

Fig. 2.19. Carnival Mask Example.

Supplies

Thick posterboard (any color)
Scissors
White glue
Glitter
Sequins
Feathers
Craft sticks

Trace and cut the sample mask in figure 2.20 on thick posterboard for each child. Where indicated on the mask pattern, have each child securely attach a craft stick to the back of the mask. Children glue feathers around the back edge of the mask so that the ends of the quills are not visible from the front. Decorate with sequins and glitter.

Sources for Craft Ideas and Activities

Deshpande, Chris. *Festival Crafts.* Photographs by Zul Mukhida. Worldwide Crafts series. Milwaukee, WI: Gareth Stevens, 1994. (pages 4–5)
Make papier-mâché maracas to celebrate Carnival in Rio de Janeiro, Brazil.

Everix, Nancy. *Ethnic Celebrations Around the World: Festivals, Holidays, and Celebrations.* Carthage, IL: Good Apple, 1991. (page 19)
Create a disguise to celebrate Carnival.

Hart, Avery, and Paul Mantell. *Kids Make Music! Clapping and Tapping from Bach to Rock.* Charlotte, VT: Williamson, 1993. (page 65)
Make paper-bag maracas to celebrate Carnival.

Thomson, Ruth. *The Rainforest Indians.* Footsteps in Time series. Danbury, CT: Children's Press, 1996. (24 pages)
Discusses the history of the Yanomani, a native culture of the rain forest. Included are crafts and activities that represent various aspects of Yanomani life.

Whitacre, Deborah, and Becky Radtke. *Multicultural Crafts from Recycled Materials.* Choose to Reuse series. Carthage, IL: Teaching & Learning, 1995. (pages 15–16)
Design a brimmed hat similar to those that Brazilian children wear to festivals.

attach craft stick to back

Fig. 2.20. Carnival Mask.

Let's Visit the

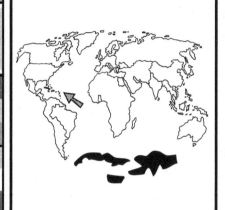

Caribbean Islands

Sample Story Times

Story Time for Preschool

Song: "Hello Song"

Book: *Caribbean Alphabet* by Frané Lessac

Fingerplay: "Five Little Coconuts"

Oral Story: "The Squeaky Old Bed" from *Crocodile! Crocodile! Stories Told Around the World* by Barbara Baumgartner

Song: "Tingalayo" from *One Light One Sun* by Raffi

Flannel Board Presentation: "A Tower for the King"

Filmstrip: *Come Away from the Water, Shirley* by John Burningham

Craft: "Pirate's Hat"

Action Rhyme: "My Hands"

Story Time for Kindergarten Through Third Grade

Song: "Hello Song"

Book: *Caribbean Alphabet* by Frané Lessac

Song: "Day O" from *Baby Beluga* by Raffi

Book: *Tiger Soup: An Anansi Story from Jamaica* by Frances Temple

Song: "Jump Shamador" from *Shake It to the One That You Love the Best* by Cheryl Warren Mattox

Oral Story: "A Very Happy Donkey" from *The Magic Orange Tree, and Other Haitian Folktales* by Diane Wolkstein

Action Rhyme: "One Two Anancy" from *No Hickory, No Dickory, No Dock: Caribbean Nursery Rhymes* by John Agard and Grace Nichols

Flannel Board Presentation: "A Tower for the King"

Filmstrip: *Come Away from the Water, Shirley* by John Burningham

Craft: "Sandy Beach Collage"

Action Rhyme: "My Hands"

Begin the story time with the "Hello Song." Then sing the song again, substituting the word *hello* with the Dominican Republic (Spanish) greeting *hola* [OH-lah]. (See p. xxvii for "Hello Song" music.)

Hello Song

Hello ev'rybody,
And how are you? How are you?
Hello ev'rybody,
And how are you today?

OH-lah ev'rybody,
And how are you? How are you?
OH-lah ev'rybody,
And how are you today?

End the story time with the "My Hands" action rhyme, substituting the words *thank you* with the Dominican Republic (Spanish) word *gracias* [GRAH-see-ahs], and *goodbye* with *adios* [ah-DYOHS]. Have children stand up and follow the actions in the rhyme.

My Hands

My hands say GRAH-see-ahs. *(hold up hands)*
With a clap, clap, clap. *(clap hands)*
My feet say GRAH-see-ahs. *(point to feet)*
With a tap, tap, tap. *(stamp or tap feet)*
Clap! Clap! Clap! *(clap hands)*
Tap! Tap! Tap! *(stamp or tap feet)*
Turn myself around and bow. *(turn and bow)*
ah-DYOHS. *(wave goodbye)*

Books to Read Aloud

Bloom, Valerie. *Fruits: A Caribbean Counting Poem.* Illustrated by David Axtell. New York: Henry Holt, 1997. (25 pages)
The reader counts to the number 10 in English using Caribbean fruit such as guavas, mangoes, and oranges.

Carlstrom, Nancy White. *Baby-O.* Pictures by Suçie Stevenson. Boston: Little, Brown, 1992. (32 pages)
A family living in the Caribbean travels to market on a jitney (bus) to sell their goods.

Gershator, Phillis. *Rata-pata-scata-fata: A Caribbean Story.* Pictures by Holly Meade. Boston: Little, Brown, 1994. (32 pages)
Junjun tries saying the magic phrase "rata-pata-scata-fata" to make his chores do themselves.

———. *Sambalena Show-Off.* Illustrated by Leonard Jenkins. New York: Simon & Schuster, 1995. (25 pages)
Sambalena is a big show-off. One day, he begins to show off by dancing around with a pot on his head—where it becomes stuck.

Joseph, Lynn. *Jasmine's Parlour Day.* Illustrated by Ann Grifalconi. New York: Lothrop, Lee & Shepard, 1994. (32 pages)
Spend Parlour Day with Jasmine and her mama as they sell their fresh fish and sugar cakes to tourists on the beach in Trinidad.

Lessac, Frané. *Caribbean Alphabet.* New York: Tambourine Books, 1989. (32 pages)
Introduces four Caribbean words for each letter of the alphabet. An engaging book for beginning a story time.

Linden, Ann Marie. *One Smiling Grandma: A Caribbean Counting Book.* Illustrated by Lynne Russell. New York: Dial Books for Young Readers, 1992. (25 pages)
A counting book showing 10 images of life in the Caribbean, as seen by a young girl.

Linden, Anne Marie. *Emerald Blue.* Illustrated by Katherine Doyle. New York: Atheneum, 1994. (25 pages)
The author remembers the time she spent as a child living with her brother and grandmother in the Caribbean Islands. Recommended for school-age children.

Milstein, Linda. *Coconut Mon.* Pictures by Cheryl Munro Taylor. New York: Tambourine Books, 1995. (32 pages)
Travel with the Coconut Mon as he sells his coconuts in this Caribbean counting book.

Mitchell, Rita Phillips. *Hue Boy.* Pictures by Caroline Binch. New York: Dial Books for Young Readers, 1993. (25 pages)
Hue Boy lives in the Caribbean Islands with his mama while his papa is away at sea. Everyone, including Hue Boy himself, is concerned about his size. His mama calls on many of the experts including a doctor, a healer, and the wise man of the village to help him.

Shute, Linda. *Rabbit Wishes.* New York: Lothrop, Lee & Shepard, 1995. (25 pages)
A folktale from Cuba about why Papá Dios (Father God) gave tío Conejo (Uncle Rabbit) such long ears.

Temple, Frances. *Tiger Soup: An Anansi Story from Jamaica.* New York: Orchard Books, 1994. (32 pages)

Trickster Anansi gets Tiger to swim in Blue Hole while he eats Tiger's soup. He then accuses the monkeys of eating it. (The underside of the book jacket contains a playscript, which might also be used for a puppet play.)

Williams, Karen Lynn. *Tap-Tap*. Illustrated by Catherine Stock. New York: Clarion Books, 1994. (39 pages)
Sasifi and her mama go to market to sell their oranges. They earn enough extra money to ride home on the tap-tap (a truck that carries people where they want to go—as the passengers want to stop they tap the side).

Storytelling

Flannel Board Presentation

"A Tower for the King." This is a retelling of a folktale from the Dominican Republic about a king who wanted to touch the moon. See figures 3.1–3.5 for patterns. Trace the patterns on felt, or photocopy and color them. If photocopying, glue small pieces of felt to the backs of the paper figures so they will hold to the flannel board. Make seven boxes for the king to stand on (using figures 3.4 and 3.5, or by simply cutting seven felt squares of various sizes). Place the figures on the flannel board as they are introduced in the story.

A Tower for the King
retold by Dee Ann Corn

Many years ago, there lived a king who was known throughout his kingdom as being very commanding. He always thought he was right, and no one was to question his authority. *(place the king on the flannel board)*

One evening, the king stepped out onto his balcony to enjoy the evening breeze. He looked up at the sky and saw the moon. *(place the moon on the flannel board)* He watched it and admired how large and wonderful it was. Oh how he wanted to reach up and touch it! For days, the king could not stop thinking about the moon and all its splendor. He lost sleep because he could not stop thinking about the moon. He wouldn't eat because he thought about the moon. He finally decided he had to find a way to touch the moon. So he sent for his royal carpenter. *(place the royal carpenter on the flannel board)*

"Find a way for me to touch the moon!" the king commanded of the carpenter.

The carpenter could not understand why the king had commanded his help. Of all the wise people in the kingdom, surely there were others with better ideas. The carpenter only knew about building things out of wood. He certainly didn't know anything about the moon! In fact, the only thing he knew was that the moon was very far away. It seemed impossible that the king would be able to reach it.

Still, the king had given him a command, so the carpenter went home and tried to think of a way for the king to touch the moon. He was not able to come up with any ideas that he believed would work. *(remove the royal carpenter from the flannel board)* A couple of days had passed when the king sent for the carpenter. *(place the royal carpenter on the flannel board)*

The king asked the carpenter if he had found a way for him to reach the moon. And the carpenter said, "Your Royal Highness, I don't believe it is possible for you to touch the moon."

"Nonsense!" shouted the king. "Find a way or you will die!"

So the carpenter left the palace fearing for his life. He didn't sleep at all that night, trying to think of a way to please the king. *(remove the royal carpenter from the flannel board)*

After a few days, the king again sent for the carpenter. *(place the royal carpenter on the flannel board)* The carpenter came before the king once again, but this time he had an idea. He told the king that he was a carpenter and knew only about building things out of wood. Would the king want a tower to the moon built out of wooden boxes?

The king liked the idea, and summoned everyone in the kingdom to bring him their boxes. As all the boxes were collected, the carpenter stacked them, one on top of another, until all the boxes were stacked. However, there were not enough. *(place three boxes on the flannel board and stack them)*

The carpenter returned to the king and told him that they were out of boxes and the tower was not yet tall enough. The king commanded that all the wood in the kingdom be delivered to him to make more boxes.

The carpenter built more boxes and then began to stack them on top of the others, making the tower taller and taller. Sadly, the tower was still too short. *(place two more boxes on the flannel board and stack them on the other boxes)*

The royal carpenter went back to the king and told him that he had now used all the wood in the kingdom, yet the tower was still not tall enough to touch the moon. The king then ordered that all the trees in the kingdom were to be cut down and made into more boxes.

The carpenter became concerned. "My King, should we really cut down all the trees in the kingdom?" asked the carpenter.

"Cut down every last one, from the beautiful, flamboyant tree to the stately palm tree!" demanded the king.

The carpenter, remembering that the king did not like to be questioned, left the palace to have every tree cut down and made into boxes. When the work was done, the new boxes were stacked onto the tower. *(place the two remaining boxes on the flannel board and stack them on the other boxes)*

The carpenter returned to the king and told him that his tower was complete. Excited, the king rushed to the tower and began to climb. He climbed and climbed and climbed, until he was above the clouds and could no longer be seen. The king reached the top of the tower, stood up, and reached out. His fingers were almost touching the moon, but not quite. *(place the king on top of the boxes)*

"I need one more box!" called the king from above the clouds.

"But Your Highness, we have no more boxes, no more wood, and no more trees. There is nothing to give you!" shouted the carpenter, up to the king.

The king did not care to hear this. He was determined to touch the moon. "Then take one from the bottom!" commanded the king.

The carpenter wondered if he was hearing the king correctly. Surely the king did not want him to take one of the boxes from the bottom of the tower.

The king called down again, "I order you to take a box from the bottom, immediately! With one more box on my tower, I will be able to touch the moon!"

The carpenter shook his head and took a box from the bottom of the tower, just as he was ordered. *(remove the bottom box from the flannel board)* You can guess what happened next: The tower came tumbling down, along with the king. And the king never bothered the carpenter again.

Fig. 3.1. King. Fig. 3.2. Royal Carpenter. Fig. 3.3. Moon.

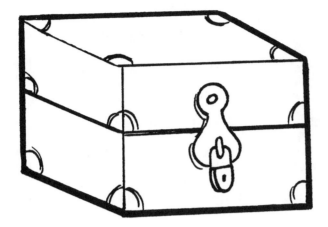

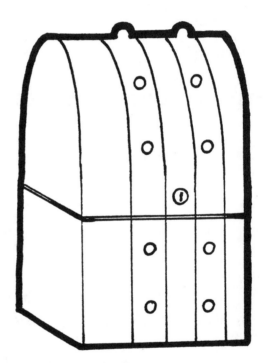

Fig. 3.4. Box. Fig. 3.5. Box.

Source for Flannel Board Presentations

Sierra, Judy. "Little Cockroach Martina." In *The Flannel Board Storytelling Book*. New York: H. W. Wilson, 1987. (pages 95–102)
   In this Puerto Rican tale, several suitors propose marriage to Martina. Includes patterns and instructions.

Sources for Oral Stories

Baumgartner, Barbara. "The Squeaky Old Bed." In *Crocodile! Crocodile! Stories Told Around the World*. Illustrated by Judith Moffatt. New York: Dorling Kindersley, 1994. (pages 16–20)
   A cumulative folktale from Puerto Rico about a young boy who gets scared when his bed squeaks.

Wolkstein, Diane. *The Magic Orange Tree, and Other Haitian Folktales*. Illustrated by Elsa Henriquez. New York: Alfred A. Knopf, 1978. (212 pages)
   A selection of Haitian folktales collected by the author during her travels in Haiti. Each story includes background information for the storyteller. Recommended for school-age children.

Fingerplays, Songs, Action Rhymes, and Games

I'm a Little Palm Tree
(sung to "I'm a Little Teapot")
by Dee Ann Corn

I'm a little palm tree, standing tall, *(stand with arms above head)*
Here on an island, round and small. *(make a circle with arms)*
When I start to see the wind begin, *(wave hands above head)*
They just blow me around, see me bend. *(bend back and forth at the waist)*

Five Little Coconuts
by Dee Ann Corn

(put up five fingers and count down one finger at a time as you tell the rhyme)

Five little coconuts on de seashore;
One washed away, an' den der was four.
Four little coconuts hanging in de tree;
One fell down, an' den der was three.
Three little coconuts admiring the view;
One rolled away, an' den der was two.
Two little coconuts playing in de sun;
One got lost, an' den der was one.
One little coconut sitting by de sea;
He put down his roots, an' den became a tree.

Sources for Fingerplays, Songs, Action Rhymes, and Games

Agard, John, and Grace Nichols. *No Hickory, No Dickory, No Dock: Caribbean Nursery Rhymes.* Illustrated by Cynthia Jabar. Cambridge, MA: Candlewick, 1991. (41 pages)
An enjoyable book of new and old nursery rhymes influenced by the Caribbean life and rhythm.

Charles, Faustin. *A Caribbean Counting Book.* Illustrated by Roberta Arenson. Boston: Houghton Mifflin, 1996. (24 pages)
A collection of traditional counting rhymes from the countries in the Caribbean.

Gunning, Monica. *Not a Copper Penny in Me House: Poems from the Caribbean.* Illustrated by Frané Lessac. Honesdale, PA: Wordsong/Boyds Mills Press, 1993. (32 pages)
Fifteen poems about the daily life of people who live in the Caribbean.

Jekyll, Walter, comp. *I Have a News: Rhymes from the Caribbean.* Compiled by Neil Philip. Illustrated by Jacqueline Mair. New York: Lothrop, Lee & Shepard, 1994. (26 pages)
Traditional songs and rhymes from the Caribbean, including musical scores.

Mattox, Cheryl Warren. "Jump Shamador," "There's a Brown Girl in the Ring," and "Go In and Out the Window." In *Shake It to the One That You Love the Best: Play Songs and Lullabies from Black Musical Traditions.* Illustrated by Varnette P. Honeywood and Brenda Joysmith. El Sobrante, CA: Warren-Mattox, 1989. Book with audiocassette. Includes lyrics and instructions for these songs and games from the Caribbean area.

Raffi. "Day O." In *Baby Beluga.* Universal City, CA: Troubadour Records, 1980. Audiocassette. "Day O" is a traditional work song from the island of Trinidad.

———. "Tingalayo." In *One Light One Sun.* Universal City, CA: Troubadour Records, 1985. Audiocassette.
Raffi sings this traditional Caribbean song about a little donkey.

Weissman, Jackie. "The Caribbean Mango Song." In *Joining Hands with Other Lands: Multicultural Songs and Games.* Long Branch, NJ: Kimbo Educational, 1993. Audiocassette.
Have children clap to the rhythm of this Caribbean song about sweet, juicy mangoes.

Media Choices

Show a video or filmstrip as a transition between storytelling activities and crafts. This gives children an opportunity to rest quietly for a few minutes.

Burningham, John. *Come Away from the Water, Shirley.* 4 min. Weston, CT: Weston Woods, 1984. Filmstrip with audiocassette.
Shirley visits the beach with her parents. Her adventures there include boarding a pirate's ship and finding buried treasure—while listening to her parent's warnings in the background.

Gleeson, Brian. *Anansi.* Illustrated by Steven Guarnaccia. Narrated by Denzel Washington. 30 min. Westport, CT: Rabbit Ears, 1991. Videocassette.
A Jamaican tale about Anansi the spider, who tricks the snake into giving him all the stories.

Crafts and Other Activities

Choose a craft suited for the age level of the group and the time allotted for the story time.

Sandy Beach Collage

The Caribbean beaches are among the most beautiful in the world. Tourists, as well as the residents, enjoy these beaches. Popular activities at the beach include sunning, swimming, snorkeling, and searching for shells.

Supplies

8½-by-11-inch posterboard
White glue
Water
Bowl
Paintbrush
Sand
Blue construction paper
Scissors
Seashells
Crayons

Fig. 3.6. Sandy Beach Collage Example.

In a bowl, mix white glue with enough water that the glue can be spread on the posterboard using a paintbrush. Paint a thin coat of the glue-and-water mixture onto the posterboard. While the glue is wet, sprinkle sand over the posterboard; shake or tap off the excess. Using figure 3.7 as a pattern, cut three blue strips and glue them to the lower border of the posterboard to make the waves. Photocopy figures 3.8–3.12 for children to color and cut out (to save time, photocopy the patterns on colored paper). Have children glue the pictures into place to create a beach scene. If desired, photocopy figures 3.4 and 3.5 (the boxes from the flannel board story "A Tower for the King"), which resemble treasure chests, for children to add to the collage. Finally, glue seashells to the collage to add depth.

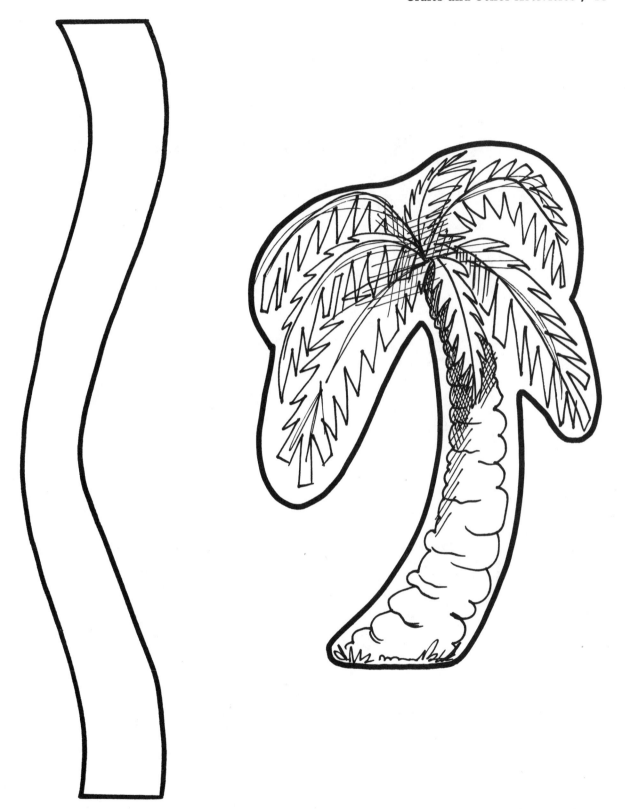

Fig. 3.7. Ocean Wave (cut three). Fig. 3.8. Palm Tree.

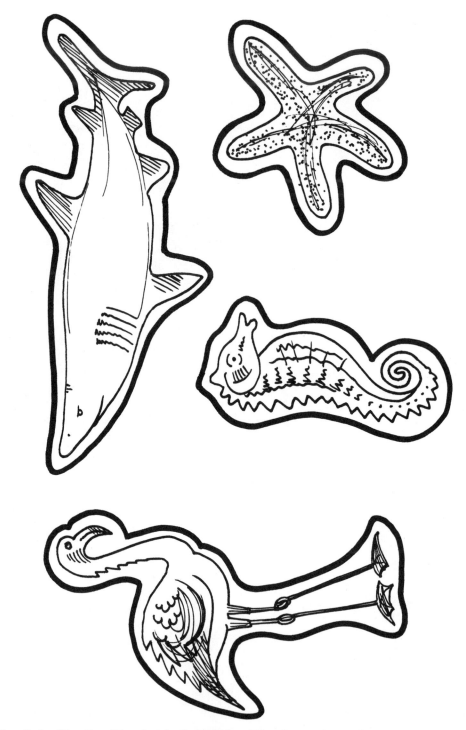

Fig. 3.9. Shark. Fig. 3.10. Starfish. Fig. 3.11. Sea Horse. Fig. 3.12. Flamingo.

Pirate's Hat

From the sixteenth century to the eighteenth century, pirates made their homes in the Caribbean Islands. During this period, Spain controlled the islands, and French, Dutch, and English pirates attacked and robbed the Spanish ships. Many of these ships were bringing supplies and treasures from Spain to the new land. Later, during the seventeenth century, pirates began to attack ships from all nations. Many of the pirate ships raised a black flag that featured a white skull and crossbones, known as the "Jolly Roger."

Making pirate hats with skull and crossbones is a quick and easy craft project, ideal for preschoolers.

Supplies

Scissors
Stapler
Black construction paper
White construction paper
Pencil
Glue sticks

Trace and cut figures 3.14–3.16 to make the hat, skull, and crossbones. Trace the hat pattern on black construction paper, and the skull and crossbones on the white construction paper. Glue the skull and crossbones to the front of the hat. Staple a 2-by-18-inch strip of paper to the ends of the hat to make a headband.

Fig. 3.13. Pirate Hat Example.

Sources for Craft Ideas and Activities

Corwin, Judith Hoffman. *Latin American and Caribbean Crafts.* New York: Franklin Watts, 1992. (48 pages)
   Includes crafts, recipes, and information about the Caribbean Islands.

Schuman, Jo Miles. *Art from Many Hands: Multicultural Art Projects for Home and School.* Englewood Cliffs, NJ: Prentice-Hall, 1981. (pages 178–82)
   Make a seed necklace similar to those that Puerto Rican children make and wear.

Wright, Rachel. *Pirates.* New York: Franklin Watts, 1991. (32 pages)
   Discusses the facts and history of pirates in the Caribbean. Includes craft ideas for making treasure maps and chests.

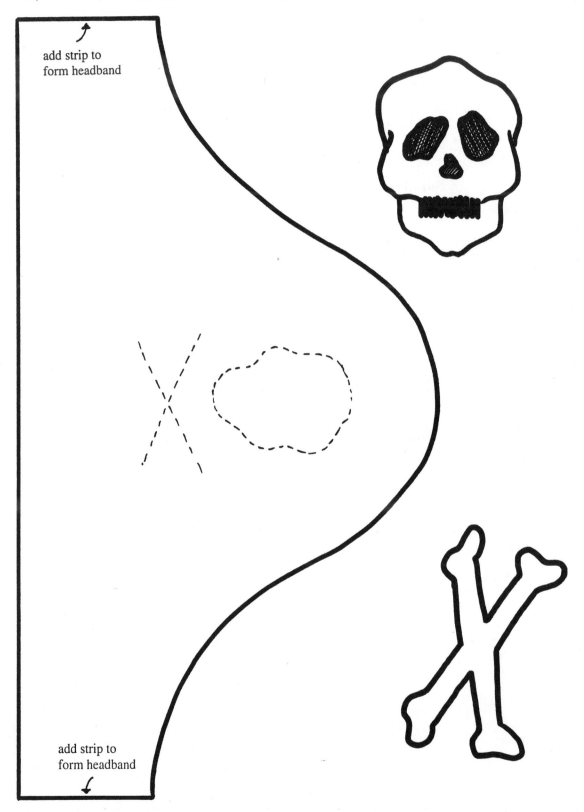

add strip to
form headband

add strip to
form headband

Fig. 3.14. Pirate Hat. Fig. 3.15. Pirate Hat Skull. Fig. 3.16. Pirate Hat Crossbones.

From *Travel the Globe.* © 1998. Desiree Lorraine Webber, et al. Libraries Unlimited. (800) 237-6124.

Let's Visit

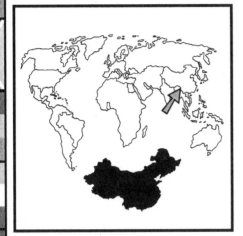

China

Sample Story Times

Story Time for Preschool

Song: "Hello Song"

Book: *In the Snow* by Huy Voun Lee

Book: *Count Your Way Through China* by James Haskins

Action Rhyme: "Mayling's Hammer"

Action Rhyme: "Two Little Eyes" from *The Laughing Baby: Remembering Nursery Rhymes and Reasons* by Anne Scott

Flannel Board Presentation: *Two of Everything* by Lily Toy Hong

Action Rhyme: "Thistle-Seed" from *The Laughing Baby: Remembering Nursery Rhymes and Reasons* by Anne Scott

Fingerplay: "Chinese New Year Dragon" from *1001 Rhymes and Fingerplays* by Jean Warren

Overhead Projector Story: "The Dragon Who Ate the Sun"

Craft: "Dragon Puppet"

Action Rhyme: "My Hands"

Story Time for Kindergarten Through Third Grade

Song: "Hello Song"

Book: *Lon Po Po: A Red Riding Hood Story from China* by Ed Young

Book: *Count Your Way Through China* by James Haskins

Action Rhyme: "Mayling's Hammer"

Tangram Story: *Grandfather Tang's Story* by Ann Tompert

Flannel Board Presentation: *Two of Everything* by Lily Toy Hong

Overhead Projector Story: "The Dragon Who Ate the Sun"

Video: *Five Chinese Brothers* by Claire Bishop

Craft: "Dragon Puppet" or "Chinese New Year Dragon"

Action Rhyme: "My Hands"

Begin the story time with the "Hello Song." Then sing the song again, substituting the word *hello* with the Mandarin Chinese greeting 你好 [KNEE-how]. (See p. xxvii for "Hello Song" music.)

Hello Song

Hello ev'rybody,
And how are you? How are you?
Hello ev'rybody,
And how are you today?

KNEE-how ev'rybody,
And how are you? How are you?
KNEE-how ev'rybody,
And how are you today?

End the story time with the "My Hands" action rhyme, substituting the words *thank you* with the Chinese word 謝謝 [SHAY shay], and *goodbye* with 再见 [shy JEN]. Have children stand up and follow the actions in the rhyme.

My Hands

My hands say SHAY shay. *(hold up hands)*
With a clap, clap, clap. *(clap hands)*
My feet say SHAY shay. *(point to feet)*
With a tap, tap, tap. *(stamp or tap feet)*
Clap! Clap! Clap! *(clap hands)*
Tap! Tap! Tap! *(stamp or tap feet)*
Turn myself around and bow. *(turn and bow)*
shy JEN. *(wave goodbye)*

Books to Read Aloud

Lee, Huy Voun. *In the Snow.* New York: Henry Holt, 1995. (28 pages)
Xiao Ming and his mother introduce the reader to 10 simple Chinese characters, which they write in the snow.

Mahy, Margaret. *The Seven Chinese Brothers.* Illustrated by Jean Tseng and Mou-sien Tseng. New York: Scholastic, 1990. (38 pages)
Seven brothers, each with a remarkable talent, save their brother from trouble with the emperor. Recommended for school-age children.

Mosel, Arlene. *Tikki Tikki Tembo.* Illustrated by Blair Lent. New York: Henry Holt, 1968. (46 pages)
A humorous tale about giving children short, simple names.

Steckman, Elizabeth. *Silk Peony, Parade Dragon.* Illustrated by Carol Inouye. Honesdale, PA: Boyds Mills Press, 1997. (32 pages)
Silk Peony, a dragon, leads the New Year's parade and prevents her mistress from being cheated by the ruler.

Wyndham, Robert. *Chinese Mother Goose Rhymes.* Illustrated by Ed Young. New York: Philomel, 1982. (48 pages)
A collection of Chinese nursery rhymes.

Yolen, Jane. *The Emperor and the Kite.* Illustrated by Ed Young. New York: Philomel Books, 1988. (31 pages)
The emperor's youngest daughter uses her kite to save her father.

Young, Ed. *Cat and Rat: The Legend of the Chinese Zodiac.* New York: Henry Holt, 1995. (32 pages)
A race determines the 12 animals of the zodiac, as well as who will be the first animal in the 12-year cycle.

———. *Lon Po Po: A Red Riding Hood Story from China.* New York: Philomel Books, 1989. (32 pages)
Three children outsmart a wolf who comes to the door pretending to be their grandmother.

Storytelling

Overhead Projector Story

"The Dragon Who Ate the Sun." This story is based on an ancient belief that a solar eclipse was caused by a giant dragon eating the sun. People would come out into the streets, pounding on their cooking pots to scare away the dragon. Of course, they were "successful" in their efforts because the sun always returned.

The following retelling is designed for use with an overhead projector. The figures, which should be made from colored transparency paper (except the moon), are manipulated on the screen of the overhead projector while the story is told. See figures 4.1–4.3 for patterns. Use yellow transparency paper for the sun, white construction paper for the moon because it must be opaque, and green transparency paper for the dragon. To make water, representing the Yellow Sea, cut a rectangle of blue transparency paper the width of the projector screen; scallop the top edge to create waves. Place the water on the overhead before beginning the narration.

Attach a thin piece of florist wire to both the dragon and the sun using a small piece of tape. This will allow easy manipulation of the figures as the story is told. The water and the moon can be easily placed on the screen by hand (the moon is used only in the prelude to the story).

The moon, when placed on the overhead projector, will appear as a dark circle because it is cut from construction paper. When laid on top of the sun, the overhead projector will show a halo of yellow around a dark circle—just as the moon has a halo of sunlight during a total eclipse.

This story calls for audience participation. At the appropriate time, have children clap their hands or drum on coffee cans or oatmeal containers (whatever is available) to scare away the dragon. Before the presentation, explain that an eclipse is caused by the moon moving between the sun and the earth, blocking our vision of the sun. Place the sun on the overhead projector and slowly move the moon across it. Pause when the moon completely covers the sun and discuss how dark it would be on earth without the sun's light.

Note: In the absence of an overhead projector, "The Dragon Who Ate the Sun" can be told as a flannel board story. Make the figures from felt, or photocopy and color the patterns. (If photocopying, glue small pieces of felt to the backs of the paper figures so they will hold to the flannel board.)

The Dragon Who Ate the Sun
by Desiree Webber

A long time ago, in the depths of the Yellow Sea near China, there lived a young dragon. *(place the dragon on the water, and make him swim about)* Although the dragon was young, he was the size of 10 skyscrapers. He had four legs, a pair of strong wings, and large paws with claws like a tiger. His body was covered with fish scales, and he had two long whiskers which grew from each side of his wide, wide mouth. His parents named him Zhenshu [zen-chew], which means "pearl."

Zhenshu loved to swim in the sea among the other creatures. But often, Zhenshu would swim close to the surface of the water, watching the sunlight glitter and dance upon the waves. Zhenshu would look up into the sky *(place the sun on overhead)* at the warm, round sun.

"I wish the sun lived in the Yellow Sea," Zhenshu told his parents.

"But the sun belongs in the sky," they answered. "Without the sun, the plants and trees would wither and die, and the people would starve."

Still, everyday, Zhenshu would watch the sun, until one day when he decided that the sun must come to live with him. Zhenshu flew out of the water and into the sky. *(move the dragon up to the sun)* Up into the atmosphere he flew, until he was next to the sun.

Afraid that he would not be able to hold the sun safely in his paws, Zhenshu decided to swallow it. *(move the dragon close to the sun)* He opened his mouth wider and wider and began to swallow the sun. *(slowly slide the sun into the dragon's mouth and throat as you continue the story)*

Down on earth, in cities such as Peking and Qingdao, people pointed to the sky: A dragon was eating the sun! Everyone ran into their houses and grabbed their cooking pots and brass kettles. They began to bang loudly on their cookery. *(have children clap their hands or bang their drums)*

Bang! Bong! Bang!

Bang! Bong! Bang! went all the pots and kettles.

Then, suddenly, everyone stopped: The sun was gone! *(slide the sun into the dragon's belly)* Bright stars twinkled in the purple-black sky, and flowers closed their petals.

Up in the sky, Zhenshu was uncertain what to do. He wanted the sun, but the loud clamoring of cooking pots frightened him.

Bang! Bong! Bang! went the pots and kettles again. *(have children clap their hands or bang their drums)*

Bang! Bong! Bang!

Reluctantly, Zhenshu opened his mouth and released the sun. *(move the sun up through the dragon's neck and out through his mouth)* He returned to the sea and was no longer afraid. *(move the dragon down to the water)* Deep in the water, Zhenshu could no longer hear the bang, bong, bang of the pots and kettles.

Flannel Board Presentation

Hong, Lily Toy. *Two of Everything.* Morton Grove, IL: Whitman, 1993. (31 pages)
Mr. Haktak finds a magic pot that doubles everything that falls inside, including Mrs. Haktak.

This story adapts well to a flannel board presentation. Use the story as a guide to creating flannel board characters and props. Use a small container as a "magic pot" to hold the figures. As you tell the story, pull the characters and props from the pot, as called for in the story, and place them on the flannel board.

Before telling this story, arrange the figures inside your pot in the order they appear in the story. For example, a second Mrs. Haktak and a second Mr. Haktak will be at the bottom of the pot, while the hairpin and the purse will be at the top. Hold the container so that the audience cannot see inside. Children will think the pot truly is magical as duplicate items are retrieved while the story is told.

Tangram Story

Tompert, Ann. *Grandfather Tang's Story.* Illustrated by Robert Andrew Parker. New York: Crown, 1990. (32 pages)
Grandfather Tang and young Soo use tangrams to tell a story about fox fairies.

Tangrams are an ancient Chinese puzzle game. School-age children enjoy creating figures using tangram puzzle pieces. Give each child a tangram set made from posterboard or construction paper. Refer to figure 4.4 for a tangram pattern. Use 11-by-14-inch sheets of paper, or larger, to make a flip chart of tangram figures from the book *Grandfather Tang's Story.*

Read the story aloud, showing the book's illustrations. Read the story aloud a second time, stopping to show each tangram character on the flip chart. Ask children to duplicate each character using their tangram puzzle pieces. Explain that all seven pieces must be used, and that each piece must touch at least one other puzzle piece.

Note: This activity may be more appropriate as the basis for an entire story time or as an extending activity for the media center or classroom. It can require 30 to 40 minutes, depending upon the age of the group and their familiarity with tangrams.

Fig. 4.1. Dragon.

From *Travel the Globe.* © 1998. Desiree Lorraine Webber, et al. Libraries Unlimited. (800) 237-6124.

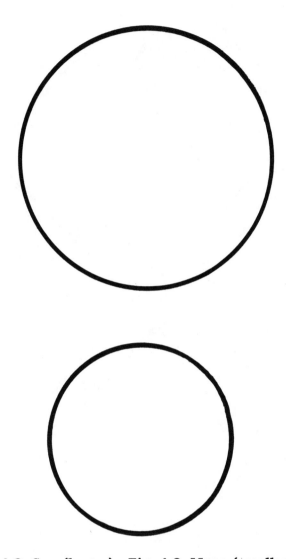

Fig. 4.2. Sun (larger).   Fig. 4.3. Moon (smaller).

Fig. 4.4. Tangram.

Fingerplays, Songs, Action Rhymes, and Games

Haskins, Jim. *Count Your Way Through China.* Illustrated by Dennis Hockerman. Minneapolis, MN: Carolrhoda Books, 1987. (24 pages)

The Mandarin Chinese characters for numbers 1–10 are introduced alongside information about the culture, government and history of China. A pronunciation guide is provided.

"Mayling's Hammer." Share the book Count Your Way Through China *with children. Teach them the Chinese words for the numbers 1 through 10 (see below), and then present this action rhyme, which is based on a children's verse known as either "Johnny's Hammer" or "Peter's Hammer" (author unknown).*

This action rhyme can be performed two ways. One method is to have children show the number of hammers with their fingers. Then they pound their fists on the palms of their other hands as they hammer.

Another method is to have the children stand and use their arms, legs, and heads as hammers. For example, first you hammer with your right arm, moving your arm up and down in a hammering motion (one hammer); then you hammer with your right and left arms (two hammers); then you hammer with both arms and your right leg by stamping your foot (three hammers); then you hammer with both arms and both legs (four hammers); finally, you hammer with both arms, both legs, and your head, by nodding the head up and down (five hammers).

Note: *This exercise usually leaves the group laughing; a fingerplay such as "Two Little Eyes" is an appropriate activity to regain the group's attention and provide a few minutes for resting quietly.*

1	一	"Ee"
2	二	"Rr"
3	三	"sahn"
4	四	"zuh"
5	五	"wuu"

Mayling's Hammer
(Desiree Webber)

Mayling pounds with one (Ee) hammer,
One (Ee) hammer, one (Ee) hammer,
Mayling pounds with one (Ee) hammer,
Then she pounds with two (Rr).
Mayling pounds with two (Rr) hammers,
Two (Rr) hammers, two (Rr) hammers,
Mayling pounds with two (Rr) hammers,
Then she pounds with three (sahn).
Mayling pounds with three (sahn) hammers,
Three (sahn) hammers, three (sahn) hammers,
Mayling pounds with three (sahn) hammers,
Then she pounds with four (zuh).
Mayling pounds with four (zuh) hammers,
Four (zuh) hammers, four (zuh) hammers,
Mayling pounds with four (zuh) hammers,
Then she pounds with five (wuu).
Mayling pounds with five (wuu) hammers,
Five (wuu) hammers, five (wuu) hammers,
Mayling pounds with five (wuu) hammers,
Then she goes to sleep.

Dragon Tag

Corbett, Pie, comp. "Dragon Tag." In *The Playtime Treasury: A Collection of Playground Rhymes, Games, and Action Songs.* New York: Doubleday, 1989. (page 91)
A collection of action rhymes and games. Instruction is included for a group game called "Dragon Tag."

"Dragon Tag" might be used as an extending activity following a craft project related to the "Parade of the Dragon," part of the New Year's Eve celebrations in China (see "Crafts and Other Activities" or refer to the book *Silk Peony, Parade Dragon* by Elizabeth Steckman, listed under "Books to Read Aloud"). In this game of tag, four children form the body of the dragon by holding hands. As the dragon tags others, those tagged must join the body of the dragon, until one long dragon is formed with all members of the group. Refer to *The Playtime Treasury* for instructions.

Sources for Fingerplays, Songs, Action Rhymes, and Games

"Chinese Fan." In *Ring a Ring o' Roses: Stories, Games and Finger Plays for Pre-School Children.* Flint, MI: Flint Public Library, 1977. (page 88)
An action rhyme that will have everyone giggling at the end as the children fan with both hands, both feet, and their head.

Scott, Anne. "Two Little Eyes," "Thistle-Seed," and "Old Chang the Crab." In *The Laughing Baby: Remembering Nursery Rhymes and Reasons.* South Hadley, MA: Bergin & Garvey, 1987. (pages 53, 88, and 93)
"Thistle-Seed" is identified as a song to sing when rocking one's baby; however, it easily lends itself to an action rhyme, as do the songs "Two Little Eyes" and "Old Chang the Crab."

Warren, Jean. "Chinese New Year Dragon." In *1001 Rhymes and Fingerplays: For Working with Young Children.* Everett, WA: Warren, 1994. (page 266)
This rhyme calls for the group to form a line, dance, and weave as they pretend they are in a New Year's parade.

Weissman, Jackie. "Chinese New Year." In *Joining Hands with Other Lands: Multicultural Songs and Games.* Long Branch, NJ: Kimbo Educational, 1993. Audiocassette.
An action song in which participants form two lines facing each other and follow the simple instructions on the audiocassette: Take eight steps forward; take eight steps back; and bow.

Media Choices

Show a video or filmstrip as a transition between storytelling activities and crafts. This gives children an opportunity to rest quietly for a few minutes.

Bishop, Claire. *Five Chinese Brothers.* 10 min. Weston, CT: Weston Woods, 1993. Videocassette.
Five Chinese brothers use their special abilities to save their brother from execution.

Flack, Marjorie. *The Story About Ping.* 10 min. Weston, CT: Weston Woods, 1993. Videocassette.
Ping, a duck, becomes separated from his family as they sail down the Yangtze River.

Mosel, Arlene. *Tikki Tikki Tembo.* 9 min. Weston, CT: Weston Woods, 1993. Videocassette.
A humorous tale about giving children short, simple names.

Crafts and Other Activities

Choose a craft suited for the age level of the group and the time allotted for the story time.

Chinese New Year

In China, people perform the "Parade of the Dragon" to celebrate New Year's Eve. The dragon has a large head made of wood or papier-mâché and is brightly painted. Attached to the dragon's head is a large piece of colorful cloth, representing its body. Several people hold the dragon's body as they walk, making it sway and dance through the parade.

The "Dragon Puppet" craft is an individual project—each child makes a New Year's Eve dragon. The "Chinese New Year Dragon" craft is a group project—children make a dragon similar to those seen in the Chinese parades.

Dragon Puppet

Supplies

Green posterboard or construction paper
Tissue paper—various colors (cut into 1-inch squares)
Glue sticks
Pencils
Scissors
Drinking straws or large craft sticks (two per child)
Clear tape

Enlarge figure 4.5 to 200 percent to create the pattern for this craft. Make a copy for each child. Have children trace their pattern on green posterboard or construction paper and cut out the dragon (for young children, supply pre-cut dragons). Tape two straws or two large craft sticks to the back of the dragon (where indicated in fig. 4.5), leaving enough room between the straws or sticks for manipulation of the puppet with both hands. Glue various colors of tissue-paper squares to the front of the puppet, creating the appearance of dragon scales.

Children can manipulate their dragon puppets like miniature New Year's Eve dragons on parade: Moving the straws or sticks backward and forward creates a rippling effect.

Chinese New Year Dragon

Supplies

Cardboard box
Large grocery sacks (paper)
Clear tape
White glue
Decorative materials (construction paper, washable tempera paints, washable markers, streamers, feathers, buttons, tissue paper, etc.)

See figure 4.6 for a sample illustration of the Chinese New Year Dragon. Create the dragon's head using a cardboard box large enough to fit over a child's head but not too heavy to carry. An adult should pre-cut the eyes, and cut slots in the side of the box to be used as handles. Have two or three children either paint the box or cover with construction paper. Then use streamers, feathers, buttons, tissue paper, and so on to decorate the head. (If desired, an adult can paint and decorate the box beforehand to save time.)

attach straws
or craft sticks
to back at arrows

Fig. 4.5. Dragon Puppet.

From *Travel the Globe.* © 1998. Desiree Lorraine Webber, et al. Libraries Unlimited. (800) 237-6124.

Cut off the bottom and one side of each grocery sack. Give each child a sack to decorate (have children lay the sacks flat when decorating) to create a colorful body for the dragon. After all the sacks are decorated, tape them together top-to-bottom to form the body of the dragon. Tape should be applied on the inside for a cleaner appearance. Then tape the body to the top of the dragon's head.

One child holds the head by the handles while the other children support the dragon's body above their heads. Have children move around the room (or any other large space) and perform their own "dragon dance."

Fig. 4.6. Chinese New Year Dragon Example.

Sources for Craft Ideas and Activities

Multicultural Crafts for Kids. Carson, CA: Lakeshore Learning Materials, 1992.
Make a "carp" kite using small paper bags, tissue paper, yarn, and crayons.

Ritter, Darlene. *Multicultural Art Activities: From the Cultures of Africa, Asia and North America.* Edited by Judy Urban. Illustrated by Diane Valko. Cypress, CA: Creative Teaching Press, 1993. (pages 52–55)
Includes instructions for creating a colorful dragon hat and for a butterfly paper-cut project using construction paper.

Terzian, Alexandra M. *The Kids' Multicultural Art Book: Art and Craft Experiences from Around the World.* Kids Can! series. Charlotte, VT: Williamson, 1993. (pages 146–47)
Learn how to make traditional paper-cuts.

Warren, Jean, and Elizabeth McKinnon. *Small World Celebrations: Around the World Holidays to Celebrate with Young Children.* Illustrated by Marion Hopping Ekberg. Everett, WA: Warren, 1988. (page 21)
Make New Year's scrolls and Chinese fans.

Let's Visit the Commonwealth of Independent States (formerly the Soviet Union)

Sample Story Times

Story Time for Preschool

Song: "Hello Song"

Book: *The Bun: A Tale from Russia* by Marcia Brown

Book: *The Mitten: A Ukrainian Folktale* by Jan Brett

Fingerplay: "Five Little Turnips"

Puppet Play: "Grandfather and the Enormous Turnip"

Audience Participation: *The Clay Pot Boy* by Cynthia Jameson

Video: *Rechenka's Eggs* by Patricia Polacco

Craft: "Decorated Paper Eggs"

Action Rhyme: "My Hands"

Story Time for Kindergarten Through Third Grade

Song: "Hello Song"

Book: *The Wooden Doll* by Susan Bonners

Book: *Babushka's Doll* by Patricia Polacco

Fingerplay: "Five Little Turnips"

Puppet Play: "Grandfather and the Enormous Turnip"

Audience Participation: *The Clay Pot Boy* by Cynthia Jameson

Video: *The Keeping Quilt* by Patricia Polacco

Craft: "Matroshka Dolls (Stacking Dolls)"

Action Rhyme: "My Hands"

Begin the story time with the "Hello Song." Then sing the song again, substituting the word *hello* with the Russian greeting Здравствуйте *zdravstvuyte* [ZDRA-hst-voo-yti]. (See p. xxvii for "Hello Song" music.)

Hello Song

Hello ev'rybody
And how are you? How are you?
Hello ev'rybody,
And how are you today?

ZDRA-hst-voo-yti ev'rybody,
And how are you? How are you?
ZDRA-hst-voo-yti ev'rybody,
And how are you today?

End the story time with the "My Hands" action rhyme, substituting the words *thank you* with the Russian word Спасибо *spasibo* [spa-si-ba], and *goodbye* with До свидания *do svidaniya* [DAS-fidá-hniya]. Have children stand up and follow the actions in the rhyme.

My Hands

My hands say spa-si-ba. *(hold up hands)*
With a clap, clap, clap. *(clap hands)*
My feet say spa-si-ba. *(point to feet)*
With a tap, tap, tap. *(stamp or tap feet)*
Clap! Clap! Clap! *(clap hands)*
Tap! Tap! Tap! *(stamp or tap feet)*
Turn myself around and bow. *(turn and bow)*
DAS-fidá-hniya. *(wave goodbye)*

Books to Read Aloud

Brett, Jan. *The Mitten: A Ukrainian Folktale.* New York: G. P. Putnam's Sons, 1989. (32 pages)
A new telling of an old tale in which all the animals find a warm sleeping place in Nicki's lost mitten—until the bear sneezes. Children will enjoy the detailed illustrations, including side panels for predicting what might happen next.

Brown, Marcia. *The Bun: A Tale from Russia.* New York: Harcourt Brace Jovanovich, 1972. (32 pages)
A bun comes alive and escapes from a man and a woman and a variety of animals, but not from the cunning fox.

Cech, John. *My Grandmother's Journey.* Illustrated by Sharon McGinlry-Nally. New York: Bradbury Press, 1991. (32 pages)
Korie's grandmother tells of her eventful life and how she journeyed halfway around the world, coming to America after World War II.

Domanska, Janina. *A Scythe, a Rooster, and a Cat.* New York: Greenwillow Books, 1981. (32 pages)
It is time for three brothers to go out into the world and seek their fortunes. With only the help of a cat, a rooster, and a scythe, they go on their way in this retelling of an old Russian folktale. Recommended for school-age children.

Franklin, Kirstine. *The Wolfhound.* Illustrated by Kris Waldherr. New York: Lothrop, Lee & Shepard, 1996. (32 pages)
Pavel saves the life of an enormous dog he finds nearly frozen to death in the snow. Fearing he will be punished for having a wolfhound that belongs to a noble, he tries to return the dog to her home, but with surprising results.

Hall, Amanda. *The Gossipy Wife.* New York: Bedrick/Blackie, 1984. (26 pages)
The story of a husband who must keep his wife from gossiping about a chest of gold he has found.

Haskins, Jim. *Count Your Way Through Russia.* Illustrated by Vera Medinkov. Minneapolis, MN: Carolrhoda Books, 1987. (24 pages)
Book introduces the numbers 1 through 10 in Russian, alongside an introduction to Russian culture.

Jackson, Ellen. *The Impossible Riddle.* Illustrated by Alison Winfield. Danvers, MA: Whispering Coyote Press, 1995. (32 pages)
Princess Katrina thinks that it is time to marry, but her father, the tsar, does not want to lose his beloved daughter. He decrees that to win his daughter's hand, her suitor must answer a seemingly impossible riddle. Recommended for school-age children.

Polacco, Patricia. *The Keeping Quilt.* New York: Simon and Schuster Books for Young Readers, 1988. (32 pages)
A homemade quilt ties together four generations of an immigrant Jewish family from Russia.

——. *Rechenka's Eggs.* New York: Philomel Books, 1988. (32 pages)
Babushka becomes very attached to the injured goose she rescues and cares for. When the goose Rechenka goes to join her own kind, she leaves behind a miracle egg.

——. *Thunder Cake.* New York: Philomel Books, 1990. (32 pages)
Babushka (Grandmother) helps her granddaughter overcome her fear of thunderstorms.

Prokofiev, Sergei. *Peter and the Wolf.* Translated by Maria Carlson. Illustrated by Charles Mikolaycak. New York: Viking Press, 1982. (32 pages)
Peter captures the wolf, ignoring his grandfather's warning about the danger.

———. *Peter and the Wolf.* Illustrated by Barbara Cooney. New York: Viking Penguin, 1985. (5 pages)
This classic tale springs to life in Cooney's three-dimensional pop-up book. Enchanting scenes of old Russia show Peter's adventure, from lassoing the wolf's tail to parading through the village as the captor.

Stories About Baba Yaga, a Russian Witch

Ayres, Becky Hickox. *Matreshka.* Illustrated by Alexi Natchev. New York: Doubleday, 1992. (32 pages)
Baba Yaga, an evil witch, captures Katy. With the help of Matreshka, her little wooden doll, Katy manages to escape.

Kimmel, Eric A. *Baba Yaga: A Russian Folktale.* Illustrated by Megan Lloyd. New York: Holiday House, 1991. (30 pages)
Marina is captured by Baba Yaga, but the witch's cat feels sorry for her and helps her escape.

Mayer, Marianna. *Baba Yaga and Vasilisa the Brave.* Illustrated by K. Y. Craft. New York: Morrow Junior Books, 1994. (30 pages)
Vasilisa's special doll helps her escape from the evil Baba Yaga.

Stories About Babushka and Matroshka Dolls

Bonners, Susan. *The Wooden Doll.* New York: Lothrop, Lee & Shepard, 1991. (32 pages)
Stephanie's curiosity gets her into trouble but also encourages her grandfather to tell an important story about his wooden dolls.

Polacco, Patricia. *Babushka's Doll.* New York: Simon and Schuster Books for Young Readers, 1990. (32 pages)
Natasha plays with her grandmother's Babushka doll while grandmother is shopping. The doll comes to life—and is even more rambunctious than Natasha.

———. *Babushka's Mother Goose.* New York: Philomel Books, 1995. (64 pages)
Russian characters and scenes are shared in traditional rhymes. The poem "Matroishka" is included.

Storytelling

Puppet Presentation

"Grandfather and the Enormous Turnip." This a retelling of a well-known Russian folktale about a giant turnip. Use figures 5.1–5.7 to make figures for the play. Photocopy the patterns on white posterboard and color them with bright oranges, reds, and yellows, in the old Russian tradition. Cut them out and attach paint sticks to the backs.

The storyteller might have children from the group hold the stick puppets, or the storyteller might hold the puppets while telling the story. For larger groups, enlarge the puppet patterns for better visibility. Introduce the play by showing *children a real turnip. Ask, "Has anyone ever eaten a turnip? Can you tell us what it tastes like?" Then tell children, "I know a Russian grandfather who loved to grow turnips. He had a problem, though—sometimes they grew too big!"*

The following Russian words are used for the characters in the play. Introduce the words to children as the story is told:

grandfather	diadushka	[DYEH-doosh-kah]
grandmother	babushka	[BAH-bush-kah]
granddaughter	dyevachka	[DYE-VUS-kah]
dog	sobaka	[sah-BAH-kah]
cat	kot	[KAWT]
mouse	mwishka	[mwihsh-kah]

Grandfather and the Enormous Turnip
retold by Donna Norvell

Out in his garden, Grandfather (Diadushka) spent a lot of time growing vegetables: green cabbages, cucumbers, peas, carrots, onions, beets, and potatoes. Of all the vegetables he grew, however, his favorite was the turnip. *(hold up the grandfather puppet)* From tiny seeds, the vegetables grew and grew. Grandfather (Diadushka) was anxious to harvest them and make a fine stew. Then one day he saw an incredible sight. One turnip had grown to a wondrous height, and its leafy top rose high into the sky.

Grandfather (Diadushka) pulled and pulled and then gave a great sigh. Help was needed, so he called for Grandmother (Babushka) to come quick and see this strange sight—an enormous turnip holding tight. *(hold up the grandmother puppet)* Grandmother (Babushka) grabbed Grandfather (Diadushka) by his belt, and they pulled and pulled, while chanting:

(children may chant the verse with the storyteller)

"Pull and tug as hard as you can.
This turnip is as stubborn as stubborn can be.
But so are we, so are we!"

But the enormous turnip held on tight.

However, Grandmother (Babushka) was not ready to give up the fight. She called for Granddaughter (Dyevachka) to come quick and see this strange sight—an enormous turnip holding tight. *(hold up the granddaughter puppet)* Granddaughter (Dyevachka) grabbed Grandmother (Babushka) by her waist, Grandmother (Babushka) grabbed Grandfather (Diadushka) by the belt, and they pulled and pulled while chanting:

[repeat verse]

But the enormous turnip held on tight.

However, Granddaughter (Dyevachka) was not ready to give up the fight. She called for Dog (Sobaka) to come quick and see this strange sight—an enormous turnip holding tight. *(hold up the dog puppet)* Dog (Sobaka) grabbed Granddaughter (Dyevachka) by her skirt, Granddaughter (Dyevachka) grabbed

Grandmother (Babushka) by her waist, Grandmother (Babushka) grabbed Grandfather (Diadushka) by his belt, and they pulled and pulled while chanting:

[repeat verse]

But the enormous turnip held on tight.

However, Dog (Sobaka) was not ready to give up the fight. He called for Cat (Kot) to come quick and see this strange sight—an enormous turnip holding tight. *(hold up the cat puppet)* Cat (Kot) grabbed Dog (Sobaka) by his tail, Dog (Sobaka) grabbed Granddaughter (Dyevachka) by her skirt, Granddaughter (Dyevachka) grabbed Grandmother (Babushka) by her waist, Grandmother (Babushka) grabbed Grandfather (Diadushka) by his belt, and they pulled and pulled while chanting:

[repeat verse]

But the enormous turnip held on tight.

However, Cat (Kot) was not ready to give up the fight. He called for Mouse (Mwishka) to come quick and see this strange sight—an enormous turnip holding tight. *(hold up the mouse puppet)* Mouse (Mwishka) grabbed Cat (Kot) by his back paw, Cat (Kot) grabbed Dog (Sobaka) by his tail, Dog (Sobaka) grabbed Granddaughter (Dyevachka) by her skirt, Granddaughter (Dyevachka) grabbed Grandmother (Babushka) by her waist, Grandmother (Babushka) grabbed Grandfather (Diadushka) by his belt, and they pulled and pulled while chanting:

[repeat verse]

Then, much to their surprise, the enormous turnip no longer held on tight. It was lying there, in plain sight. *(hold up the giant turnip puppet)* They had won the final fight!

Other Versions of "The Turnip" Story

Champlin, Connie. "The Big, Big Turnip." In *Storytelling with Puppets*. Chicago: American Library Association, 1985. (pages 211–14)

Morgan, Pierr. *The Turnip: An Old Russian Folktale*. New York: Philomel Books, 1990. (32 pages)

Polacco, Patricia. "Diadushka Planted a Turnip." In *Babushka's Mother Goose*. New York: Philomel Books, 1995. (pages 16–17)

Sierra, Judy. "Turnip: A Russian Story." In *The Flannel Board Storytelling Book*. New York: H. W. Wilson, 1987. (pages 50–55)

Fig. 5.1. Mouse. Fig. 5.2. Cat. Fig. 5.3. Dog. Fig. 5.4. Granddaughter.

Fig. 5.5. Grandmother. Fig. 5.6. Grandfather.

Fig. 5.7. Giant Turnip.

From *Travel the Globe.* © 1998. Desiree Lorraine Webber, et al. Libraries Unlimited. (800) 237-6124.

Audience Participation

Jameson, Cynthia. *The Clay Pot Boy.* Illustrated by Arnold Lobel. New York: Coward, McCann & Geoghegan, 1973. (64 pages)

A story about an old man and woman who never had children. They make a clay pot in the shape of a boy. When they remove him from the oven, he begins asking for things to eat. He eats a number of characters whole before a billy goat saves the day.

This story is appropriate for audience participation. The storyteller narrates the story while playing the part of the Clay Pot Boy. Children selected from the audience play the characters who are swallowed whole by the Clay Pot Boy.

To give a visual appearance of swallowing characters, the storyteller wears a floor-length robe constructed of two sheets sewn together. As the Clay Pot Boy swallows the story's characters, the children duck through the opening and underneath the sheets. As more characters enter through the opening, the larger the Clay Pot Boy grows—with hilarious results. In the end, the billy goat bumps the Clay Pot Boy and all the characters tumble out through the side slit.

To create the robe, sew two full-size sheets together at the top. Leave an opening in the middle for the head. For the best results, sew in elastic or a drawstring at the neck. This will gather the material around the neck and shoulders, making it easier for the storyteller to move about. The robe should be long enough to reach the floor. Next, sew along one side leaving an opening for the hand and arm to come through. The other side is left open.

Using colored construction paper, make a replica of the Clay Pot Boy for a mask (refer to the illustrations in *The Clay Pot Boy* by Cynthia Jameson). Attach a paint stick or craft stick to the back of the mask. The storyteller holds the mask to his or her face when the Clay Pot Boy speaks and away from the face when narrating the remainder of the story.

Sources for Oral Stories

Milord, Susan. "The Clever Maiden." In *Tales Alive! Ten Multicultural Folktales with Activities.* Illustrated by Michael A. Donato. Charlotte, VT: Williamson, 1995. (pages 25–29)

The daughter of a poor farmer impresses the czar with her clever wisdom. Four extending activities follow the story, including how to make a puzzle using beans or pebbles.

Pellowski, Anne. "Naughty Marysia." In *The Story Vine: A Source Book of Unusual and Easy-to-Tell Stories from Around the World.* Illustrated by Lynn Sweat. New York: Macmillan, 1984. (pages 80–83)

The story "Naughty Marysia" might be told using a set of matroshka nesting dolls. During this story the dolls are taken apart as they are introduced.

Fingerplays, Songs, Action Rhymes, and Games

"Five Little Turnips." Teach children the Russian numbers 1 through 5 and substitute them in the following fingerplay. Or, Count Your Way Through Russia *by Jim Haskins (see "Books to Read Aloud") can be used to introduce counting in Russian.*

1	odin	[ah-DEEN]	Один (одна́, одно́)
2	dva	[DVAH]	Два (две)
3	tri	[TREE]	Три
4	chetire	[cheh-TI-ree]	Четы́ре
5	pyaht	[PYAHT]	Пять

For this fingerplay, begin with five turnip puppets, one on each finger; remove a puppet each time a turnip is pulled by Babushka in the fingerplay. The storyteller will wear the turnip finger puppets. The children will hold up five fingers and follow along. To make the finger puppets, photocopy figures 5.8 and 5.9 on white tagboard or construction paper. Use markers to color the turnip tops green and the bodies of the turnips white and purple. Laminate and cut out the turnips and finger attachments. Tape together the three flaps of each finger attachment. This will fit over the tip of each finger like a thimble. Tape a turnip to each attachment.

Five Little Turnips
by Donna Norvell

Five (pyaht) little turnips planted in a row.
Water them a lot, and watch them grow.
Along comes Babushka ready to make stew.
Pulled up a turnip, now only four (chetire) grew.
Four (chetire) little turnips planted in a row.
Water them a lot, and watch them grow.
Along comes Babushka ready to make stew.
Pulled up a turnip, now only three (tri) grew.
Three (tri) little turnips planted in a row.
Water them a lot, and watch them grow.
Along comes Babushka ready to make stew.
Pulled up a turnip, now only two (dva) grew.
Two (dva) little turnips planted in a row.
Water them a lot, and watch them grow.
Along comes Babushka ready to make stew.
Pulled up a turnip, now only one (odin) grew.
One (odin) little turnip growing in the row.
Water it good, and watch it grow.
Along comes Babushka ready to make stew.
Pulled the last turnip, and finished her stew.
Yum, yum, it's ready for me and you.

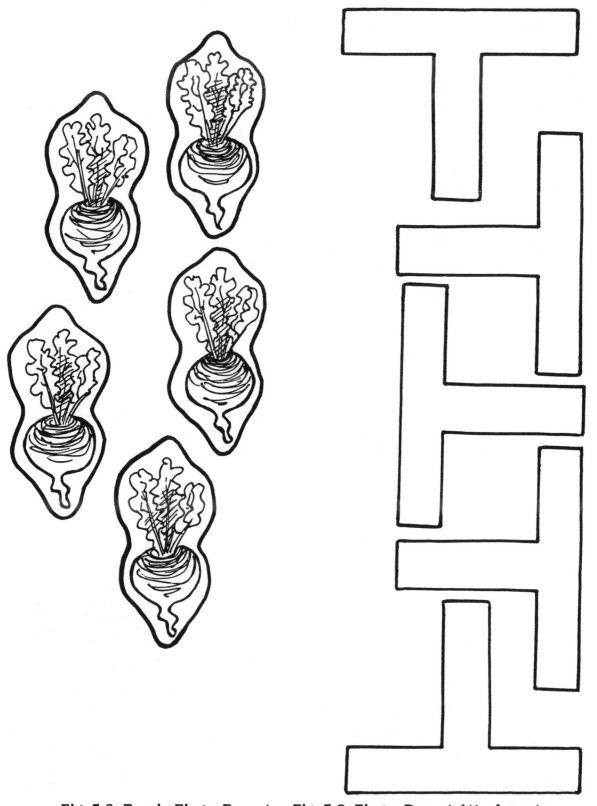

Fig. 5.8. Turnip Finger Puppets.   Fig. 5.9. Finger Puppet Attachments.

Sources for Fingerplays, Songs, Action Rhymes, and Games

Music from Russia. Los Angeles: Delta Music, 1990. Compact disc.
>   Traditional Russian music performed by well-known Russian singers and orchestras. Play this music to set the mood for a story time.

Salidor, Susan. *Little Voices in My Head: Music for Children and Their Families.* Chicago: Sing with Me, 1995. Compact disc.
>   Includes the Russian folk song "Tumbalalaika."

Scott, Anne. *The Laughing Baby: Remembering Nursery Rhymes and Reasons.* South Hadley, MA: Bergin & Garvey, 1987. (116 pages)
>   Includes the fingerplays and action rhymes "Bliny" (Pat-a-Cake), "Edu-Edu" (Here I Go), "Zalika Belen kii sidit" (Little White Rabbit Sits), "Pal chik-mal chik" (Little Boy-Finger).

Stewart, Georgiana. "Trepak" (Nutcracker Suite). In *Multicultural Rhythm Stick Fun.* Long Branch, NJ: Kimbo Educational, 1992. Audiocassette.
>   Children tap rhythm sticks (or clap hands) and move side-to-side to the beat of this song.

————. "A Visit to My Friend." In *Children of the World: Multicultural Rhythmic Activities.* Long Branch, NJ: Kimbo Educational, 1991. Audiocassette.
>   Children move in a circle while they clap, wave, and hop to this song. The lyrics tell of visiting friends in Mexico, Russia, and Greece.

Warren, Jean, and Elizabeth McKinnon. *Small World Celebrations.* Illustrated by Marion Hopping Ekberg. Everett, WA: Warren, 1988. (157 pages)
>   "Dancing Bears," "Troika, Troika," and "Dance, Little Snow Girl" are a few of the songs and action rhymes included in the chapter about Russia.

Weissman, Jackie. "Sasha and Natasha." In *Joining Hands with Other Lands: Multicultural Songs and Games.* Long Branch, NJ: Kimbo Educational, 1993. Audiocassette.
>   "Sasha and Natasha" inspires movement—have children clap their hands and stomp. This song is played on the balalaika, a popular stringed instrument in Russia.

Media Choices

Show a video or filmstrip as a transition between storytelling activities and crafts. This gives children an opportunity to rest quietly for a few minutes.

Ginsburg, Mira. *Mushroom in the Rain.* 7 min. Weston, CT: Weston Woods, 1989. Filmstrip with audiocassette.
>   An old Russian folktale about a group of animals who are not always friendly to each other but manage to fit themselves together under a mushroom while waiting out a rainstorm.

Polacco, Patricia. *The Keeping Quilt.* 11 min. Columbus, OH: Varsity Reading Services, 1993. Videocassette.
>   Author Patricia Polacco narrates a story about the "Keeping Quilt," a story about how the author's immigrant family arrived and settled in New York City.

————. *Rechenka's Eggs.* 11 min. New Rochelle, NY: Spoken Arts, 1991. Videocassette.
>   Old Babushka (Grandmother), preparing her colored eggs for the Easter Festival, helps an injured goose, who later repays her kindness in an extraordinary way.

————. *Thunder Cake.* 13 min. New Rochelle, NY: Spoken Arts, 1990. Videocassette.
>   A grandmother helps her granddaughter overcome her fear of thunderstorms.

Prokofiev, Sergei. *Peter and the Wolf.* Illustrated by Charles Mikolaycak. 7 min. Ancramdale, NY: Live Oak Media, 1982. Filmstrip with audiocassette.
    The story of a young boy who sets out to play in the forest, accompanied by a bird, a duck, and a cat. Peter captures a wolf and displays him in the local zoo.

Crafts and Other Activities

Choose a craft suited for the age level of the group and the time allotted for the story time.

Matroshka Dolls (Stacking Dolls)

Begin this craft project by introducing author and illustrator Patricia Polacco. Patricia Polacco was born to parents of Russian heritage; many of her stories reflect this heritage and convey Russian traditions. Show or read one of the following works by Polacco: *Babushka's Doll* or the poem "Matroishka" in *Babushka's Mother Goose* (see "Books to Read Aloud"). Matroshka (MAH-trohsh-kah) dolls—a sequence of brightly colored wooden dolls that fit inside of one another—are a favorite toy of Russian children. Some matroshka dolls have as many as 20 dolls, the tiniest one being a wooden bead with eyes.

In this craft project, children will each make a set of matroshka dolls. For younger children, adapt this craft project as a coloring activity: Photocopy the largest doll (fig. 5.10) and have children create their own designs.

Supplies

White tagboard paper (vellum-bristol cover) or construction paper
Colored markers, colored pencils, or crayons
Stapler or clear tape
Scissors

Photocopy figures 5.10–5.18 on white tagboard paper. The children color the dolls using markers, colored pencils, or crayons. Suggested colors: scarf—orange; hair—yellow; cheeks—pink; eyes—blue; mouth—red; flower petals—red; flower center—yellow; leaves—green; dress—blue. Cut out the dolls and the pockets. With help from an adult, children staple the pockets onto the backs of the dolls, matching sizes (have younger children use clear tape). Staple as close to the edges as possible so the dolls will fit inside the pockets.

Decorated Paper Eggs

Decorated Easter Eggs are created by pysanky, a beautiful form of folk art. A pysanky egg is created using a kistka (a small tool), a lighted candle, shavings of beeswax, and several brilliant dyes. Pysanky eggs may take several hours to complete and have several layers of wax and dyes.

To introduce this craft project, have available a basket of colored eggs to show children. Share the story *Rechenka's Eggs* by Patricia Polacco (see "Books to Read Aloud") and discuss the eggs that Babushka painted for the Easter Festival in Moskava (Moscow). Have available samples of eggs that have been "blown" to show children how fragile they are (blown eggs have small holes at each end, through which the whites and yolks have been blown out).

There are many books available that show full-color photographs of beautifully decorated eggs from many countries; for example, *Decorative Eggs* by Candace Ord Manroe (New York: Crescent Books, 1992). Share the photographs with children, as well as information about Fabergé Eggs (Karl Fabergé was the jeweler to the Imperial Family of prerevolutionary Russia and created beautiful, jeweled eggs).

Fig. 5.10. Matroshka Doll A.

From *Travel the Globe*. © 1998. Desiree Lorraine Webber, et al. Libraries Unlimited. (800) 237-6124.

Fig. 5.11. Matroshka Doll B.

Fig. 5.12. Matroshka Doll C.

Fig. 5.13. Matroshka Doll D. Fig. 5.14. Matroshka Doll E. Fig. 5.15. Pocket A.

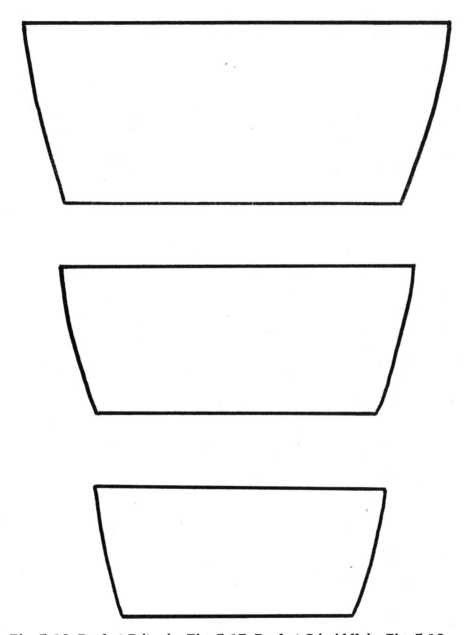

Fig. 5.16. Pocket B (top). Fig. 5.17. Pocket C (middle). Fig. 5.18. Pocket D (bottom).

Supplies

Crayons or brightly colored markers
White tagboard or construction paper
Scissors
White glue

Photocopy figure 5.20 on white tagboard or construction paper. The designs and colors of decorated pysanky eggs are based on symbols. Divide the egg into geometric shapes (see fig. 5.19), and then decorate with borders and designs (see fig. 5.21). Before coloring the eggs, refer to the "Symbols" list on page 82, which notes the meanings for symbols and colors. Encourage children to create original borders and designs. For younger children, simplify this activity by having them glue pieces of fabric and yarn, sequins, and rickrack to their eggs.

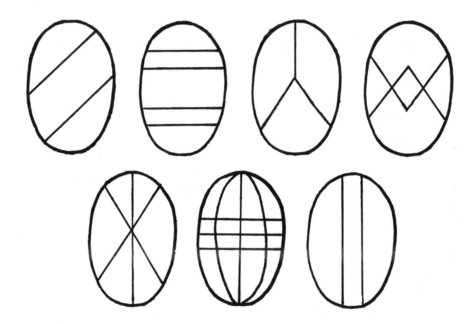

Fig. 5.19. Pysanky Egg Geometric Designs Examples.

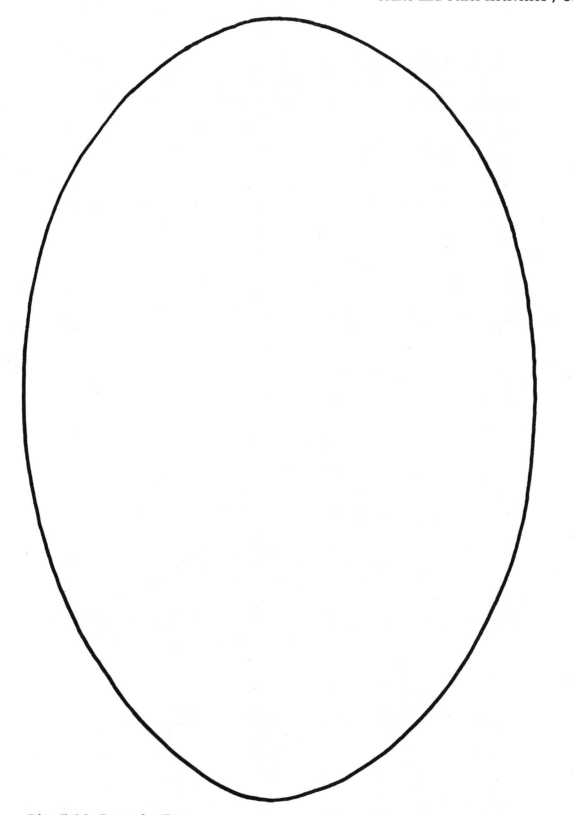

Fig. 5.20. Pysanky Egg.

Symbols

Animal: Prosperity; wealth
Bee: Hard work; pleasantness
Bird: Fulfillment of wishes; protection; a good harvest
Flower: Beauty; children; wisdom; love; charity; goodwill
Fruit: Knowledge; health; wisdom; a good life
Spider: Good fortune
Star: Success
Sun: Growth; good fortune
Tree: Long life; good health; strength; youthfulness
Water: Health
Waves and ribbons: Closed circle around the egg symbolizes eternity
Wheat: Bountiful harvest

Colors

Blue: Good health; sky; air
Brown: Prosperity
Green: Hope; wealth; happiness
Orange: Power; endurance
Pink: Success
Purple: Faith; trust
Red: Love; happiness; hope; life
White: Purity
Yellow: Spirituality; wisdom

Fig. 5.21. Pysanky Egg Symbols, Patterns, and Borders Examples.

Russian Ballet

Russia takes special pride in the ballet, and many Russian cities have their own ballet troupes. Share with children Kate Castle's book *Ballet* (see "Sources for Crafts and Other Activities"). Invite someone from the community to demonstrate for children the basic ballet movements. Ask the dancers to wear their ballet costumes. After the presentation, play Russian ballet music; for example, Peter Tchaikovsky's "Swan Lake," "The Sleeping Beauty," or "The Nutcracker." Invite children to dance on their tiptoes, moving their arms and bodies gracefully to the music.

Sources for Crafts Ideas and Activities

Castle, Kate. *Ballet.* New York: Kingfisher, 1996. (32 pages)
  A history of the ballet, including costumes and performers.

Cole, Ann, et al. *Children Are Children Are Children: An Activity Approach to Exploring Brazil, France, Iran, Japan, Nigeria, and the U.S.S.R.* Illustrated by Lois Axeman. Boston: Little, Brown, 1978. (page 187)
  Includes craft activities for New Year's Day, May Day, and Easter celebrations in Russia, along with recipes, pysanky egg decorating, and directions for creating a miniature circus.

Franco, Betsy. *Russia: A Literature-Based Multicultural Unit.* Illustrated by Jo Supancich. Monterey, CA: Evan-Moor, 1993. (48 pages)
  Craft activities include decorating onion domes, designing a cathedral, and making matroshka dolls. Also included are instructions for growing a vegetable garden, plus the recipe "Bliny" (Russian pancakes), which are eaten in celebration of "Maslinitsa." Maslinitsa is a celebration that marks the end of winter and the beginning of spring.

Gomez, Aurelia. *Crafts of Many Cultures: 30 Authentic Craft Projects from Around the World.* New York: Scholastic, 1992. (pages 96–97)
  Includes instructions for making flax dolls, a popular craft from western Russia.

Tuma-Church, Deb. *The Storytime Handbook.* Lincoln, NE: Media, 1988. (pages 52–53)
  Includes gardening activities for extending the story "The Turnip" (see "Puppet Presentation"), instructions for planting a miniature garden in egg cartons, and the songs "Farmer's Garden" and "Dig a Little Hole."

Let's Visit

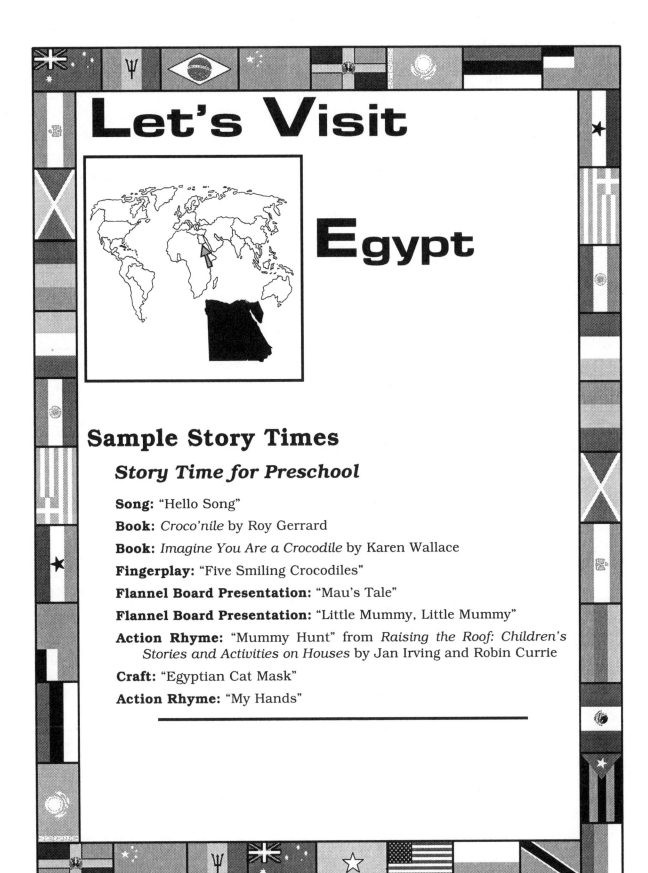

Egypt

Sample Story Times

Story Time for Preschool

Song: "Hello Song"

Book: *Croco'nile* by Roy Gerrard

Book: *Imagine You Are a Crocodile* by Karen Wallace

Fingerplay: "Five Smiling Crocodiles"

Flannel Board Presentation: "Mau's Tale"

Flannel Board Presentation: "Little Mummy, Little Mummy"

Action Rhyme: "Mummy Hunt" from *Raising the Roof: Children's Stories and Activities on Houses* by Jan Irving and Robin Currie

Craft: "Egyptian Cat Mask"

Action Rhyme: "My Hands"

Story Time for Kindergarten Through Third Grade

Song: "Hello Song"

Book: *The Egyptian Cinderella* by Shirley Climo

Book: *Croco'nile* by Roy Gerrard

Action Rhyme: "Mummy Hunt" from *Raising the Roof: Children's Stories and Activities on Houses* by Jan Irving and Robin Curry

Book: *The Egyptian Polar Bear* by JoAnn Adinolfi

Flannel Board Presentation: "Mau's Tale"

Filmstrip: *Pyramid* by David Macaulay

Craft: "Paper Pyramid" or "Egyptian Cat Mask"

Action Rhyme: "My Hands"

Begin the story time with the "Hello Song." Then sing the song again, substituting the word *hello* with the Egyptian (Arabic) greeting أهلا *Ahalan* [A-hal-an]. (See p. xxvii for "Hello Song" music.)

Hello Song

Hello ev'rybody,
And how are you? How are you?
Hello ev'rybody,
And how are you today?

A-hal-an ev'rybody,
And how are you? How are you?
A-hal-an ev'rybody,
And how are you today?

End the story time with the "My Hands" action rhyme, substituting the words *thank you* with the Egyptian (Arabic) word شكراً *shokran* [SHOK-ran], and *goodbye* with مع السلامة *Ma'a ElSalama* [MAE-aes-sae-LAE-mae]. Have children stand up and follow the actions in the rhyme.

My Hands

My hands say SHOK-ran. *(hold up hands)*
With a clap, clap, clap. *(clap hands)*
My feet say SHOK-ran. *(point to feet)*
With a tap, tap, tap. *(stamp or tap feet)*
Clap! Clap! Clap! *(clap hands)*
Tap! Tap! Tap! *(stamp or tap feet)*
Turn myself around and bow. *(turn and bow)*
MAE-aes-sae-LAE-mae. *(wave goodbye)*

Books to Read Aloud

Adinolfi, JoAnn. *The Egyptian Polar Bear*. Boston: Houghton Mifflin, 1994. (32 pages)
Egypt's boy king Rahotep has a very unusual pet, a polar bear, who arrives in Egypt on an iceberg.

Aliki. *Mummies Made in Egypt*. New York: HarperCollins, 1979. (32 pages)
Explains why the ancient Egyptians made mummies and describes the process and technique. Recommended for school-age children.

Clements, Andrew. *Temple Cat*. Illustrated by Kate Kiesler. New York: Clarion Books, 1996. (32 pages)
A temple cat, tired of being pampered and worshipped, finds the love and affection he is seeking from a fisherman's family.

Climo, Shirley. *The Egyptian Cinderella*. Illustrated by Ruth Heller. New York: HarperCollins, 1989. (32 pages)
In this Egyptian version of Cinderella, Rhodopis, a slave girl, is chosen to be queen by the Pharaoh. Recommended for school-age children.

dePaola, Tomie. *Bill and Pete Go down the Nile*. New York: G. P. Putnam's Sons, 1987. (32 pages)
While on a class trip to a Cairo museum, Little William Crocodile and his friend Pete, his toothbrush, are involved in mystery.

Gerrard, Roy. *Croco'nile*. New York: Farrar, Straus & Giroux, 1994. (32 pages)
Set sail for adventure with Hamut and his sister, Nekatu, as they stow away on a sailboat, paint a pyramid, and win the favor of a pharaoh.

Grant, Joan. *The Monster That Grew Small*. Illustrated by Jill Karla Schwarz. New York: Lothrop, Lee & Shepard, 1987. (32 pages)
In this Egyptian folktale, a young boy finds courage to save the people in his village as he faces a monster that becomes smaller when confronted.

Greger, C. Shana. *Cry of the Benu Bird: An Egyptian Creation Story*. New York: Houghton Mifflin, 1996. (32 pages)
A beautiful creation story in which Nun brings forth Benu, a magnificent glowing bird, and the other creatures of the sky and earth. Recommended for school-age children.

Haskins, Jim. *Count Your Way Through the Arab World*. Rev. ed. Illustrated by Dana Gustafson. Minneapolis, MN: Carolrhoda Books, 1990. (24 pages)
The author uses the Egyptian dialect, a form of Arabic, to present the numbers 1 through 10, alongside information about the Arab world.

Heide, Florence Parry, and Judith Heide Gilliland. *The Day of Ahmed's Secret*. Illustrated by Ted Lewin. New York: Lothrop, Lee & Shepard, 1990. (30 pages)
Ahmed (AK-med) has a secret that he intends to tell his family on his birthday.

Mike, Jan M. *Gift of the Nile: An Ancient Egyptian Legend*. Illustrated by Charles Reasoner. Legends of the World series. [N.p.]: Troll, 1993. (32 pages)
When the Pharaoh challenges Mutemwia's love for him, she proves that her love is a gift of the heart by returning to him after being set free.

Milton, Nancy. *The Giraffe That Walked to Paris*. Illustrated by Roger Roth. New York: Crown, 1992. (32 pages)
Recounts the true story of how the first giraffe came to Europe as a gift from the Pasha of Egypt to the King of France in 1826. Recommended for school-age children.

Sabuda, Robert. *Tutankhamen's Gift.* New York: Atheneum Books for Young Readers, 1994. (32 pages)

> Tutankhamen became Pharaoh at age 10. He rebuilt the temples and was loved and respected by the people. Have children try to find his sacred cats in each illustration.

Wynne-Jones, Tim. *Zoom Upstream.* Illustrated by Eric Beddows. New York: HarperCollins, 1992. (32 pages)

> Maria and her friend Zoom, a cat, embark on a mysterious adventure to Egypt in search for her Uncle Roy. This is the final adventure in the Zoom trilogy.

Storytelling

Flannel Board Presentation

> *"Mau's Tale." Cats were first domesticated in Egypt and held a special place in Egyptian worship. They were sacred because they were associated with the Cat Goddess, Bastet. Bastet was the Goddess of Joy who loved music and dance. She had a pretty Egyptian cat's head with a narrow snout and large pointed ears. Many families, rich or poor, owned a cat. Even the Pharaoh had a pet cat.*
>
> *Share this story and discover many interesting facts about Egyptian cats. See figures 6.1–6.6 for patterns. Trace the patterns on felt, or photocopy and color them. If photocopying, glue small squares of felt to the backs of the paper figures so they will hold to the flannel board. Place the figures on the flannel board as they are introduced in the story.*

Mau's Tale
by Donna Norvell

Mau was a yellow-striped tabby kitten who lived with her mother, a brother, and a sister. *(place the mother cat with kittens on the flannel board)* One day when Mau and her family were asleep in their warm cozy basket, Mau began to dream. She was a sleek Egyptian cat. She dreamed of the exciting and strange story their mother had just told them. There were pyramids, palm trees, and pharaohs. *(take basket off and place Mau on the flannel board)*

Suddenly, Mau opened her eyes, there was sand all around, and so many strange smells. What were those large stone buildings she could see in the distance? Then she knew: She was in that far away place called Egypt that her mother had described to them. It was the home of her ancestor cats many, many years ago; in fact, about 3,500 years ago. It was in Egypt that people first made pets of cats. Cats were greatly admired by the Egyptians because they were great hunters and protected the grain storages from rats and mice.

Mau remembered her mother saying that many of her ancestors once lived in a city called Bubastis along a large river called the Nile. These cats lived with families in palaces, homes, and huts. *(place the temple on the flannel board)* At the center of the city was a grand temple where the statue of Bastet was kept. *(place the statue of Bastet on the flannel board)* Bastet was the Cat Goddess.

Then Mau heard music. She could see boats floating down the Nile, and there were people dancing, clapping their hands, and beating on drums and singing. It was the Spring Festival in honor of Bastet. *(place the Egyptian woman on the flannel board)* The Egyptian women wore glittering jewelry and lined their eyes with black makeup, like cats' eyes.

Mau's mother also told her that all cats were sacred in ancient Egypt. If a house was on fire, the cats were the first to be saved. Killing a cat was punishable by death. And it was forbidden to take cats out of Egypt. The Romans and the Greeks smuggled them out, though, and that is why cats are found all over the world today.

As Mau was prowling through the streets, she saw another strange sight: A small boy and his mother and father were crying. Their family cat had died, and they had shaved off their eyebrows out of respect and grief. They proceeded to prepare their cat for a special burial, so he would be ready for his life in the next world. They wrapped him tightly in pieces of cloth, mummifying him. *(place the cat mummy on the flannel board)* They also caught mice and mummified them so the mummy cat would have food. Mau thought this was all rather strange, but interesting. However, thinking of mice was making Mau hungry.

What was this new smell? Could it be? Kitty Chow, here in Egypt? Then Mau yawned and stretched. She woke up and realized she was in the basket with her family at home. *(remove all pieces from flannel board and place the mother cat with kittens on the flannel board)* There was her mother, her brother, and her sister, but where did Egypt go? Across the ocean—far, far away.

Source for Flannel Board Presentations

MacDonald, Margaret Read. "The Biyera Well." In *Look Back and See: Twenty Lively Tales for Gentle Tellers.* Illustrated by Roxane Murphy. New York: H. W. Wilson, 1991. (pages 90–93)

Three animals, a donkey, a goat, and a dog, become partners who decide to plant a field of clover. When the clover disappears, the three animals are put to a test! Children can participate in the story in several places. No patterns are included with this story, but the animals are common, and patterns can be found in many books with flannel board patterns (coloring books are also a good resource for patterns).

Fig. 6.1. Cat Mummy. Fig. 6.2. Bastet, Cat Goddess. Fig. 6.3. Egyptian Woman (top).

Fig. 6.4. Mau. Fig. 6.5. Mother Cat with Kittens.

Fig. 6.6. Bubastis Temple.

From *Travel the Globe.* © 1998. Desiree Lorraine Webber, et al. Libraries Unlimited. (800) 237-6124.

Fingerplays, Songs, Action Rhymes, and Games

Flannel Board Presentation

"Little Mummy, Little Mummy." Preschool children will enjoy this flannel board guessing game with a repeating rhyme. Use figures 6.7 and 6.8 to make the figures for this game. Trace the patterns on felt, or photocopy and color them. If photocopying, glue small squares of felt to the backs of the paper figures so they will hold to the flannel board. Make five pyramids, each a different color: red, yellow, orange, blue, and green.

Little Mummy, Little Mummy
by Desiree Webber and Sandy Shropshire

To play this game, the storyteller will place all the pyramids on the flannel board, hiding the cat mummy behind one of them. Do not let the children see where the mummy is placed. Have the children say the following rhyme and the storyteller will remove each colored pyramid from the flannel board. Repeat the process until the Little Mummy is found.

Little Mummy, Little Mummy are you hid
Underneath the (red, yellow, orange, blue, green) pyramid?

Fingerplay

"Five Smiling Crocodiles." The landscape of ancient Egypt was created by the Nile River, the longest river in the world. Once a year, after torrential rainstorms, the river overflowed its banks. This was a blessing for the people of Egypt because they could plant their crops in the rich soil left by the fertile river mud. Of all the wildlife found along the Nile, the crocodile was the most feared.

The crocodile was the symbol for the ancient Egyptian god Sebek. In the city Crocodopolis, one of the duties of the priests was to keep a live crocodile fat and healthy. After it died, it was mummified and placed into a special tomb. (See books about crocodiles at the end of this fingerplay, which might be used to supplement the fingerplay that follows.)

Photocopy one set of five crocodile finger puppets (fig. 6.9) and four sets of ten fish finger puppets (fig. 6.10) on white tagboard or construction paper. Use markers to color the crocodiles green; color the sets of fish red, blue, orange, and green. Cut out the crocodiles and fish and tape or glue each to a finger attachment (make six copies of fig. 6.11). Tape together the three flaps of each finger attachment. This will fit over the tip of each finger like a thimble.

Choose four children to help perform this fingerplay. Give each child a set of fish. As each color is introduced in the fingerplay, have the child with that color of fish approach the storyteller and make the fish swim around the crocodiles (the child will have a fish puppet on each finger of both hands; the storyteller will have a crocodile puppet on each finger of one hand). As each crocodile swims away, remove a finger puppet. Have all children participate when the crocodiles grunt, hiss, growl, and roar.

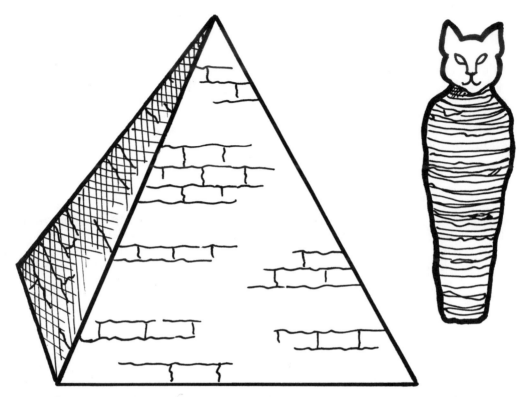

Fig. 6.7. Pyramid. Fig. 6.8. Cat Mummy.

Five Smiling Crocodiles
by Donna Norvell

Five little crocodiles,
Floating down the Nile.
Each of them had a great big smile.
GRUNT! HISSSS! GROWL! ROAR!
They were enjoying their play that sunshiny day,
When a large school of red fish swam their way.
One little crocodile forgot about play . . .
Something yummy in his tummy was his wish,
As he swam away after the red fish.

Four little crocodiles,
Floating down the Nile.
Each of them had a great big smile.
GRUNT! HISSSS! GROWL! ROAR!
They were enjoying their play that sunshiny day,
When a large school of blue fish swam their way.
One little crocodile forgot about play . . .
Something yummy in his tummy was his wish,
As he swam away after the blue fish.

Three little crocodiles,
Floating down the Nile.
Each of them had a great big smile.
GRUNT! HISSSS! GROWL! ROAR!
They were enjoying their play that sunshiny day,
When a large school of orange fish swam their way.
One little crocodile forgot about play . . .
Something yummy in his tummy was his wish,
As he swam away after the orange fish.

Two little crocodiles,
Floating down the Nile.
Each of them had a great big smile.
GRUNT! HISSSS! GROWL! ROAR!
They were enjoying their play that sunshiny day,
When a large school of green fish swam their way.
One little crocodile forgot about play . . .
Something yummy in his tummy was his wish,
As he swam away after the green fish.

One little crocodile,
Floating down the Nile.
He no longer had a great big smile.
His friends were gone and so were the fish,
So he swam back home with a swish, swish, swish.

Fig. 6.9. Crocodile Finger Puppets.

Fig. 6.10. Fish Finger Puppets.

From *Travel the Globe.* © 1998. Desiree Lorraine Webber, et al. Libraries Unlimited. (800) 237-6124.

Fig. 6.11. Finger Puppet Attachments.

From *Travel the Globe.* © 1998. Desiree Lorraine Webber, et al. Libraries Unlimited. (800) 237-6124.

Books About Crocodiles

Hogan, Paula Z. *The Crocodile.* Illustrated by Larry Mikec. Milwaukee, WI: Raintree
  Childrens Books, 1979. (32 pages)
  Discover how crocodiles live in this lively picture book.

Petty, Kate. *Crocodiles and Alligators.* Illustrated by Karen Johnson. New York: Franklin
  Watts, 1985. (30 pages)
  An informative book with a simple text about crocodiles and their relative, the
  alligator.

Tibbitts, Alison, and Alan Roocroft. *Crocodiles.* Animals, Animals, Animals series. Mankato,
  MN: Capstone Press, 1992. (32 pages)
  A simple discussion of crocodiles—what they look like, their size, their teeth, and
  how they raise their babies.

Wallace, Karen. *Imagine You Are a Crocodile.* Illustrated by Mike Bostock. New York: Henry
  Holt, 1996. (26 pages)
  What would it be like if you were a mother crocodile?

The Mummy Wrap Game

Have children pair off and then give each pair several rolls of toilet tissue paper. One
child stands straight with their arms by their sides and acts as the mummy. The other
child does the wrapping. Time the pairs: Who can wrap their mummy the quickest?

Irving, Jan, and Robin Currie. "Mummy Hunt." In *Raising the Roof: Children's Stories
  and Activities on Houses.* Englewood, CO: Teacher Ideas Press, 1991. (65 pages)
  Reprinted by permission of the author.

Mummy Hunt
by Jan Irving and Robin Currie

We're going on a mummy hunt.
We're going to swish through the sand. *(rub hands together)*
Swish, swish, swish.
Here we are at the pyramid.
Open the creaking door. *(move arm as if opening the door)*
Eeeeeek.
Look, there's writing on the walls. *(point)*
It's hieroglyphics—it says, "Walk this way."
Let's tiptoe. *(tiptoe in place)*
Shhhhh, shhhhh. *(put index finger to lips)*
Here is the inner chamber and . . .
King Tut!
He's having a party.
Let's dance! *(dance Egyptian-style)*
Time to go.
Better tiptoe out so they don't miss us. *(tiptoe)*
Read the hieroglyphics. *(point)*
It says "This way out."
Open the door.
Eeeek. *(move arm as if opening the door)*
And slam it shut.

Bang. *(clap)*
Back through the swishing sand. *(rub hands together)*
And back to our home.
Brush the sand out of your clothes. *(brush self)*
Do you remember how to dance like King Tut? *(dance as before)*

King Tut Dance

Martin, Steve. "King Tut." In *Kids Wanna Rock.* Oklahoma City: Melody House, 1996.
Compact disc.
A humorous song with a catchy tune for dancing.

Play this song after the action rhyme "Mummy Hunt" (above) and have children dance Egyptian-style. Or, play the song after the craft "Egyptian Cat Masks" (see "Crafts and Other Activities") and have children dance while holding their cat masks to their faces.

Media Choices

Show a video or filmstrip as a transition between storytelling activities and crafts. This gives children an opportunity to rest quietly for a few minutes.

Desert. Narrated by Martin Sheen. Eyewitness series. 35 min. [N.p.]: Dorling Kindersley and BBC Worldwide Americas, 1996. Videocassette.
Includes sections about the pyramids of Egypt. Selected sections can be used with preschoolers.

Macaulay, David. *Pyramid.* 27 min. Verdugo City, CA: Pied Piper, 1984. Filmstrip and audiocassette.
The filmstrip follows the steps of building a pyramid for an imagined Pharaoh of ancient Egypt. Selected sections can be used with preschoolers.

Crafts and Other Activities

Choose a craft suited for the age level of the group and the time allotted for the story time.

Egyptian Cat Mask

The children will enjoy making masks that look like "Bastet," the Egyptian Cat Goddess of Joy who loved music and dancing. After making the masks have them dance to Egyptian music, such as "King Tut." (See Fingerplays, Songs, Action Rhymes, and Games.)

Supplies

Yellow posterboard	Craft sticks
Orange construction paper	Clear tape
Black construction paper	Scissors
Hot-glue gun and glue sticks	Pencils
Black and orange markers	Hole punch

See figures 6.12–6.14 for patterns (enlarge the cat mask pattern and accompanying pieces, 20 percent if desired).

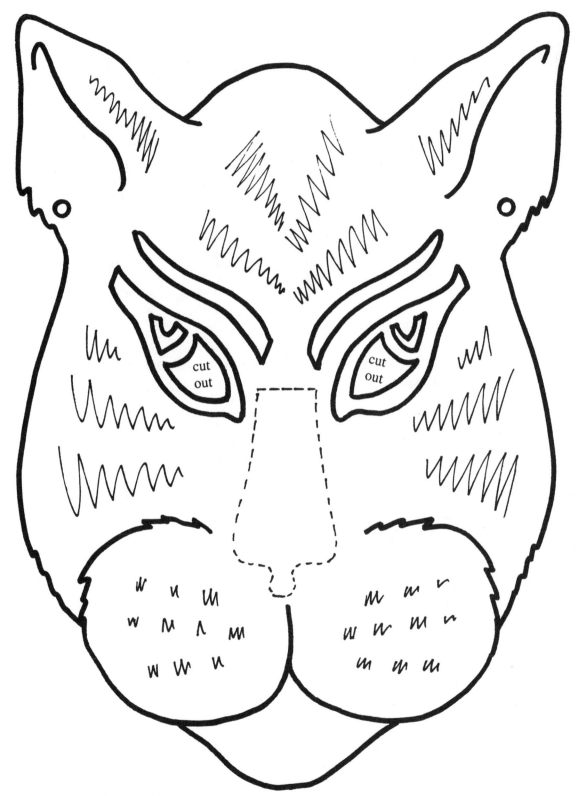

cut
out

cut
out

Fig. 6.12. Cat Mask.

From *Travel the Globe.* © 1998. Desiree Lorraine Webber, et al. Libraries Unlimited. (800) 237-6124.

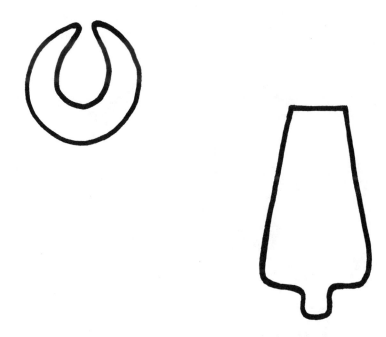

Fig. 6.13. Cat Mask Earring (left). Fig. 6.14. Cat Mask Nose (right).

Using yellow posterboard, trace and cut out the cat mask (for younger children, pre-cut the mask and eye holes). An adult should hot glue (or tape) a craft stick to the back of the mask. Using orange construction paper, trace and cut out the nose and earrings (pre-cut for younger children). Glue the nose into place. To make whiskers, glue 4-by-¼-inch strips of black construction paper to the face, beside the nose. Curl the ends if desired. Using a black marker, color the eyebrows and bold lines around the eyes. Using an orange marker, color the wavy "tabby cat" stripes. Punch a hole in each ear, where indicated, using a hole punch. Insert the earrings into the holes and attach them behind the ears with tape.

Paper Pyramid

Some of the oldest stone buildings in the world are the great pyramids of Egypt. The Pharaohs had the pyramids built to serve as their tombs after they died. The pyramids are so colossal because they had to hold all the pharaoh's treasures, which were to be with him in his next life. It took up to 20 years to build one pyramid. The largest pyramid, the Great Pyramid of Giza, the tomb of Pharaoh Cheops, is 40 stories high.

In this craft project, children make a pyramid using a piece of posterboard.

Supplies

Light-brown or tan posterboard or tagboard
Clear tape
Scissors
Fine-tipped colored markers

Use figure 6.15 as a pattern for the pyramid. On light-brown or tan tagboard, photocopy and cut out a pyramid for each child. Have children refer to the sample hieroglyphs in figure 6.15 and draw brightly colored designs on the sides of their pyramids. Fold the triangular sides upward to form a pyramid and tape them into place.

Sources for Craft Ideas and Activities

Der Manuelian, Peter. *Hieroglyphs from A to Z: A Rhyming Book with Egyptian Stencils for Kids.* New York: Scholastic, 1991. (43 pages)
Information from A to Z about the Egyptian culture, including a set of stencils to use for making ancient Egyptian hieroglyphs. The letter C is for the Egyptian cat. It also has the Egyptian symbol for C and shows how to spell cat in hieroglyphs.

Hamilton, Robyn. *Ancient Egypt Activity Book.* Illustrated by Barb Lorseyedi. Dana Point, CA: Edupress, 1994. (48 pages)
Hieroglyph patterns, a Nile crocodile pattern, instructions for making papyrus, and instructions for making Egyptian wigs are just a few of the activities found in this excellent resource.

Newbold, Patt, and Anne Diebel. *Paper Hat Tricks IV: A Big Book of Hat Patterns.* Northville, MI: Paper Hat Tricks, 1992. (page 11)
Includes a pattern for an Egyptian hat.

Terzian, Alexandra M. *The Kids' Multicultural Art Book: Art and Craft Experiences from Around the World.* Kids Can! series. Charlotte, VT: Williamson, 1993. (pages 90–91)
Includes instructions for making Egyptian paper beads.

Thomson, Ruth. *The Egyptians.* Illustrated by Cilla Eurich and Ruth Levy. Footsteps in Time series. Chicago: Childrens Press, 1995. (24 pages)
Includes instructions and patterns for making a collar necklace and a scarab amulet.

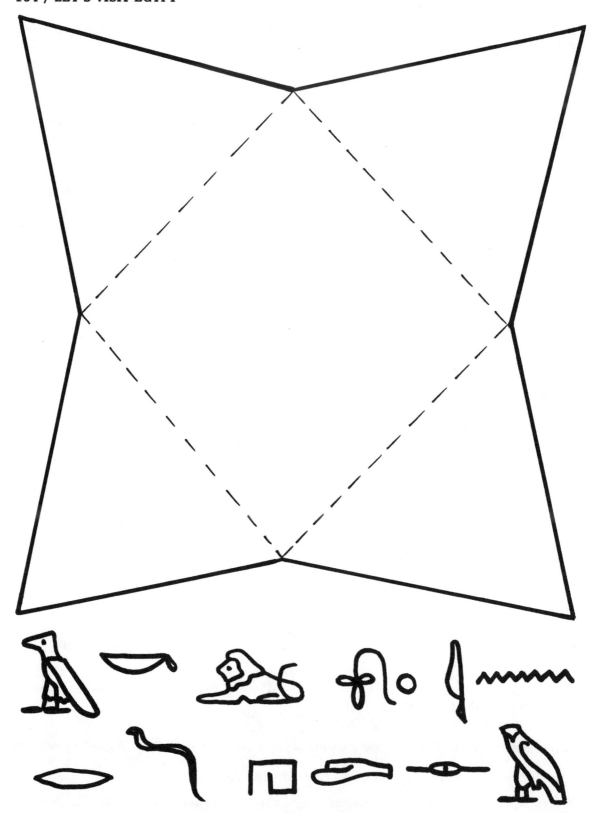

Fig. 6.15. Paper Pyramid and Hieroglyphic Examples.

Let's Visit

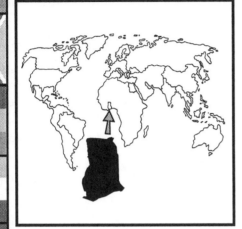

Ghana

Sample Story Times

Story Time for Preschool

Song: "Hello Song"

Book: *Kente Colors* by Debbi Chocolate

Flannel Board Presentation: "The Leopard's Drum" from Teeny-Tiny Folktales comp. by Jean Warren

Song: "The Eensy Weensy Anansi"

Book: *Anansi and the Talking Melon* by Eric A. Kimmel

Oral Story: "Why Hare Is Always on the Run" from *Tales Alive! Ten Multicultural Folktales with Activities* by Susan Milord

Song: "Anansi" from *The Corner Grocery Store, and Other Singable Songs* by Raffi

Flannel Board Presentation: "How Jerboa Tricked Lion"

Video: *Anansi and the Moss-Covered Rock* by Eric A. Kimmel

Craft: "Atumpan (Talking Drum)"

Action Rhyme: "My Hands"

Story Time for Kindergarten Through Third Grade

Song: "Hello Song"

Book: *Oh, Kojo! How Could You! An Ashanti Tale* by Verna Aardema

Flannel Board Presentation: "Anansi and the Rock" from *Multicultural Folktales: Stories to Tell Young Children* by Judy Sierra and Robert Kaminski

Action Rhyme: "Mama, Put Your Headcloth On" from *Jaha and Jamil Went down the Hill: An African Mother Goose* by Virginia Kroll

Book: *The Leopard's Drum* by Jessica Souhami

Oral Story: "How Anansi Got the Stories" from *Joining In: An Anthology of Audience Participation Stories and How to Tell Them* by Barbara Reed

Song: "Anansi" from *The Corner Grocery Store, and Other Singable Songs* by Raffi

Flannel Board Presentation: "How Jerboa Tricked Lion"

Filmstrip: *A Story, A Story* by Gail E. Haley

Craft: "Royal Ashanti Crown and Ring"

Action Rhyme: "My Hands"

Begin the story time with the "Hello Song." Then sing the song again, substituting the word *hello* with the Twi greeting *a kwaaba* [a-QUAH-bah]. (See p. xxvii for "Hello Song" music.)

Hello Song

Hello ev'rybody,
And how are you? How are you?
Hello ev'rybody,
And how are you today?

a-QUAH-bah ev'rybody,
And how are you? How are you?
a-QUAH-bah ev'rybody,
And how are you today?

End the story time with the "My Hands" action rhyme, substituting the words *thank you* with the Twi word *meda ase* [may-DAH-say], and *goodbye* with *nantew yiye* [nan-tee yee-yah]. Have children stand up and follow the actions in the rhyme.

My Hands

My hands say may-DAH-say. *(hold up hands)*
With a clap, clap, clap. *(clap hands)*
My feet say may-DAH-say. *(point to feet)*
With a tap, tap, tap. *(stamp or tap feet)*
Clap! Clap! Clap! *(clap hands)*
Tap! Tap! Tap! *(stamp or tap feet)*
Turn myself around and bow. *(turn and bow)*
nan-tee yee-yah. *(wave goodbye)*

Books to Read Aloud

Aardema, Verna. *Oh, Kojo! How Could You! An Ashanti Tale.* Pictures by Marc Brown. New York: Dial Books for Young Readers, 1984. (32 pages)
Ananse is up to his tricks again: This time he tricks Kojo into giving him his money. In the end, however, Ananse's trick is on himself.

Appiah, Sonia. *Amoko and Efua Bear.* Illustrated by Carol Easmon. New York: Macmillan, 1988. (29 pages)
Amoko lives with her family in Ghana. She has a teddy bear named Efua bear; they do everything together, until one evening when Amoko loses Efua bear.

Chocolate, Debbi. *Kente Colors.* Illustrated by John Ward. New York: Walker, 1996. (32 pages)
A rhyming picture book about the myriad of beautiful colors used in the hand-woven kente cloth made by the Ashanti and Ewe people of Ghana.

Chocolate, Deborah M. Newton. *Spider and the Sky God: An Akan Legend.* Illustrated by Dave Albers. Legends of the World series. [N.p.]: Troll, 1993. (32 pages)
A popular version of how Ananse came to be keeper of all stories, known as "Spider Stories."

———. *Talk, Talk: An Ashanti Legend.* Illustrated by Dave Albers. Legends of the World series. [N.p.]: Troll, 1993. (32 pages)
A humorous story begins when a farmer gathers his yams for market and the yams begin to speak.

Dee, Ruby. *Tower to Heaven.* Illustrated by Jennifer Bent. New York: Henry Holt, 1991. (32 pages)
Yaa spoke with the sky god every day. One day, Yaa pokes the sky god with her pestle one too many times, causing the sky god to go live in the sky. The village decides to build a tower to heaven to speak to him.

Haley, Gail E. *A Story, A Story: An African Tale.* New York: Atheneum, 1970. (34 pages)
In this Caldecott Medal award-winner, Ananse uses tricks to get three things needed for the price of the Sky God's stories.

Kimmel, Eric A. *Anansi and the Talking Melon.* Illustrated by Janet Stevens. New York: Holiday House, 1994. (32 pages)
Anansi the Spider tricks Elephant and the other animals into believing that a melon can talk.

McDermott, Gerald. *Anansi the Spider: A Tale from the Ashanti.* New York: Holt, Rinehart and Winston, 1972. (41 pages)
Anansi has six sons with special gifts, which they each use when Anansi gets into trouble.

Souhami, Jessica. *The Leopard's Drum.* Boston: Little, Brown, 1995. (29 pages)
Nyami, the Sky-God, has offered a big reward to the animal who will bring him the drum of Osebo, the leopard.

Storytelling

Flannel Board Presentation

"How Jerboa Tricked Lion." This is a folktale of the Hausa people in northern Ghana. See figures 7.1–7.5 for patterns. Trace the patterns on felt, or photocopy and color them. If photocopying, glue small pieces of felt to the backs of the paper figures so they will hold to the flannel board. If performing the story for a large group of children, enlarge the patterns 100 percent to make the figures easier to see. Place the figures on the flannel board as they are introduced in the story.

How Jerboa Tricked Lion
retold by Dee Ann Corn

Lion was the most powerful animal in all the land. *(place the lion on the right side of the flannel board)* He was eating all the other animals. So the animals got together to talk about this terrible problem. After much discussion, the animals came up with the best solution they could: They decided to choose one animal at random every day to give to Lion to eat. They hoped this would satisfy him and make him happy. They went to Lion and asked him if he would leave them alone if they brought him one animal every morning for breakfast. Lion agreed.

The first morning, they chose Gazelle and took her to Lion. *(place the gazelle on the flannel board)* Lion did not bother the other animals that day. The next morning, Roan Antelope was chosen and sent to Lion. *(place the roan antelope on the flannel board)* This continued every morning, until it was Jerboa's turn. *(remove the gazelle and the roan antelope from the flannel board)*

Jerboa had an idea. *(place the jerboa on the left side of the flannel board)* He told all the animals he would go to Lion alone. The next day, as the sun came up, Lion waited for Jerboa. But Jerboa stayed in his hole until noon. Lion was getting very impatient and decided to go look for Jerboa because he had missed his breakfast and was getting hungry. He began to walk through the forest, roaring as loud as he could, searching for Jerboa. He was extremely angry.

Jerboa heard Lion roaring a little ways down the road. Jerboa smiled and climbed a tree so he could see Lion. Lion came closer, then closer, and closer still, until he was right beneath Jerboa. *(place the lion beneath the jerboa)*

Jerboa asked, "Why are you roaring so loudly?"

Lion looked up and said, "I waited for you all morning and you never came."

"Well," Jerboa began, "I was on my way to your house with some honey for you to enjoy with your meal when the lion in the well took it."

Lion replied, "Take me to this lion."

Jerboa said, "He was in the well over there when I saw him, and he told me he was much more powerful than you." *(place the well on the flannel board)*

Lion became furious. He walked over to the well and looked in—and there was the lion, staring back at him. *(place the lion next to the well on the flannel board)* Lion didn't know it was his own reflection in the well.

"You are right, Jerboa," said Lion. "There is a lion down in the well. Lion asked the other lion in the well for the honey. But the lion in the well only mimicked him. Lion roared as loud as he could and jumped into the well to attack the lion. *(remove the lion from the flannel board)* That was the last time Lion was ever seen.

Jerboa returned to the animals and told them what had happened, and that they could live in peace once again.

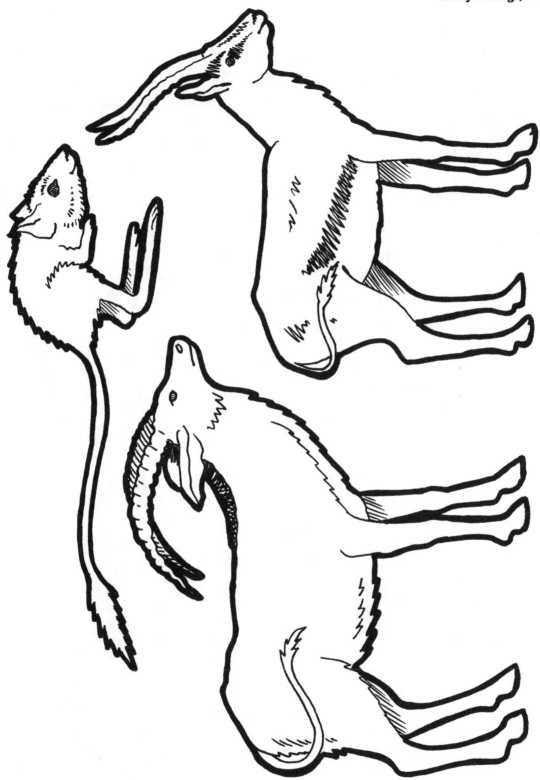

Fig. 7.1. Jerboa (left). Fig. 7.2. Gazelle (right top). Fig. 7.3. Roan Antelope (right bottom).

Fig. 7.4. Lion.   Fig. 7.5. Well.

Sources for Flannel Board Presentations

Sierra, Judy, and Robert Kaminski. "Anansi and the Rock." In *Multicultural Folktales: Stories to Tell Young Children.* Phoenix, AZ: Oryx Press, 1991. (pages 46–48)
Anansi becomes greedy after not having anything to eat. He finds a magical stone that makes millet into flour and decides to take it home for himself.

Warren, Jean, comp. "Leopard's Drum." In *Teeny-Tiny Folktales: Simple Folktales for Young Children Plus Flannelboard Patterns.* Totline Teaching Tales series. Illustrated by Marion Hopping Ekberg. Flannel board patterns by Cora Bunn. Everett, WA: Warren, 1987. (page 33)
The Ruler of the Sky wants Leopard's drum. He asks each animal to get the drum for him; however, all the animals except Turtle are too afraid.

Sources for Oral Stories

Milord, Susan. "Why Hare Is Always on the Run." In *Tales Alive! Ten Multicultural Folktales with Activities.* Illustrated by Michael A. Donato. Charlotte, VT: Williamson, 1995. (pages 47–50)
There is a drought in the land. All the animals, except Hare, come together to solve the problem.

Pellowski, Anne. "The Mosquito." In *The Story Vine: A Source Book of Unusual and Easy-to-Tell Stories from Around the World.* Illustrated by Lynn Sweat. New York: Macmillan, 1984. (pages 5–8)
A short story using string to tell about a woman catching a mosquito.

Reed, Barbara. "How Anansi Got the Stories." In *Joining In: An Anthology of Audience Participation Stories and How to Tell Them.* Compiled by Teresa Miller, with Anne Pellowski. Edited by Norma Livo. Cambridge, MA: Yellow Moon Press, 1988. (pages 75–88)
A popular version of how Anansi receives the stories from Nyamé. Recommended as an audience participation story for school-age children.

Sierra, Judy, and Robert Kaminski. "Why Do Monkeys Live in Trees?" In *Multicultural Folktales: Stories to Tell Young Children.* Phoenix, AZ: Oryx Press, 1991. (pages 111–13)
The bush cat wants the monkey to pay for his trick—and so, to this day, monkeys live in trees.

Fingerplays, Songs, Action Rhymes, and Games

Beat the Drum
(sung to "Row, Row, Row Your Boat")
by Dee Ann Corn

Beat, beat, beat the drum,
Rum, Pum, Pum, Pum, Pum.
Listen to the sounds it makes,
Watch us have some fun.
Play, play, play the drum,
Rum, Pum, Pum, Pum, Pum.
Hear it talk and tell a tale,
Listen everyone.

The Eensy Weensy Anansi (a-NAHN-see)
(sung to "The Eensy Weensy Spider")
(traditional rhyme)
*(substitute the word **spider** with the word **Anansi**)*

Eensy Weensy Anansi
Went up the waterspout. *(move one hand up opposite arm like a spider)*
Down came the rain *(raise hands and drop them while wiggling fingers)*
And washed Anansi out. *(move hands from center outwards)*
Out came the sun *(make a circle with hands above head)*
And dried up all the rain.
And Eensy Weensy Anansi *(move hand up arm again)*
Went up the spout again.

Che Che Koolay

A traditional singing game that children play in Ghana: The players stand in a circle with one person in the middle, who is the leader (or "It"). The leader places his or her hands on his or her head and sings "Che Che Koolay" (a nonsense phrase). The players in the circle follow the leader and repeat the line. The leader sings the next line, with hands on shoulders, and the players in the circle follow and repeat the phrase. The game continues, with hands on hips, hands on knees, and hands on ankles for the last phrase. When the song ends, the leader falls down and the players follow. Then, suddenly, the leader stands up and tags one of the other players before they can stand up (the players cannot stand up before the leader). The person who is tagged becomes the leader. Note: It might be more appropriate for a story time to have children stand in place and follow the leader, without forming a circle and playing tag.

Sources for Fingerplays, Songs, Action Rhymes, and Games

Beall, Pamela Conn, and Susan Hagen Nipp, with Nancy Spence Klein. "Tue Tue." In *Wee Sing Around the World*. Los Angeles: Price Stern Sloan, 1994. Book with audiocassette.
A circle game, including music and directions for playing the game.

Kroll, Virginia. *Jaha and Jamil Went down the Hill: An African Mother Goose*. Illustrated by Katherine Roundtree. Watertown, MA: Charlesbridge, 1995. (32 pages)
A collection of poems about the various countries in Africa, including two poems about Ghana. Each poem corresponds to a Mother Goose rhyme.

Raffi. "Anansi." In *The Corner Grocery Store, and Other Singable Songs*. Universal City, CA: Troubadour Records, 1979. Audiocassette.
Raffi sings this fun song about Anansi, who is half spider and half human.

Sharon, Lois, and Bram. "Che Che Koolay." In *Smorgasbord*. Toronto: Elephant Records, 1980. Audiocassette.
A traditional singing game that children play in Ghana.

Media Choices

Show a video or filmstrip as a transition between storytelling activities and crafts. This gives children an opportunity to rest quietly for a few minutes.

Aardema, Verna. *Oh, Kojo! How Could You!* Illustrated by Marc Brown. 19 min. DeSoto, TX: Random House Video, 1989. Videocassette.
In this adaptation of an Ashanti tale, Anansi attempts to trick Kojo out of his money.

Haley, Gail E. *A Story, A Story.* 10 min. Weston, CT: Weston Woods, 1970. Filmstrip with audiocassette.
A filmstrip based on the Caldecott Medal award-winning book about how stories became know as "Spider Stories."

Kimmel, Eric A. *Anansi and the Moss-Covered Rock.* Illustrated by Janet Stevens. 11 min. Pine Plains, NY: Live Oak Media, 1990. Videocassette.
Anansi, up to his tricks again, tricks all the animals but one using a magical, moss-covered rock.

——. *Anansi Goes Fishing.* Illustrated by Janet Stevens. 12 min. Pine Plains, NY: Live Oak Media, 1992. Videocassette.
Anansi plans to trick Turtle into giving him the fish he catches—but Turtle is not as dumb as Anansi thinks he is.

McDermott, Gerald. *Anansi the Spider.* 10 min. Weston, CT: Weston Woods, 1974. Filmstrip with audiocassette.
Anansi's six sons use their talents to save their father's life.

Crafts and Other Activities

Choose a craft suited for the age level of the group and the time allotted for the story time.

Atumpan (Talking Drum)

Atumpan drumming is one of the oldest traditions in Ghana. Atumpan drums are used in celebrations, ceremonies, and storytelling, as well as for sending messages. It is said that a good drummer can make the drums "talk" by imitating the pitch patterns of the language.

In this craft project, children create their own talking drums. Children will enjoy playing their drums while listening to stories about Ghana. To see an example of an atumpan drum look at: Price, Christine. *Talking Drums of Africa.* New York: Charles Scribner's Sons, 1973. (46 pages)

Supplies

Coffee cans, oatmeal containers, or baby formula cans with plastic lids
Construction paper
Scissors
Crayons or colored markers
Pencils
Clear tape
Cotton balls

Pre-cut the construction paper to fit around the cans or containers that children will be using. Have children decorate the construction paper with crayons or markers. Tape the construction paper around the cans or containers. (If the cans or containers do not have plastic lids, use masking tape to make the membrane across the top of the can or container.) Have children tape a cotton ball to a pencil to make the drumstick.

Royal Ashanti Crown and Ring

Beckwith, Carol, and Angela Fisher. "Royal Gold of the Asante Empire." *National Geographic* 190, no. 4 (October 1996): 36–47.
Includes photographs of royal jewelry.

The Ashanti people value gold above all other metals. Gold has been mined in the Ghana area since the 1300s. Gold jewelry is still worn widely throughout Ghana. At one time, however, gold jewelry was only worn by royalty.

Have children make an Ashanti crown and ring like those worn by Ashanti royalty. Refer to "Royal Gold of the Asante Empire" by Carol Beckwith and Angela Fisher for examples of this wonderful jewelry.

Supplies

Posterboard
Pasta—various shapes and sizes
Gold spray paint
White glue
Scissors
Stapler or clear tape

Pre-paint the pasta with gold spray paint. Using figures 7.7–7.9, create an Ashanti gold crown and a gold ring. Using posterboard, trace and cut out the patterns (fig. 7.7 is a half-pattern). Have children decorate the crown and the ring top by gluing the gold-colored pasta to the posterboard. Staple or tape the ring band around the child's finger, and glue the ring top, decorated with pasta, to the ring band. Staple or tape together the back of the crown so it will fit tightly around the child's head.

Note: For older children, it may be necessary to add a 2-inch-wide band to the crown to accommodate a larger head.

Fig. 7.6. Crown and Ring Example.

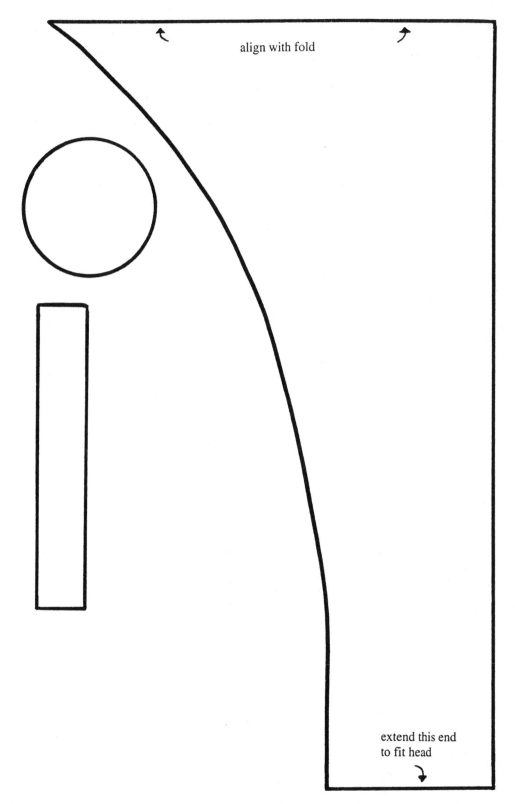

align with fold

extend this end
to fit head

Fig. 7.7. Crown. Fig. 7.8. Ring Band (left rectangle). Fig. 7.9. Ring Top (circle).

Sources for Craft Ideas and Activities

Corwin, Judith Hoffman. *African Crafts*. New York: Franklin Watts, 1990. (48 pages)
     Easy African crafts, including making Ashanti gold weights and an Ashanti doll.

MacLeod-Brudenell, Iain. *Costume Crafts*. Photographs by Zul Mukhida. Worldwide Crafts
     series. Milwaukee, WI: Gareth Stevens, 1994. (pages 18–19)
     Design a T-shirt with symbols that show your interests, similar to the adinkra cloth
     worn by royalty in Ghana.

Multicultural Crafts for Kids. Carson, CA: Lakeshore Learning Materials, 1992. (n.p.)
     Make a money bag similar to those sold at the markets in Ghana.

Ritter, Darlene. *Multicultural Art Activities: From the Cultures of Africa, Asia and North
     America*. Edited by Judy Urban. Illustrated by Diane Valko. Cypress, CA: Creative
     Teaching Press, 1993. (pages 10–11)
     Weave a basket from yarn and paper cups, similar to the baskets used in Ghana.

Terzian, Alexandra M. *The Kids' Multicultural Art Book: Art and Craft Experiences from
     Around the World*. Kids Can! series. Charlotte, VT: Williamson, 1993. (160 pages)
     Includes easy African crafts such as making a kufi (a round hat) and an akua-ba
     doll, kente paper weaving, and adinkra sponge stamping.

Let's Visit

Greece

Sample Story Times

Story Time for Preschool

Song: "Hello Song"

Book: *Max and Ruby's First Greek Myth, Pandora's Box* by Rosemary Wells

Book: *A Sip of Aesop* by Jane Yolen

Fingerplay: "Five Greek Fishing Boats"

Puppet Presentation: "The Lion and the Mouse"

Puppet Presentation: "The North Wind and the Sun"

Flannel Board Story: "The Miller, the Boy and the Donkey" from *The Flannel Board Storytelling Book* by Judy Sierra

Filmstrip: *The Town Mouse and the Country Mouse* by Lorinda Cauley

Overhead Projector Story: "The Fox and the Grapes"

Craft: " 'The Fox and the Grapes' Stick Puppet Theater"

Action Rhyme: "My Hands"

Story Time for Kindergarten Through Third Grade

Song: "Hello Song"

Book: *The Lion and the Mouse* by A. J. Wood

Fingerplay: "Five Greek Fishing Boats"

Book: *A Sip of Aesop* by Jane Yolen

Puppet Presentation: "The North Wind and the Sun"

Oral Story: "The Crow and the Pitcher"

Song: "Children's Song" from *Multicultural Rhythm Stick Fun* by Georgiana Stewart

Filmstrip: *The Town Mouse and the Country Mouse* by Lorinda Cauley

Craft: "Fish Mosaic"

Action Rhyme: "My Hands"

Begin the story time with the "Hello Song." Then sing the song again, substituting the word *hello* with the Greek greeting Γειά σας [yassas], which means both "hello" and "goodbye." (See p. xxvii for "Hello Song" music.)

Hello Song

Hello ev'rybody,
And how are you? How are you?
Hello ev'rybody,
And how are you today?

yassas ev'rybody,
And how are you? How are you?
yassas ev'rybody,
And how are you today?

End the story time with the "My Hands" action rhyme, substituting the words *thank you* with the Greek word Εὐχαριστῶ [ef-har-eesto], and *goodbye* with Γειά σας [yassas]. Have children stand up and follow the actions in the rhyme.

My Hands

My hands say ef-har-eesto. *(hold up hands)*
With a clap, clap, clap. *(clap hands)*
My feet say ef-har-eesto. *(point to feet)*
With a tap, tap, tap. *(stamp or tap feet)*
Clap! Clap! Clap! *(clap hands)*
Tap! Tap! Tap! *(stamp or tap feet)*
Turn myself around and bow. *(turn and bow)*
yassas. *(wave goodbye)*

Books to Read Aloud

Some of the books selected for reading aloud, such as *Town Mouse, Country Mouse* by Jan Brett, are based on Aesop's fables. Aesop, a freed Greek slave, lived about 620–560 B.C. He is considered the author of many popular fables that were passed along orally for several hundred years before being written down. A fable is a story that has a stated moral or lesson at the end. Children are delighted by the animal characters and simple story lines found in Aesop's fables.

Brett, Jan. *Town Mouse, Country Mouse.* New York: G. P. Putnam's Sons, 1994. (32 pages)
Brett's illustrated version of this story involves a mouse couple from the country exchanging homes with a mouse couple from town. Each couple discovers anew the pleasures of their own home. School-age children will enjoy the intricate detail of the illustrations.

Cauley, Lorinda Bryan. *The Town Mouse and the Country Mouse.* New York: G. P. Putnam's Sons, 1984. (32 pages)
A country mouse visits his city cousin and discovers that he prefers his own simple pleasures. (Available in filmstrip format from Weston Woods; see "Media Choices.")

Delton, Judy. *My Uncle Nikos.* Illustrated by Marc Simont. New York: Thomas Y. Crowell, 1983. (32 pages)
A little girl visits her uncle, who lives in a small Greek village.

Hague, Michael. *Aesop's Fables.* New York: Holt, Rinehart and Winston, 1985. (28 pages)
A selection of well-known and lesser-known fables, illustrated by the author.

Haskins, Jim, and Kathleen Benson. *Count Your Way Through Greece.* Illustrated by Janice Lee Porter. Minneapolis, MN: Carolrhoda Books, 1996. (24 pages)
The Greek numbers 1 through 10 are introduced alongside information about modern and ancient Greece. A pronunciation guide is provided.

Rockwell, Anne. *The One-Eyed Giant and Other Monsters from the Greek Myths.* New York: Greenwillow Books, 1996. (32 pages)
Ten illustrated stories of monsters and fantastical creatures from Greek myths. A pronunciation guide is included.

Waldherr, Kris. *Persephone and the Pomegranate: A Myth from Greece.* New York: Dial Books for Young Readers, 1993. (32 pages)
A richly illustrated version of the Greek myth explaining the origins of winter and spring.

Walker, Barbara. *Pigs and Pirates: A Greek Tale.* Illustrated by Harold Berson. New York: David White, 1969. (48 pages)
Three young swineherds train their pigs to do tricks, which help the pigs avoid capture by pirates. Appropriate for school-age children.

Wells, Rosemary. *Max and Ruby's First Greek Myth, Pandora's Box.* New York: Dial Books for Young Readers, 1993. (24 pages)
Wells uses the well-known and well-loved Max to retell the myth of Pandora whose curiosity unleashes a hoard of insects. However, a friendly spider saves the day.

———. *Max and Ruby's Midas: Another Greek Myth.* New York: Dial Books for Young Readers, 1995. (24 pages)
Max and Ruby return with a new twist on the story of King Midas. Everything Midas touches becomes a rich, frothy dessert—including his family.

Wood, A. J. *The Lion and the Mouse.* Illustrated by Ian Andrew. Brookfield, CT: Millbrook Press, 1995. (32 pages)
A richly illustrated retelling of Mouse who helps the mighty Lion.

Yolen, Jane. *A Sip of Aesop.* Illustrated by Karen Barbour. New York: Blue Sky Press, 1995. (32 pages)
A selection of Aesop's fables, told in rhyme, that will appeal to children of all ages.

Storytelling

Puppet Presentation

"The Lion and the Mouse" and "The North Wind and the Sun" are retellings of Aesop's fables using stick puppets. Photocopy the puppet patterns on poster-board, cut them out, and hot glue craft sticks or paint sticks to the backs of the puppets (paint sticks, available at paint supply stores, are sturdier than craft sticks). The storyteller may hold the puppets, or have children from the group hold them.

Note: If performing the story for a large group of children, enlarge the patterns 100 percent to make the figures easier to see. Lamination (after coloring the puppets) can add brightness, and it makes the puppets more durable.

"The Lion and the Mouse." Two puppets and one prop are needed for this puppet play: the mouse, the lion, and a 12-by-12-inch net made by weaving and hot gluing macramé string. Use figures 8.1 and 8.2 to make the lion and mouse puppets.

Ask three children to help tell the story. Have one child hold the lion puppet, another child the mouse puppet, and a third child the net. At the appropriate time during the narration, have the child with the net throw it over the lion. Have the child with the mouse make the puppet nibble at the net, freeing the lion.

The Lion and the Mouse
retold by Desiree Webber

Now, as you know, the lion is the king of beasts—mighty and fearsome. One day, the lion was resting in the shade of a tree after walking through his domain. Suddenly, a little mouse scurried across the lion's paw. The lion trapped the mouse, picked him up by his tail, and brought the mouse close to his face.

"Please," begged the mouse. "I did not see you. Let me go and someday I will do a favor for you."

The lion did not think the little mouse could ever do anything for him, but he was in a generous mood. So he let the mouse go.

Several days later, the lion was walking through the jungle when a net from a hunter's trap fell upon him without warning. The lion roared out in anger and fear. Deep in the jungle, the little mouse heard the lion's roar and ran quickly to help. When he saw the ropes that entangled the lion, the little mouse began to chew through the net, and soon the king of beasts was free.

"See," said the mouse. "Even a little one can help a great one."

Fig. 8.1. Lion.   Fig. 8.2. Mouse.

"The North Wind and the Sun." Use figures 8.3 and 8.4 to make wind and sun puppets for this puppet play. Ask three children to help tell the story. Have one child hold the North Wind puppet, another child the Sun puppet, and have a third child, wearing a piece of cloth as a cloak, play the role of the traveler.

The North Wind and the Sun
retold by Desiree Webber

One day, the North Wind and the Sun were arguing as to which one was stronger. Looking down from the sky, the North Wind and the Sun saw a traveler on horseback who was wearing a cloak upon his shoulders. The Sun said, "Whoever can make the traveler remove his cloak first will be named the strongest."

The North Wind tried first. Gathering up his forces, he blew down with all his strength upon the man. Cold air swirled around the man, tugging furiously at his cloak, but the man just gathered his cloak closer around his body. The harder the North Wind blew, the tighter the man clutched his cloak.

"My turn," said the Sun, coming out from behind the clouds. He began to shine warm, gentle rays upon the earth. The man opened his cloak, and continued riding. The Sun shone warmer and warmer until, finally, the man tossed off his cloak, glad to be free of it.

Moral: Persuasion is better than force.

Oral Story

"The Crow and the Pitcher." Use a small, clear pitcher (or jar) and marbles as props to tell this Aesop's classic fable. Fill the pitcher halfway full with water. While telling the story, drop the marbles into the pitcher, one by one, letting children watch as the water rises to the top.

The Crow and the Pitcher
retold by Desiree Webber

A thirsty crow found a pitcher halfway full with water. It tried and tried to drink but was unable to reach the water with its beak. The crow stopped to think of a plan to save itself. At last, an idea struck: Taking pebbles lying nearby, the crow dropped one pebble *(begin dropping marbles into the pitcher)* after another into the pitcher until, finally, the water reached the top, where the crow was able to drink.

Moral: Little by little a goal is reached.

Fig. 8.3. North Wind.

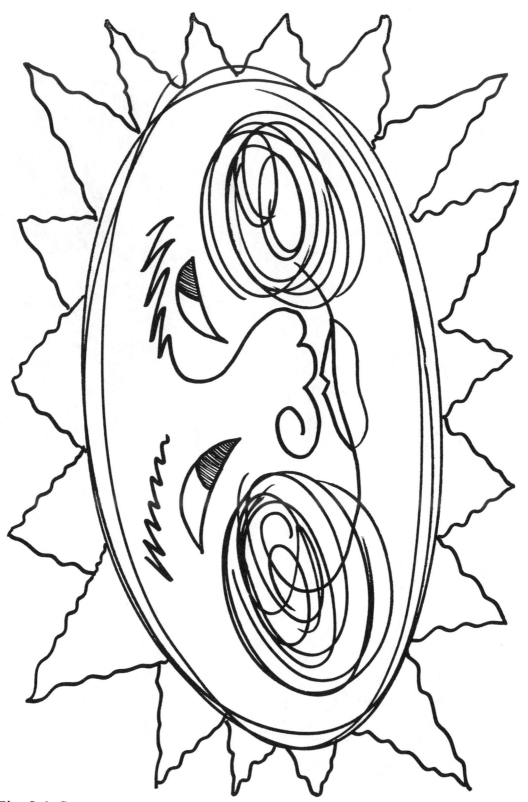

Fig. 8.4. Sun.

From *Travel the Globe.* © 1998. Desiree Lorraine Webber, et al. Libraries Unlimited. (800) 237-6124.

Overhead Projector Story

Tell Aesop's fable "The Fox and the Grapes" using an overhead projector. This fable can be found in *Aesop's Fables* by Michael Hague (see "Books to Read Aloud").

On a piece of clear transparency paper, draw a grape arbor using permanent markers. On construction paper, draw and cut out a small fox and attach a piece of florist wire to one side. (Refer to fig. 8.7 on page 128, " 'The Fox and the Grapes' Stick Puppet Theater," for a sample illustration.) Place the transparency picture of the grape arbor on the overhead projector. While telling the story, manipulate the wire to make the fox jump at the grapes.

Sources for Flannel Board Presentations

Sierra, Judy. "The Miller, the Boy and the Donkey." In *The Flannel Board Storytelling Book*. New York: H. W. Wilson, 1987. (pages 190–95)
   A miller and his son lose their donkey when they follow the advice of others. Patterns and instructions are included.

Fingerplays, Songs, Action Rhymes, and Games

"Five Greek Fishing Boats." For this fingerplay, the storyteller will begin with five fishing boat puppets, one on each finger. Bend down a finger each time a boat exits the poem. Children will hold up five fingers and follow along. To make finger puppets, photocopy figures 8.5 and 8.6 on white tagboard or construction paper. Use markers to color the boats. Laminate and cut out the boats and finger attachments. Tape together the three flaps of each finger attachment. This will fit over the tip of each finger like a thimble. Tape a boat to each finger attachment.

Five Greek Fishing Boats
by Desiree Webber

Five Greek fishing boats looking to moor;
One found a harbor, then there were four.
Four Greek fishing boats trolling the sea;
One caught its limit, then there were three.
Three Greek fishing boats sailing the blue;
One saw Poseidon, then there were two.
Two Greek fishing boats up before dawn;
One sailed for Crete, then there was one.
One Greek fishing boat under the sun;
It charted for home, then there were none.

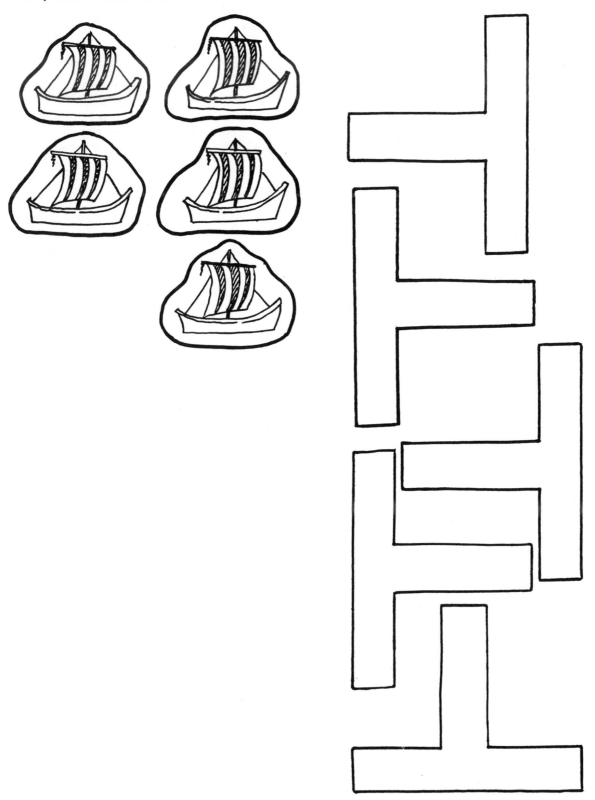

Fig. 8.5. Boat Finger Puppets.   Fig. 8.6. Finger Puppet Attachments.

From *Travel the Globe.* © 1998. Desiree Lorraine Webber, et al. Libraries Unlimited. (800) 237-6124.

Sources for Fingerplays, Songs, Action Rhymes, and Games

All the Best from Greece: 20 Great Favorites. St. Laurent, Quebec: L.D.M.I., n.d. Audiocassette.
Engaging songs to set the mood for a story time. Includes songs to play while teaching the traditional folk dance step known as the "Grapevine." Check with a dance teacher for instructions, or invite a guest presenter to show the group. If local music stores cannot supply the audiocassette, write to L.D.M.I., P.O. Box 1445, St. Laurent, Quebec, Canada H4L 4Z1.

Beall, Pamela Conn, and Susan Hagen Nipp, with Nancy Spence Klein. "Pou'n-Do To Dachtilidi—Where Is the Ring?" In *Wee Sing Around the World.* Los Angeles: Price Stern Sloan, 1994. Book with audiocassette.
Presents instructions for a group game played while singing "Pou'n-Do To Dachtilidi."

Stewart, Georgiana. "Children's Song." In *Multicultural Rhythm Stick Fun.* Long Branch, NJ: Kimbo Educational, 1992. Audiocassette.
Children use rhythm sticks (or clap their hands) to this song about Greece.

——. "A Visit to My Friend." In *Children of the World: Multicultural Rhythmic Activities.* Long Branch, NJ: Kimbo Educational, 1991. Audiocassette.
Children move in a circle and clap, wave, hop, and so forth to music from Mexico, Russia, and Greece.

Media Choices

Show a video or filmstrip as a transition between storytelling activities and crafts. This gives children an opportunity to rest quietly for a few minutes.

Cauley, Lorinda Bryan. *The Town Mouse and the Country Mouse.* 9 min. Weston, CT: Weston Woods, 1987. Filmstrip and audiocassette.
A country mouse visits his city cousin and discovers that he prefers his own simple pleasures.

The Lion and the Rat/The Hare and the Tortoise. 7 min. Illustrated by Brian Wildsmith. Weston, CT: Weston Woods, 1963. Filmstrip and audiocassette.
Both stories, Aesop's fables as retold by Jean de la Fontaine, are combined on one filmstrip.

Crafts and Other Activities

Choose a craft suited for the age level of the group and the time allotted for the story time.

"The Fox and the Grapes" Stick Puppet Theater

The Greeks are well known for their theater. During the 4th century B.C., the actors were always male and wore character masks that showed the emotions they were expressing.

In this craft project, children create a puppet theater for Aesop's fable "The Fox and the Grapes."

Supplies

Light-yellow or light-blue posterboard   White glue
Brown construction paper   Scissors
Purple or dark-blue construction paper   Pencils
Colored markers or crayons

Introduce the fable "The Fox and the Grapes" (see *Aesop's Fables* by Michael Hague under "Books to Read Aloud") before beginning this craft project. Each child needs an 8½-by-11-inch piece of light-yellow or light-blue posterboard, with a slit cut 1 inch from the bottom and 2 inches from each side (see fig. 8.7).

Use figures 8.8 and 8.9 to make the fox puppet and the grapes for the arbor. The fox puppet is two-sided, and should be pre-cut or pre-drawn for younger children. Have older children trace and cut out their puppet, using brown construction paper. Glue a ½-by-6-inch strip of posterboard between the two fox pattern pieces (a craft stick or straw can be substituted for the posterboard strip).

Make the grape arbor by gluing strips of brown construction paper onto the poster-board (see fig. 8.7). Cut an outline of hanging grapes from purple or dark-blue construction paper (or photocopy the grape pattern on white paper and have children color them). Glue the grapes in the middle and upper corners of the arbor.

To perform the fable, insert the fox puppet through the slit from the back of the posterboard. Children make the fox jump up at the grapes as they tell the story.

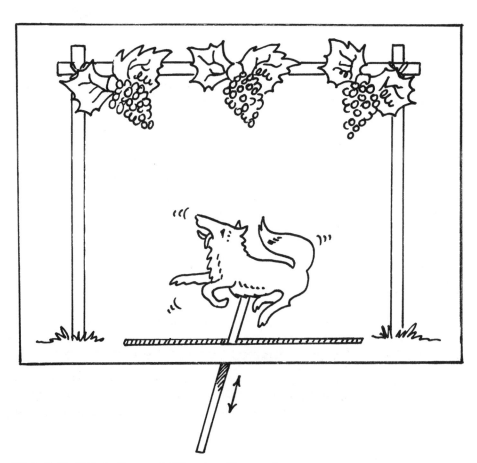

Fig. 8.7. Stick Puppet Theater Example.

Fig. 8.8. Foxes. Fig. 8.9. Grapes.

From *Travel the Globe.* © 1998. Desiree Lorraine Webber, et al. Libraries Unlimited. (800) 237-6124.

Fish Mosaic

Archeologists have found mosaics in Greece that date back to the fourth century B.C. These early mosaics often had only two colors and were created using pebbles. For example, a typical background was created using black or blue pebbles, while the figure was created using white or light-brown pebbles. Later mosaics were created from cut glass, stones, or clay tiles. Some Greeks decorated the floors of their homes with mosaics.

In this craft project, children create mosaics using posterboard and construction paper. The fish design was chosen because of the importance of fishing as an industry in Greece. It is also a simple design for most children. However, depending upon the age and abilities of the group, other designs for mosaics might include mythological creatures, such as the Cyclops or Medusa, or a simple graphic arrangement using two or more colors.

Supplies

Brown posterboard	White glue
White or light-yellow construction paper	Paper cutter
Blue construction paper	

See figure 8.10 for an example of a fish mosaic. An adult should pre-cut an 8½-by-11 piece of white or light-yellow posterboard for each child. This will serve as the background for the mosaic. Pre-cut the white construction paper into 1-inch squares. Then cut some of the blue construction paper into 1-inch squares, and some into ½-by-1-inch rectangles.

The children create the fish mosaic by gluing squares of paper to the posterboard in the shape of a fish. Use white squares for the body and blue squares for the eyes and fins.

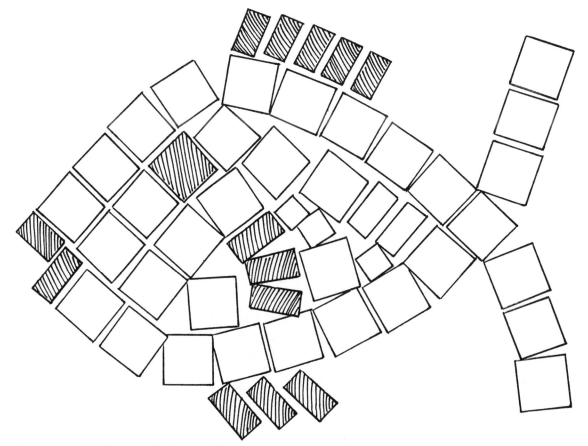

Fig. 8.10. Fish Mosaic Example.

Sources for Craft Ideas and Activities

Hewitt, Sally. *The Greeks.* Footsteps in Time series. Chicago: Childrens Press, 1995. (pages 4–5 and 16–17)
Learn the Greek alphabet. Construct an Olympic torch using construction paper.

Purdy, Susan, and Cass R. Sandak. *Ancient Greece.* Illustrated by Bert Dodson. Civilization Project Book series. New York: Franklin Watts, 1982. (pages 14–15 and 25–26)
Make a Greek lyre using a coat hanger and rubber bands. Play the game "Knucklebones."

Wright, Rachel. *Greeks: Facts, Things to Make, Activities.* Craft Topics series. New York: Franklin Watts, 1992. (pages 16–19 and 23)
Make a mask of Medusa; create a musical pipe using drinking straws.

Let's Visit

India

Sample Story Times

Story Time for Preschool

Song: "Hello Song"

Book: *Seven Blind Mice* by Ed Young

Action Rhyme: "An Elephant Goes Like This"

Action Rhyme: "Elephant"

Book: *The Monkey and the Crocodile* by Paul Galdone

Action Rhyme: "Five Little Monkeys"

Flannel Board Presentation: "What Is an Elephant?"

Video: *Once a Mouse* by Marcia Brown

Craft: "Pongal Cow Mask"

Action Rhyme: "My Hands"

Story Time for Kindergarten Through Third Grade

Song: "Hello Song"

Book: *The Story of Wali Dâd* by Kristina Rodanas

Action Rhyme: "An Elephant Goes Like This"

Action Rhyme: "Elephant"

Book: *In the Heart of the Village: The World of the Indian Banyan Tree* by Barbara Bash

Puppet Presentation: "The Pearl Thief"

Video: *Once a Mouse* by Marcia Brown

Craft: "Rakhi (Bracelet)"

Action Rhyme: "My Hands"

Begin the story time with the "Hello Song." Then sing the song again, substituting the word *hello* with the Hindi greeting नमस्ते *namaste* [nah-MAH-stee], which means both "hello" and "goodbye." (There are many languages in India, but Hindi is the country's official language.) When greeting someone, place your hands together, as if praying, and bow your head as you say the word *namaste*. (See p. xxvii for "Hello Song" music.)

Hello Song

Hello ev'rybody,
And how are you? How are you?
Hello ev'rybody,
And how are you today?

nah-MAH-stee ev'rybody,
And how are you? How are you?
nah-MAH-stee ev'rybody,
And how are you today?

End the story time with the "My Hands" action rhyme, substituting the words *thank you* with the Hindi word शुक्रिया *sûkriyā* [SHOE-crea], and *goodbye* with नमस्ते *namaste* [nah-MAH-stee]. Have children stand up and follow the actions in the rhyme.

My Hands

My hands say SHOE-crea. *(hold up hands)*
With a clap, clap, clap. *(clap hands)*
My feet say SHOE-crea. *(point to feet)*
With a tap, tap, tap. *(stamp or tap feet)*
Clap! Clap! Clap! *(clap hands)*
Tap! Tap! Tap! *(stamp or tap feet)*
Turn myself around and bow. *(turn and bow)*
nah-MAH-stee. *(wave goodbye)*

Books to Read Aloud

Arnold, Marsha Diane. *Heart of a Tiger.* Illustrated by Jamichael Henterly. New York: Dial Books for Young Readers, 1995. (32 pages)
A kitten seeks the company of a Bengal tiger to learn what name he should choose for the "Name Day Celebration." This fictional story illustrates the ritual Namakarana, the naming ceremony.

Bash, Barbara. *In the Heart of the Village: The World of the Indian Banyan Tree.* San Francisco: Sierra Club Books for Children, 1996. (32 pages)
A nonfiction picture book with large, colorful illustrations about the animals and people found among a village's banyan tree. Recommended for school-age children but can be paraphrased for preschoolers.

Brown, Marcia. *Once a Mouse . . . A Fable Cut in Wood.* New York: Charles Scribner's Sons, 1961. (32 pages)
In this Caldecott Medal-winner, a hermit saves the life of a mouse and magically changes the rodent into larger and larger animals until finally it becomes an arrogant tiger.

Galdone, Paul. *The Monkey and the Crocodile: A Jataka Tale from India.* New York: Clarion Books, 1969. (32 pages)
A monkey cleverly outwits a crocodile who tries more than once to make a meal of him.

Haskins, Jim. *Count Your Way Through India.* Illustrated by Liz Brenner Dodson. Minneapolis, MN: Carolrhoda Books, 1990. (24 pages)
Presents the numbers 1 through 10 in Hindi, alongside information about India. Includes an introductory note about the many languages spoken in India, as well as a pronunciation guide.

Hodges, Margaret. *Hidden in the Sand.* Illustrated by Paul Birling. New York: Charles Scribner's Sons, 1994. (32 pages)
A trader takes his son with him on a caravan crossing the desert. The boy wants to ride with the pilot to learn how he navigates by the stars, but the pilot is unfriendly. Along the way, the pilot makes a dangerous error, and the boy saves everyone's life. Recommended for school-age children.

Kipling, Rudyard. *Rikki-Tikki-Tavi.* Illustrated by Lambert Davis. San Diego, CA: Harcourt Brace Jovanovich, 1992. (37 pages)
A little mongoose saves a family from two dangerous cobras, Nag and Nagaina. A richly illustrated story, recommended for school-age children.

Lewin, Ted. *Sacred River.* New York: Clarion Books, 1995. (34 pages)
A beautiful picture book, illustrated with water colors, about the brightly clothed pilgrims who visit the Ganges River to offer jai flowers.

Rodanas, Kristina. *The Story of Wali Dâd.* New York: Lothrop, Lee & Shepard, 1988. (32 pages)
Wali Dâd is a grass-cutter who does not need much material wealth to be happy. The more he gives, the more he receives—much to his dismay!

Skurzynski, Gloria. *The Magic Pumpkin.* Illustrated by Rocco Negri. New York: Four Winds Press, 1971. (47 pages)
Mother Parvati travels through the jungle in a magic pumpkin. She meets a tiger and a wolf who want to make a meal of her. Includes a pronunciation guide.

Young, Ed. *Seven Blind Mice.* New York: Philomel Books, 1992. (40 pages)
A retelling of the fable "The Blind Men and the Elephant." The story also relates the days of the week and colors.

Storytelling

Flannel Board Presentation

"What Is an Elephant?" This is a retelling of a fable from India about four men (sometimes it is six men), blind from birth, who want to touch an elephant so that they can understand what type of animal it is. The ancient meaning of this story has religious significance. One age-old version ends with the moral that we are all blind in religious matters because we see the parts but not the whole.

See figures 9.1–9.6 for patterns. Trace the patterns on felt, or photocopy and color them. If photocopying, glue small pieces of felt to the backs of the paper figures so they will hold to the flannel board. Place the figures on the flannel board as they are introduced in the story.

What Is an Elephant?
retold by Desiree Webber

There were once four blind men who lived in a small village in India. The four were good friends and often discussed things under the shade of a large tree. *(place the four blind men on the flannel board.)*

One day, an elephant driver came to the village riding an elephant. *(place the elephant on the flannel board and the elephant driver on the elephant)* Although there were many elephants in India, the four men had never seen one. They asked the elephant driver if they could examine the beast. *(remove the elephant driver from the flannel board)* The driver agreed and the four blind men approached the elephant, exploring it with their hands.

The first man felt the foot of the elephant and said, "The elephant is like a mortar for pounding rice." *(pound fist on palm of hand)*

The second man felt the tail of the elephant and said, "No, my friend, the elephant is like a broom." *(make sweeping motions)*

"You are both wrong," said the third man feeling the ear of the elephant. "The animal is like a broad, flat leaf. *(fan one hand back and forth)*

"I do not know what you can be thinking," said the fourth, feeling the sides of the elephant. "This magnificent beast is like a mountain—huge and endless." *(bring hands together and make a point with fingers)*

The four friends began to argue among themselves, each thinking his opinion was right, until they were interrupted by the elephant driver. *(place elephant driver on elephant)*

"You are each right, but also, each of you is wrong! When one of you says the elephant is like a mortar, you are speaking of the elephant's foot. When another of you says the elephant is like a broom, you are speaking of the elephant's tail. And when another describes the elephant as being like a broad, flat leaf, you are speaking of the elephant's ear. When the last of you describes the elephant as being like a mountain—huge and endless, you are speaking of it's sides."

The four men understood the wisdom of elephant driver's words. They had been arguing about the whole when they each knew only a portion.

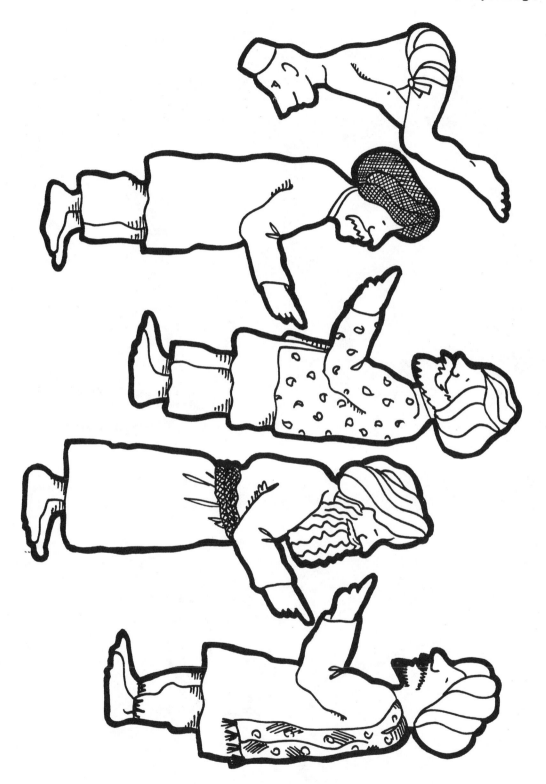

Fig. 9.1. Elephant Driver (sitting). Fig. 9.2. First Blind Man. Fig. 9.3. Second Blind Man. Fig. 9.4. Third Blind Man. Fig. 9.5. Fourth Blind Man.

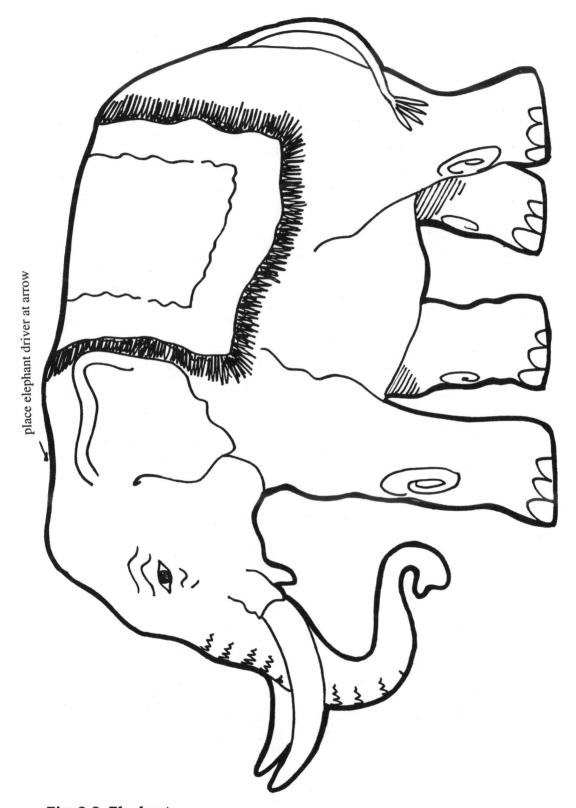

place elephant driver at arrow

Fig. 9.6. Elephant.

From *Travel the Globe.* © 1998. Desiree Lorraine Webber, et al. Libraries Unlimited. (800) 237-6124.

Sources for Flannel Board Presentations

Sierra, Judy. "The Cat and the Parrot." In *The Flannel Board Storytelling Book*. New York: H. W. Wilson, 1987. (pages 140–45)
The cat goes to the parrot's house for dinner but ends up eating the parrot, the spicy cakes, and several other characters. Includes patterns and a note about children acting out the story.

——. "The Monkey and the Crocodile." In *The Flannel Board Storytelling Book*. New York: H. W. Wilson, 1987. (pages 196–201)
A monkey outwits a crocodile who wants to make a meal of him. Includes patterns.

Puppet Presentation

Supplies

Three bags, cloth or paper, approximately 6 inches wide and 9 inches long (if cloth, sew in a drawstring)
Hot glue or needle and thread
Package of white pony beads (available at craft stores) (need 20 beads to tell the story)
One strand of white plastic cord, 8 inches in length (available at craft stores)
One strand of pink (or some other color) plastic cord, 8 inches in length
One small bowl

Fig. 9.7. Pearl Bag Example.

"The Pearl Thief." This puppet presentation is performed using three 6-by-9-inch cloth bags with drawstrings. Sew or hot-glue the picture of each man (figs. 9.8–9.10) to each of the three bags—see figure 9.7. (Lunch-size paper sacks, with the pictures of the three men glued to the front, can be substituted for the cloth bags.) Use a thin piece of cord or fold the bag closed as needed within the story.

Two of the men in this story are neighbors. One of the men is called the "kind man"; the second is called the "greedy neighbor," who later becomes known as the "pearl thief"; the third man is called the "judge."

Put two pony beads (pearls) into the kind man's bag; the pink plastic cord (strong thread), with a knot tied at one end, into the greedy neighbor's bag; and a strand of 18 pearls, strung on white plastic cord (rotten thread), into the judge's bag. When the time comes, restring the judge's 18 pearls onto the greedy neighbor's thread, plus the kind man's two pearls.

Lay the three bags on your lap and have the bowl close at hand. As each character is introduced in the story, raise the appropriate bag, with the face toward the audience.

Fig. 9.8. Judge.

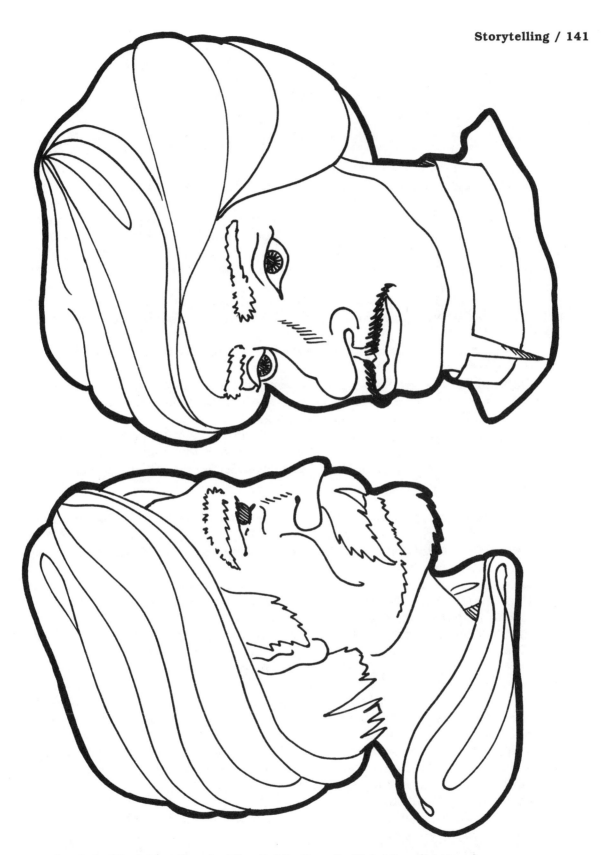

Fig. 9.9. Kind Man (top).   Fig. 9.10. Greedy Neighbor (bottom).

The Pearl Thief
retold by Desiree Webber

Once there was a kind and trusting man who owned two pearls. *(show the kind man)* He was about to leave on a long journey and did not want to take his treasure with him, in case he should be robbed. So he asked his neighbor, *(show the greedy neighbor)* whom he thought was honest, to watch over his two pearls. *(take the two pearls from the kind man's bag and drop them, one at a time, into the greedy neighbor's bag)*

The man said goodbye to his neighbor and began his long journey. During the several months he was gone, his neighbor thought and thought about the two pearls he had been trusted to protect. Slowly, greed filled his heart, and he decided to keep the pearls for himself. *(close the greedy neighbor's bag by pulling the drawstring)*

When the kind man finally returned home, he went straight-away to his neighbor. The man thanked his neighbor for caring for his pearls and asked for their return.

The neighbor looked astonished and said, "No pearls did you entrust to me. My friend, you are mistaken."

The kind man begged his neighbor for the return of the two pearls. They were the only wealth he possessed. But the greedy neighbor only said, "No pearls did you entrust to me. You are mistaken."

The kind man went immediately to the judge *(show the judge)* and told him his story. The judge summoned the greedy neighbor and asked for his version of what had happened. Again, the neighbor said, "No pearls did he entrust to me. He is mistaken."

The judge was a wise man and could read the guilt upon the greedy neighbor's face, but the judge knew he needed proof. So he sent the kind man and the greedy neighbor away and thought about the situation. *(lay the kind man and greedy neighbor down)* Finally, he came up with a plan to catch the greedy neighbor, whom he now called "the pearl thief."

The judge went to his safe, removed 18 pearls, and strung them onto a piece of rotten thread. *(take the strand of 18 pearls out of the judge's bag and count them aloud with the children)*

The next day, the judge called for the pearl thief *(show pearl thief)* and said, "I trust an honest face such as yours. Please take these 20 pearls and restring them onto a strong piece of thread." *(place the strand of 18 pearls into the pearl thief's bag and lay the judge down)*

The pearl thief was pleased that the judge trusted him with the 20 pearls. He was sure it was a sign that the judge thought him to be innocent, and that he would get away with the crime against his neighbor.

"Tonight I will restring the pearls, and tomorrow return them to the judge," the pearl thief told himself. "Then I will again be considered an honest man by all, and I will still possess my neighbor's two pearls!"

After eating his fill of dinner, the pearl thief sat down by his fire and threaded his needle with a strong piece of thread. *(take the pink cord from the pearl thief's bag)* Then he removed the pearls from the rotten thread and placed them into a bowl. *(slide the 18 pearls from the judge's strand into the bowl)*

"Now I shall restring these 20 pearls," said the thief, and he began to count each pearl as he threaded it onto the needle. *(thread the pearls onto the thief's pink thread while counting them aloud with the children)* "One, two, three, four, five . . . sixteen, seventeen, eighteen . . . Where did the other two go?!" exclaimed the thief. Frantically, he jumped up from his seated position and began to search about the floor. He looked in the bowl again, among his clothes, around the furniture, in the entrance to his home—everywhere he had been.

"The judge will accuse me of stealing two of his pearls. What am I to do?" he moaned. Then the thief remembered the two stolen pearls he possessed. He hated to part with his treasure, but he was afraid of the judge. So he added the two stolen pearls to the strand of eighteen. *(add the two pearls from the pearl thief's bag to the strand)*

Again he counted the strand to make sure that he indeed had 20 pearls. *(count the pearls with the children)* "One, two, three, four, five . . . sixteen, seventeen, eighteen, nineteen, and twenty." Breathing a heavy sigh of relief, the thief placed the pearls into his pocket and went to bed. *(place the strand into the pearl thief's bag)*

Early the next morning, the pearl thief hurried to the judge's house to deliver the pearls. Waiting for him was the judge, and the kind man whose pearls had been stolen. *(show all 3 bags)*

Handing the strand of pearls to the judge, the thief loudly proclaimed, "Here are the 20 pearls you asked me to restring upon a strong piece of thread. Now you know me to be a honest man and wrongly accused by my neighbor."

"Let me count these pearls," said the judge. *(take the strand of pearls from the thief's bag and hold it up)* "I asked you to restring 20 pearls, but *in reality*, I gave you only *18* pearls. I knew that in your fear of me you would add the stolen pearls."

The pearl thief knew he had been cleverly tricked and quietly went away to prison. The kind man received his two pearls *(remove two of the pearls from the strand and place them into the kind man's bag; return the strand to the judge's bag)*, and the judge remained one of the wisest men in India.

Source for Oral Stories

Milord, Susan. "A Drum." In *Tales Alive! Ten Multicultural Folktales with Activities.* Illustrated by Michael A. Donato. Charlotte, VT: Williamson, 1995. (pages 37–45)
The wonderful story of a young boy who helps others by giving them something he possesses. In return, he receives a desired gift.

Fingerplays, Songs, Action Rhymes, and Games

The following is a sampling of fingerplays and action rhymes which introduce animals from India.

Elephant
(author unknown)

Right foot, left foot, see me go. *(step in rhythm and sway like an elephant)*
I am gray and big and slow.
I come walking down the street,
With my trunk and four big feet. *(stretch out arm by face and swing
like an elephant's trunk)*

An Elephant Goes Like This
(author unknown)

An elephant goes like this and that. *(lift feet up and down)*
He's terribly big, *(hold arms up high)*
And he's terribly fat. *(hold arms out to the side)*
He has no fingers, *(wiggle fingers)*
And he has no toes, *(bend over and touch toes)*
But goodness gracious, what a nose! *(stretch out arm by face and swing
like an elephant's trunk)*

Five Little Monkeys
(author unknown)

Five little monkeys, sitting in a tree. *(show five fingers)*

[chorus]
Teasing Mr. Crocodile, *(shake index finger)*
"You can't catch me, You can't catch me!"
Along comes Mr. Crocodile, quiet as can be. *(with palms together,
slowly stretch out arms to represent the crocodile)*
SNAP! *(clap hands)*

Four little monkeys, sitting in a tree. *(show four fingers)*
[chorus]
Three little monkeys, sitting in a tree. *(show three fingers)*
[chorus]
Two little monkeys, sitting in a tree. *(show two fingers)*
[chorus]
One little monkey, sitting in a tree. *(show one finger)*
[chorus]
No more monkeys, sitting in the tree. *(shake head back and forth)*

Sources for Fingerplays, Songs, Action Rhymes, and Games

"Monkey See—Monkey Do." In *Ring a Ring o' Roses: Stories, Games and Finger Plays for Pre-School Children*. Flint, MI: Flint Public Library, 1977. (page 43)
A fun action rhyme in which monkeys in the song mimic the children's clapping, stamping, and other movements. Encourage children to suggest other movements the monkeys can copy.

Scott, Anne. "Hati Jhulare." In *The Laughing Baby: Remembering Nursery Rhymes and Reasons*. South Hadley, MA: Bergin & Garvey, 1987. (page 34)
While reading aloud this lullaby, have children pretend to be elephants.

———. "Namo Ganesha." In *The Laughing Baby: Remembering Nursery Rhymes and Reasons*. South Hadley, MA: Bergin and Garvey, 1987. (page 64)
Have children clap their hands and lift them to the sky while reading aloud this Sanskrit chant.

Scott, Louise Bender. "Tiger Walk." In *Rhymes for Learning Times: Let's Pretend Activities for Early Childhood*. Minneapolis, MN: T. S. Denison, 1983. (page 137)
Have children pretend to be tigers as they follow the words of this action rhyme.

Stewart, Georgiana. "Wonders of the World." In *Children of the World: Multicultural Rhythmic Activities*. Long Branch, NJ: Kimbo Educational, 1991. Audiocassette.
An action song about the wonders of the world, including the Taj Mahal of India.

Yolen, Jane, ed. "Wave Your Hand" and "Moon, Moon, Come to Me." In *Street Rhymes Around the World*. Honesdale, PA: Boyds Mills Press, 1992. (pages 8–9)
Two rhymes written in both the Tamil and English languages.

Media Choice

Show a video or filmstrip as a transition between storytelling activities and crafts. This gives children an opportunity to rest quietly for a few minutes.

Brown, Marcia. *Once a Mouse*. 6 min. DeSoto, TX: American School, 1986. Videocassette.
A hermit saves the life of a mouse and magically changes the rodent into larger and larger animals until it finally becomes an arrogant tiger. Based on the Caldecott Medal-winning book.

Crafts and Other Activities

Choose a craft suited for the age level of the group and the time allotted for the story time.

Rakhi (Bracelet)

Raksha Bandhan [raksha BUND-end] is a Hindu festival honoring sisters and brothers. It is celebrated mainly in the northern part of India during the month of August. A sister ties a rakhi [raw-key] (bracelet) on her brother's arm to show her love and affection. In return, he gives her a gift and promises to protect her.

For more information about Raksha Bandhan, see *Gopal and the Temple's Secret* by Bridget Daly (Morristown, NJ: Silver Burdett, 1985) or *Festivals Together: A Guide to*

Multi-Cultural Celebration by Sue Fitzjohn, Minda Weston, and Judy Large (Stroud, Gloucestershire: Hawthorn Press, 1993).

Supplies

Posterboard (orange, yellow or pink)
Aluminum foil
Construction paper (use bright colors)
Buttons (metallic, if possible)
Yarn
Glue stick
Scissors
Pencil
Hole punch
White glue or hot-glue gun and glue sticks

Fig. 9.11. Rakhi (Bracelet) Example.

Use figures 9.12–9.16 to make a rakhi. An adult should pre-cut all pieces for the rakhi. Each child should receive one of each piece with the exception of the leaf-shaped piece. Give each child eight leaf-shaped pieces.

Trace and cut the large circle, figure 9.12, from orange posterboard. Using a multitude of brightly colored construction paper, trace and cut the leaf-shaped pieces (fig. 9.13). The small round circle (fig. 9.14), and the flower-shaped piece (fig. 9.15) are traced from yellow and pink posterboard, respectively. Figure 9.16 is cut from aluminum foil. Cut a fringe around the edge of the foil using scissors. Lastly, cut a 15-inch strand of yarn for each child.

The teacher or librarian should glue the large circle (fig. 9.12) to the center of the foil (fig. 9.16). The foil piece will be the bottom of the bracelet. The fringed edge of the foil will extend beyond the edge of the posterboard circle. These two pieces, glued together, form the main part of the rakhi. When dry, punch two holes at the center, ½-inch apart, with a single-hole punch.

Children can now use the main part of the rakhi and the remaining pieces to create their bracelets. Each child should begin by threading the 15-inch length of yarn through the two holes. Thread up through the bottom and down through the other hole, looping across the top of the posterboard.

Glue the leaf-shaped pieces on top of the posterboard circle in a flower petal design. Next, glue the flower-shaped piece (fig. 9.15) at the center of the circle, covering the yarn looped across. At the center of figure 9.15, glue the small circle. Finish the bracelet with a decorative button glued at the center of the small circle. (If using hot-glue, have an adult perform this step.) The rakhi is now ready to tie around the child's wrist.

Fig. 9.12. Bracelet (cut from posterboard) (upper left). Fig. 9.13. Bracelet (cut from construction paper) (leaf). Fig. 9.14. Bracelet (cut from construction paper) (upper right circle). Fig. 9.15. Bracelet (cut from construction paper) (bottom left). Fig. 9.16. Bracelet (cut from foil) (bottom right circle).

Pongal Cow Mask

In the state of Tamil Nadu, in southern India, the Tamils celebrate Pongal [pon-GAL] during the middle of January. Pongal is a thanksgiving festival which lasts three days. On the first day of Pongal, bonfires are lit and a sweet rice pudding is made. On the second day, the sun is thanked; and on the third day cows and bullocks are honored as sacred animals. Their horns are brightly painted and tipped with brass ornaments. Garlands of flowers are hung around their necks. Once decorated, the cows and bullocks are paraded through the village as people play music and drum loudly.

In this craft project, children make cow masks representing the animals honored during Pongal. As a follow-up activity, have children make drums using coffee cans or oatmeal containers. Lead children in a procession around the room or library. Have some children play the drums (or other musical instruments) while the other children hold cow masks to their faces.

Supplies

Yellow posterboard	Scissors
Yellow construction paper	Pencils
White posterboard	Jumbo craft sticks
Glue sticks	Colored markers or crayons
Clear tape	Foil

Use figures 9.17–9.19 to make the mask. An adult should pre-cut one cow's head, two ears, and two horns per child.

Using yellow posterboard, trace and cut out the cow's head (fig. 9.17 is a half-pattern). Cut out the openings for the eyes and nose. Trace and cut two horns (fig. 9.18) from the white posterboard and two ears (fig. 9.19) from the yellow construction paper. Fold the ears in half along the dashed lines.

Children will glue the horns and ears into place and decorate. Glue the folded ears at the top of the head, behind the mask. Color the horns using markers or crayons and glue at the top of the head, behind the mask, where indicated. Fold small pieces of foil around the tips of the horns to represent the brass ornaments.

Either an adult or child can tape a craft stick to the back of the mask, at the base, to be used as a handle.

Sources for Craft Ideas and Activities

Deshpande, Chris. *Festival Crafts.* Photographs by Zul Mukhida. Worldwide Crafts series. Milwaukee, WI: Gareth Stevens, 1994. (page 10)
Do splatter painting; make a paper flower garland to celebrate Holi, the most boisterous of India's celebrations. Everyone celebrates by throwing colored water and powder on one another.

———. *Food Crafts.* Photographs by Zul Mukhida. Worldwide Crafts series. Milwaukee, WI: Gareth Stevens, 1994. (page 22)
Use paper and colored glitter to create rangoli patterns, which are used to decorate the floor or ground for various Hindu celebrations.

MacLeod-Brudenell, Iain. *Costume Crafts.* Photographs by Zul Mukhida. Worldwide Crafts series. Milwaukee, WI: Gareth Stevens, 1994. (page 22)
Trace and cut out paper hand shapes and decorate them with mehndi designs. Mehndi is a temporary body decoration that looks like a tattoo.

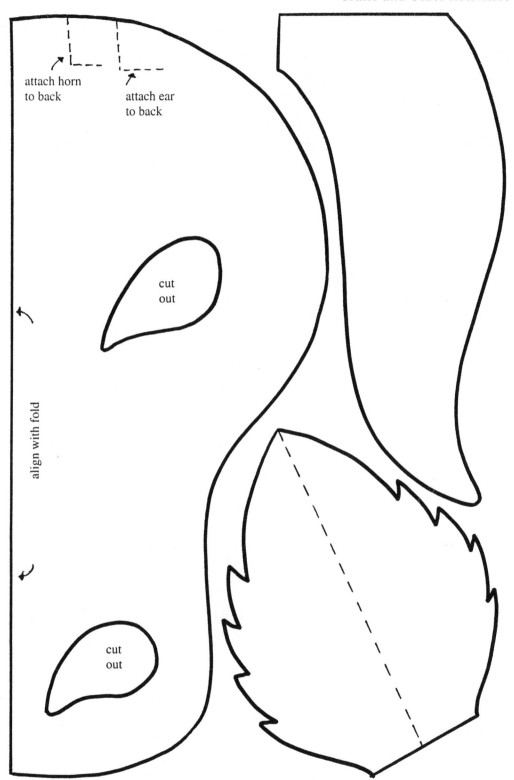

attach horn
to back

attach ear
to back

cut
out

align with fold

cut
out

Fig. 9.17. Cow Mask (left). Fig. 9.18. Cow Mask Horn (cut 2) (top right).
Fig. 9.19. Cow Mask Ear (cut 2) (top bottom).

Newbold, Patt, and Anne Diebel. *Paper Hat Tricks IV: A Big Book of Hat Patterns*. Northville, MI: Paper Hat Tricks, 1992.
Make a trace-and-cut turban attached to a headband.

Press, Judy. *The Little Hands Big Fun Craft Book: Creative Fun for 2- to 6-Year-Olds*. Illustrated by Loretta Trezzo Braren. Little Hands series. Charlotte, VT: Williamson, 1996. (pages 90–91)
Create a floating (but nonburning) Diwali candle using a sturdy paper bowl and a toilet-tissue tube. Diwali, a Hindu festival, is celebrated throughout India for five days.

Let's Visit

Ireland

Sample Story Times

Story Time for Preschool

Song: "Hello Song"

Book: *Market Day* by Eve Bunting

Action Rhyme: "I'm a Little Leprechaun"

Book: *Count Your Way Through Ireland* by Jim Haskins and Kathleen Benson

Song: "This Old Man" from *Mel Bay's Action Songs for Children* by Pamela Cooper Bye

Book: *Jamie O'Rourke and the Big Potato: An Irish Folktale* by Tomie dePaola

Filmstrip: *The Selkie Girl* by Susan Cooper

Craft: "Illuminated Manuscript Border"

Action Rhyme: "My Hands"

Story Time for Kindergarten Through Third Grade

Song: "Hello Song"

Book: *Clever Tom and the Leprechaun* retold by Linda Shute

Song: "Wee Falorie Man" from *Wee Sing Around the World* by Pamela Conn Beall and Susan Hagen Nipp, with Nancy Spence Klein

Oral Story: "Children of Lir" from *Irish Legends for Children* by Yvonne Carrol

Flannel Board Presentation: "Billy Beg and the Bull"

Fingerplay: "Do Your Ears Point Up?" from *1001 Rhymes and Fingerplays* by Totline Staff

Flannel Board Presentation: "Five Little Instruments"

Video: *Fin McCoul* by Brian Gleeson

Craft: "Brooches"

Action Rhyme: "My Hands"

Begin the story time with the "Hello Song." Then sing the song again, substituting the word *hello* with the Gaelic greeting *dia duit* [djiah gwich]. (See p. xxvii for "Hello Song" music.)

Hello Song

Hello ev'rybody,
And how are you? How are you?
Hello ev'rybody,
And how are you today?

djiah gwich ev'rybody,
And how are you? How are you?
djiah gwich ev'rybody,

And how are you today?

End the story time with the "My Hands" action rhyme, substituting the words *thank you* with the Gaelic word *go raibh maith agat* [guramahhagut], and *goodbye* with *sl&aacuten* [shlahn]. Have children stand up and follow the actions in the rhyme.

My Hands

My hands say guramahhagut. *(hold up hands)*
With a clap, clap, clap. *(clap hands)*
My feet say guramahhagut. *(point to feet)*
With a tap, tap, tap. *(stamp or tap feet)*
Clap! Clap! Clap! *(clap hands)*
Tap! Tap! Tap! *(stamp or tap feet)*
Turn myself around and bow. *(turn and bow)*
shlahn. *(wave goodbye)*

Books to Read Aloud

Bunting, Eve. *Clancy's Coat.* Illustrated by Lorinda Bryan Cauley. New York: Frederick Warne, 1984. (44 pages)
Tippitt the tailor and Clancy the farmer have not spoken for a long time because of a disagreement. When Clancy brings his coat to Tippitt for repair, their friendship, slowly but surely, is also repaired.

——. *Market Day.* Illustrated by Holly Berry. New York: HarperCollins, 1996. (32 pages)
When Tess and Wee Boy get together on market day, they see all the sights, including a sword swallower, pipe players, and farm animals.

——. *The Traveling Men of Ballycoo.* Illustrated by Kaethe Zemach. New York: Harcourt Brace Jovanovich, 1983. (28 pages)
A story of three men who have grown too old to be traveling musicians. They think of a new and creative way to stay in one place and still share their great talent with others.

Cooper, Susan. *The Selkie Girl.* Illustrated by Warwick Hutton. New York: Macmillan, 1986. (30 pages)
While at the beach one day, Donallan sees the love of his life. The only problem is that she is part woman and part seal. He decides to trick her by stealing her seal skin, which forces her to stay with him.

dePaola, Tomie. *Fin M'Coul: The Giant of Knockmany Hill.* New York: Holiday House, 1981. (32 pages)
Fin, the giant of Knockmany Hill, is afraid of the giant Cucullin. Fin's wife, Oonagh, helps Fin to prepare for Cucullin's visit.

——. *Jamie O'Rourke and the Big Potato: An Irish Folktale.* New York: G. P. Putnam's Sons, 1992. (28 pages)
When Jamie, a lazy farmer, captures a leprechaun, he is offered a magic potato seed in exchange for the leprechaun's freedom.

——. *Patrick: Patron Saint of Ireland.* New York: Holiday House, 1992. (28 pages)
Tomie dePaola describes the life and legends of Patrick, the Patron Saint of Ireland.

Haskins, Jim, and Kathleen Benson. *Count Your Way Through Ireland.* Illustrated by Beth Wright. Minneapolis, MI: Carolrhoda Books, 1996. (24 pages)
Count from 1 to 10 in Gaelic while learning about Ireland.

McDermott, Gerald. *Daniel O'Rourke: An Irish Tale.* New York: Viking Kestrel, 1986. (28 pages)
The mythological Irish character Pooka takes Daniel on an amazing journey.

Shute, Linda. *Clever Tom and the Leprechaun.* New York: Lothrop, Lee & Shepard, 1988. (34 pages)
Tom thinks that he is very clever when he captures a leprechaun. Tom forces the leprechaun to tell him where he hides his gold, but the leprechaun has a trick up his sleeve.

Storytelling

Flannel Board Presentation

"Billy Beg and the Bull." This is the story of how the loyal friendship of an animal helps a boy find happiness. See figures 10.1–10.8 for patterns. Trace the patterns on felt, or photocopy and color them. If photocopying, glue small squares of felt to the backs of the paper figures so they will hold to the flannel board. Place the figures on the flannel board as they are introduced in the story.

Billy Beg and the Bull
retold by Elaine Harrod

In the green pastures of Ireland lived Billy Beg and his bull. *(place Billy Beg and the bull on the flannel board)* They were best friends. The bull had been a gift from Billy's mother, who had died a few years before. When Billy's father remarried, the stepmother soon made it clear that she did not like Billy spending all his time with the bull. She wanted Billy to do not only his chores but also her children's chores. Billy was so unhappy that he would quickly finish his chores and run to be with his bull. They spent many hours together and were great friends.

One day, Billy overheard his stepmother say she was going to get rid of his bull. Billy knew he would never let anything happen to his bull, for it was all he had left to remind him of his mother. He told the bull of his plan for them to leave their home. The bull was a friend and agreed to follow Billy anywhere. Billy and the bull set off on their journey, not knowing where the road would take them.

As Billy and his bull traveled, they met with many challenges. The bull was wise and taught Billy many things. Billy's bull was an extraordinary animal with very special abilities. When Billy was hungry, he would reach into the bull's right ear and pull out a cloth. When Billy laid it out upon the ground, it would magically become covered with food. *(place the cloth with food on the flannel board)* After supper every evening, the bull would have the boy take a stick out of his other ear. *(place the magic stick on the flannel board)* The bull would have Billy practice with the stick as if it were a sword, and in this way Billy was learning to take care of himself.

One day as the two approached a forest, they saw another bull. The strange bull approached and told Billy and the bull they could not pass through his forest. Billy and the bull did not want to turn back, for they had come so far. Billy's bull told Billy that he would fight the other bull. He explained to Billy that if he were to lose, Billy was to make a belt from his hide. This special belt would help give Billy strength. This was, unfortunately, the outcome of the fight between the two bulls. Before the bull died, he told Billy to take the stick from his ear, and after he had made the belt from his hide, he was to wave the stick above his head.

Billy was very sad, but he did what the bull had asked him to do. He made the belt out of the hide of the bull and waved the stick above his head. Magically, the stick turned into a sword. *(place the sword on the flannel board and remove the magic stick)* After the fight, the strange bull watched in fear as Billy turned the stick into a sword. When the bull saw this, he ran away. Billy then made his way into the forest. As Billy traveled through the forest, he became a brave hunter.

One day as Billy was walking, he saw smoke. As he approached, he could see that there was an outdoor celebration. (*place the princess on the flannel board*) Many people were dancing and having a feast. Billy was invited to join the celebration. Suddenly, he noticed something coming out of the forest: It was a dragon! (*place the dragon on the flannel board*) The dragon was reaching out to grab a young princess. Billy took his sword and quickly slew the dragon. He had saved the princess. The people rushed in to make sure the princess was all right, and when they did, Billy slipped away into the forest. (*remove the dragon and Billy from the flannel board*)

When the princess realized that the young man who saved her was gone, she looked down and saw that, during the struggle with the dragon, the young man had lost one of his boots. (*place Billy's boot on the flannel board*) She quickly ordered the king's men to bring all the men within a 10-mile range back to the celebration to try on the boot.

Many men came to the celebration hoping that the boot would fit them, making them a hero. (*place Billy on the flannel board*) After many tries, the boot was finally slipped onto Billy's foot. The princess was so happy that she asked Billy to be her husband. At last, Billy knew his journey had come to an end. He and the princess lived a very happy life together!

Flannel Board Presentation

"Five Little Instruments." The people of Ireland have a rich musical history. Today, music continues to be an important part of Irish culture. Some of the common instruments played in Ireland are the bodhran [BAH-rahn] (drum), the fiddle (violin), the penny whistle (flute), the accordion, and the harp, which are featured in this flannel board presentation. See figures 10.9–10.13 for patterns. Photocopy, color, and laminate the patterns. Glue small pieces of felt to the backs of the figures so they will hold to the flannel board. Place the figures on the flannel board as the instruments are introduced in the poem. (Optionally, reduce the size of the patterns and make puppets for a fingerplay; use fig. 6.11 to make finger attachments for the puppets.)

Five Little Instruments
by Elaine Harrod and Sandy Shropshire

Here are Irish instruments to blow, to pound, to strum.
Beat the bodhran [BAW-rahn] hard and strong; it's a Celtic drum.
(Place drum on flannel board.)

Now play a penny whistle, a flute with sweetest sound.
Blow it soft; blow it loud; great music will abound!
(Place the penny whistle/flute on flannel board.)

Next we'll hear the fiddle, it's a violin to some.
The notes they blend together—join in; have some fun!
(Place the violin on flannel board.)

Time for the accordion with buttons, keys and folds.
Listen to the music; hear ancient tales retold.
(Place the accordion on flannel board.)

Last we add the Gaelic harp—Ireland's ancient treasure.
Our Irish band is now complete; the music is such pleasure.
(Place the harp on flannel board.)

Fig. 10.1. Billy Beg. Fig. 10.2. Princess.

Fig. 10.3. Bull.   Fig. 10.4. Cloth with Food.   Fig. 10.5. Sword.   Fig. 10.6. Billy's Boot.   Fig. 10.7. Magic Stick.

Fig. 10.8. Dragon (place edge marked by arrows against outside edge of flannelboard).

From *Travel the Globe*. © 1998. Desiree Lorraine Webber, et al. Libraries Unlimited. (800) 237-6124.

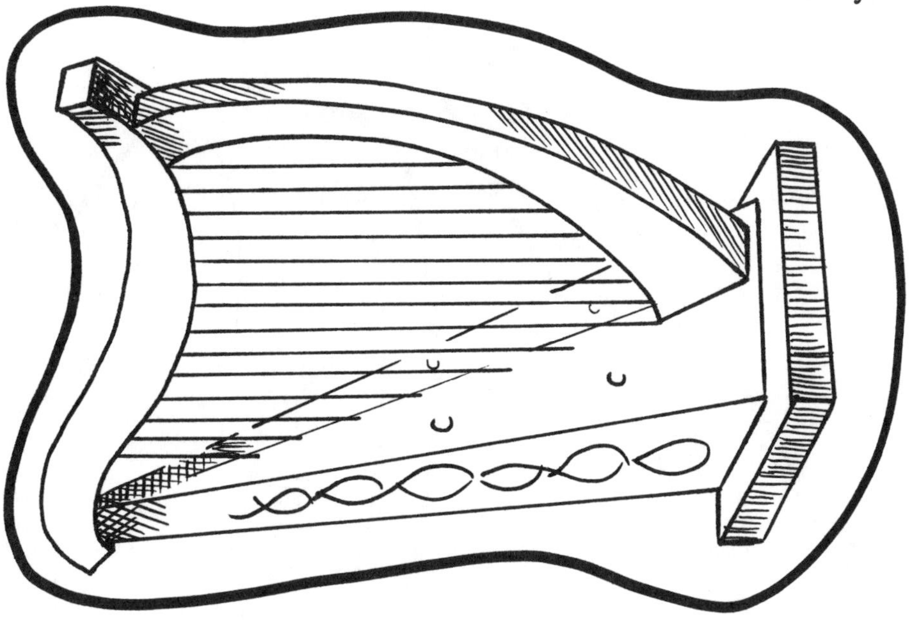

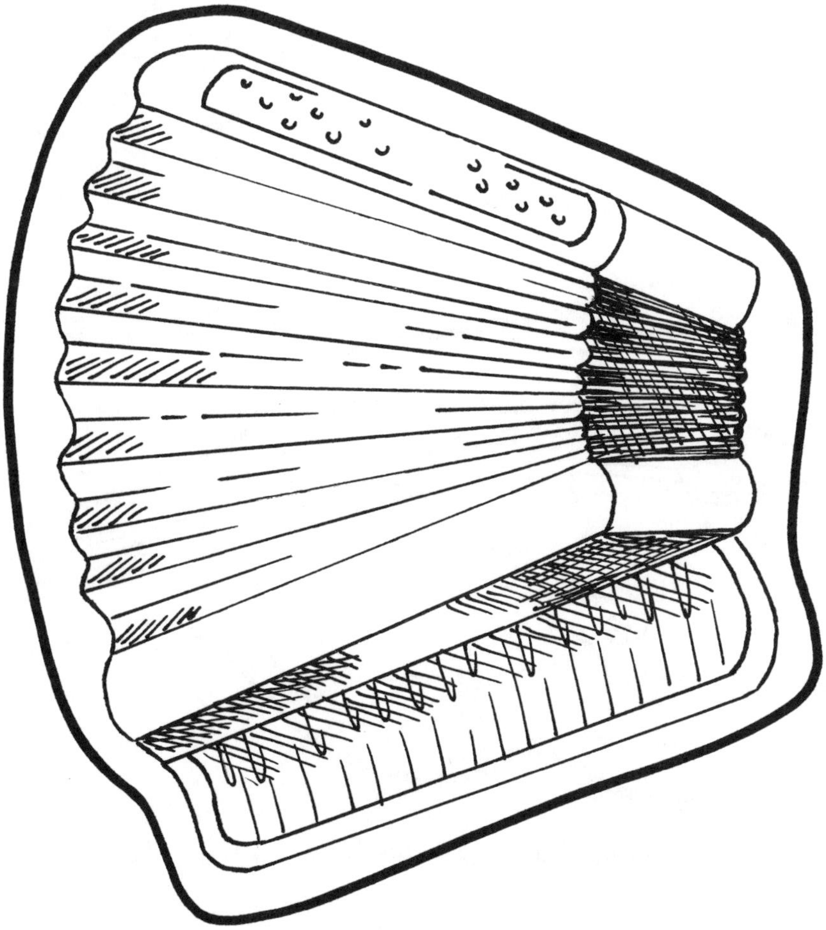

Fig. 10.9. Harp. Fig. 10.10. Accordion.

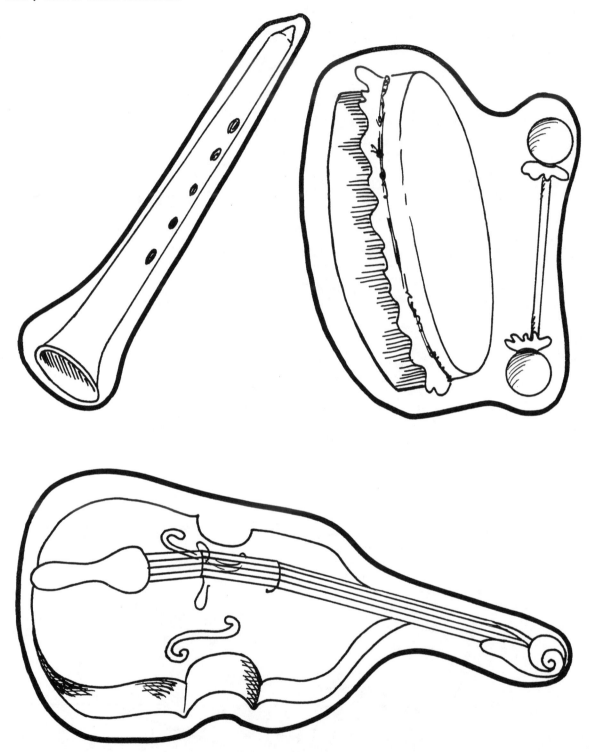

Fig. 10.11. Fiddle (Violin). Fig. 10.12. Bodhran (Drum). Fig. 10.13. Penny Whistle (Flute).

Sources for Flannel Board Presentations

Sierra, Judy. "Munachar and Manachar." In *Multicultural Folktales for the Feltboard and Readers' Theater*. Phoenix, AZ: Oryx Press, 1996. (pages 85–92)
In this cumulative story, Munachar seeks a way to stop Manachar from eating all the raspberries.

Warren, Jean, comp. "The Little Old Lady and the Leprechaun." In *Teeny-Tiny Folktales: Simple Folktales for Young Children Plus Flannelboard Patterns*. Totline Teaching Tale series. Illustrated by Marion Hopping Ekberg. Flannel board patterns by Cora Bunn. Everett, WA: Warren, 1987. (pages 19 and 54–55)
A little old lady catches a leprechaun and tries to force him to reveal where he hides his gold. Patterns for characters are included.

Sources for Oral Stories

Carrol, Yvonne. *Irish Legends for Children*. Illustrated by Lucy Su. New York: Random House, 1994. (63 pages)
Includes many traditional Irish stories in picture-book form, such as "Children of Lir." Each is about 10 pages in length.

Fingerplays, Songs, Action Rhymes, and Games

A picture of a shillelagh and a description can be found by referring to "Count Your Way Through Ireland" by Jim Haskins and Kathleen Benson. (See "Books to Read Aloud.")

I'm a Little Leprechaun
(sung to "I'm a Little Teapot")
by Elaine Harrod

I'm a little leprechaun, bold and wee. *(walk in place)*
Here is my gold and my shillelagh [sha-LAY-lee]. *(hold up one fist, then the other)*
When I hide my pot of precious gold, *(pretend to hold pot)*
Keep your eyes on the Irish rainbows. *(hold hand above eyes as if looking into the sun)*

Sources for Fingerplays, Songs, Action Rhymes, and Games

Beall, Pamela Conn, and Susan Hagen Nipp, with Nancy Spence Klein. "Wee Falorie Man." In *Wee Sing Around the World*. New York: Price Stern Sloan, 1994. Book with audiocassette. This song is about an Irish Wee Falorie Man. Falorie means a unique and interesting fellow.

Bye, Pamela Cooper. "This Old Man." In *Mel Bay's Action Songs for Children*. Pacific, MO: Mel Bay, 1992. (page 22)
A collection of songs for young children. "This Old Man" is a song that the children of Ireland have enjoyed for many years.

Graham, Steve. *Dear Old Donegal*. Illustrated by John O'Brien. New York: Clarion Books, 1996. (30 pages)
A picture book about an Irish man who immigrates to the United States and then later returns to his homeland. The words of a song form the text; the music is included at the beginning of the book.

Oakley, Ruth. "Jacks." In *The Marshall Cavendish Illustrated Guide to Games Children Play Around the World: Games with Sticks, Stones and Shells.* Illustrated by Steve Lucas. New York: Marshall Cavendish, 1989. (page 41)
Explains the Irish version of the game "Jacks," known as "Jackstones," which is played to the tune "This Old Man."

Stewart, Georgiana. "Piper Piper." In *Multicultural Rhythm Stick Fun.* Long Branch, NJ: Kimbo Educational, 1992. Audiocassette.
"Piper Piper" is a song about following the piper. Children keep time by tapping rhythm sticks (or clapping).

Totline Staff, comps. "Eensy Weensy Leprechaun" and "Do Your Ears Point Up?" In *1001 Rhymes and Fingerplays: For Working with Young Children.* Illustrated by Gary Mohrmann. Everett, WA: Warren, 1994. (page 256)
Contains more than a dozen fingerplays and rhymes about St. Patrick's Day.

Warren, Jean, and Elizabeth McKinnon. "Leprechaun, Leprechaun" and "If You're Wearing Green Today." In *Small World Celebrations: Around the World Holidays to Celebrate with Young Children.* Illustrated by Marion Hopping Ekberg. Everett, WA: Warren, 1988. (pages 43–44)
Contains Irish fingerplays, songs, and poems, as well as activities and craft ideas.

Yolen, Jane. "Wild Mountain Thyme." In *Jane Yolen's Songs of Summer.* Music Arranged by Adam Stemple. Illustrated by Cyd Moore. Honesdale, PA: Boyds Mills Press, 1993. (pages 22–24)
A colorfully illustrated book of songs about summer for young children. Includes music and lyrics.

Media Choices

Show a video or filmstrip as a transition between storytelling activities and crafts. This gives children an opportunity to rest quietly for a few minutes.

Cooper, Susan. *The Selkie Girl.* 14 min. Weston, CT: Weston Woods, 1987. Filmstrip with audiocassette.
The story of a young man and his love for a woman who is a human when on land and a seal when in the sea.

Gleeson, Brian. *Fin McCoul.* Illustrated by Peter de Sève. Music by Boys of the Lough. 30 min. Rowayton, CT: Rabbit Ears, 1991. Videocassette.
Fin McCoul, a legendary Irish giant, and his wife, Oonagh, outwit the giant Cucullin.

Crafts and Other Activities

Choose a craft suited for the age level of the group and the time allotted for the story time.

Illuminated Manuscript Border

Between the fifth and seventh century, monasteries in Ireland were built for monks. Many people in Ireland did not know how to write, but the monks knew how to write in Latin and even developed a written language for Gaelic, which many people spoke (some people still speak Gaelic today). In those days, books were written and copied by hand. This became a large portion of the monks' day-to-day work. They turned their books into wonderful works of art by illustrating the pages. The colors were so bright and beautiful that the works seemed to glow. They became known as "illuminated manuscripts." Many of these manuscripts are kept in the Trinity College Library in Dublin for all the world to see.

Because storytelling is such an important part of Irish culture, the following craft project will allow children to combine two aspects of Irish culture—illuminated manuscripts and storytelling. Show children pictures of illuminated manuscripts, which can be found in encyclopedias.

Supplies

Colored pencils	Crayons
Markers	Pencils

Make a copy of figure 10.15 for each child. Have children tell a story inside the illuminated manuscript border. The border pattern allows space for writing and drawing pictures. The border can be enlarged to give the child a larger space for their art or story. If the children are old enough to use the border to write a story, the child can be given two copies. One copy to write their story and another to draw a picture to go with their story. The child can also color the border with colored pencils or markers.

Brooches

The Celts were an ancient people who came to Ireland centuries ago. They brought their language, known as Gaelic, which is still used to this day by about 30 percent of Irish people. All school children are taught to read and write Gaelic. The Celts also brought with them a clothing adornment, the brooch, worn by males and females alike. It was used to hold clothes together. It consisted of an open metal disk and a long pin. The clothing was pushed together through the hole; then the pin was stuck through the clothing, holding it in place inside the brooch.

In this craft project, children make brooches similar to those worn by the Celts. Make a sample brooch to show children before beginning the project.

Supplies

Pencils
Scissors
Posterboard
Sequins, buttons, glitter, and beads
Craft knife
Glue (strong-bonding craft glue)
Safety pin or brooch pin (available at craft stores)

Fig. 10.14. Brooch Example.

Use figures 10.16 and 10.17 to make a brooch. School-age children can trace the patterns on posterboard and cut out the two pieces. For younger children, a teacher or librarian may want to pre-cut pieces. Cut two slits into the brooch, where indicated, using a craft knife (an adult should complete this task). Slide the posterboard brooch pin through the slits (see fig. 10.14). Have children glue decorative materials to the brooch, such as sequins, buttons, and glitter. Glue a brooch pin (from a craft store) to the back of the brooch, or pin the brooch to the child's shirt with a safety pin. Allow the glue to dry completely before wearing.

Fig. 10.15. Illuminated Manuscript Border.

From *Travel the Globe.* © 1998. Desiree Lorraine Webber, et al. Libraries Unlimited. (800) 237-6124.

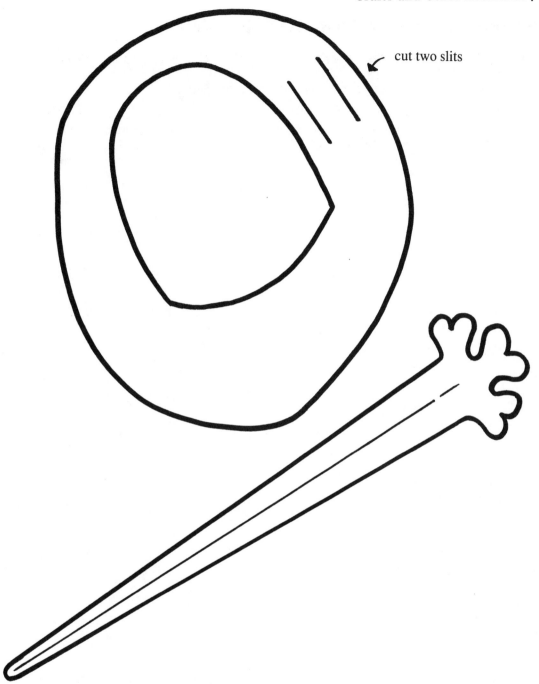

cut two slits

Fig. 10.16. Brooch (left). Fig. 10.17. Brooch Pin (right).

Sources for Craft Ideas and Activities

Newbold, Patt, and Anne Diebel. *Paper Hat Tricks IV: A Big Book of Hat Patterns.* Northville,
    MI: Paper Hat Tricks, 1992. (pages 12 and 21)
    Includes patterns for an elf/dwarf hat and a leprechaun hat.

Warren, Jean, and Elizabeth McKinnon. *Small World Celebrations: Around the World
    Holidays to Celebrate with Young Children.* Illustrated by Marion Hopping Ekberg.
    Everett, WA: Warren, 1988. (page 41)
    Includes instructions for making a leprechaun ladder and a Saint Patrick's Day hat.

Let's Visit

Italy

Sample Story Times

Story Time for Preschool

Song: "Hello Song"

Book: *Papa Gatto: An Italian Fairy Tale* by Ruth Sanderson

Action Rhyme: I'm a Venetian Gondolier

Song: "Tarantella" from *Multicultural Rhythm Stick Fun* by Georgiana Stewart

Oral Story: "The One-Legged Crane" from *The Thread of Life: Twelve Old Italian Tales* by Domenico Vittorini

Song: "Mio Galletto" from *Wee Sing Around the World* by Pamela Conn Beall and Susan Hagen Nipp, with Nancy Spence Klein

Book: *Grandfather's Rock* by Joel Strangis

Video: *Strega Nonna* by Children's Circle

Craft: "Italian Mosaic Medallions"

Action Rhyme: "My Hands"

Story Time for Kindergarten Through Third Grade

Song: "Hello Song"

Book: *Count Silvernose* by Eric A. Kimmel

Song: "Funiculi, Funicula" from *Children of the World: Multicultural Rhythmic Activities* by Georgiana Stewart

Oral Story: "The Most Precious Possession" from *The Thread of Life: Twelve Old Italian Tales* by Domenico Vittorini

Flannel Board Presentation: "Lionbruno"

Book: *Caterina: The Clever Farm Girl* by Julienne Peterson

Video: *Papa Piccola*

Craft: " 'Pepitto' Marionette Puppet"

Action Rhyme: "My Hands"

Begin the story time with the "Hello Song." Then sing the song again, substituting the word *hello* with the Italian greeting *ciao* [CHOW]. (See p. xxvii for "Hello Song" music.)

Hello Song

Hello ev'rybody,
And how are you? How are you?
Hello ev'rybody,
And how are you today?

CHOW ev'rybody,
And how are you? How are you?
CHOW ev'rybody,
And how are you today?

End the story time with the "My Hands" action rhyme, substituting the words *thank you* with the Italian word *gratzie* [GRATZEE-eh], and *goodbye* with *arivederci* [ah reeveh-DAIRCHEE]. Have children stand up and follow the actions in the rhyme.

My Hands

My hands say GRATZEE-eh. *(hold up hands)*
With a clap, clap, clap. *(clap hands)*
My feet say GRATZEE-eh. *(point to feet)*
With a tap, tap, tap. *(stamp or tap feet)*
Clap! Clap! Clap! *(clap hands)*
Tap! Tap! Tap! *(stamp or tap feet)*
Turn myself around and bow. *(turn and bow)*
ah reeveh-DAIRCHEE. *(wave goodbye)*

Books to Read Aloud

Basile, Giambattista. *Petrosinella: A Neapolitan Rapunzel.* Illustrated by Diane Stanley. New York: Frederick Warne, 1981. (28 pages)
An ogress holds Petrosinella prisoner with the power of three magical acorns—until the hero arrives.

dePaola, Tomie. *The Clown of God.* New York: Harcourt Brace Jovanovich, 1978. (40 pages)
The life story of an Italian juggler whose last performance is special.

———. *Strega Nona.* Englewood Cliffs, NJ: Prentice-Hall, 1975. (30 pages)
Strega Nona has a magic pasta pot. When she leaves Big Anthony alone with the pot, he fills the village with pasta.

Ehrlich, Amy. *Pome and Peel.* Illustrated by László Gál. New York: Dial Books for Young Readers, 1990. (30 pages)
After Pome is married, Peel helps save his sister-in-law from a curse.

Kimmel, Eric A. *Count Silvernose: A Story from Italy.* Illustrated by Omar Rayyan. New York: Holiday House, 1996. (30 pages)
Assunta saves her two younger sisters from Count Silvernose.

Peterson, Julienne. *Caterina: The Clever Farm Girl.* Pictures by Enzo Giannini. New York: Dial Books for Young Readers, 1996. (28 pages)
Caterina impresses her husband with her cleverness.

Rayevsky, Inna. *The Talking Tree (an Old Italian Tale).* Illustrated by Robert Rayevsky. New York: G. P. Putnam's Sons, 1990. (30 pages)
A king wants one last thing: the famous talking tree. During his quest for the tree, the king discovers a princess.

Sanderson, Ruth. *Papa Gatto: An Italian Fairy Tale.* Boston: Little, Brown, 1995. (30 pages)
Papa Gatto, a cat who is an advisor to a prince, tries to find someone to care for his motherless kittens.

Strangis, Joel. *Grandfather's Rock: An Italian Folktale.* Illustrated by Ruth Gamper. Boston: Houghton Mifflin, 1993. (30 pages)
An Italian family works together to keep their grandfather from going to a home for the old folk.

Storytelling

Flannel Board Presentation

"Lionbruno." This is an Italian folktale about Lionbruno and his many adventures. See figures 11.1–11.8 for patterns. Trace the patterns on felt, or photocopy and color them. If photocopying, glue small squares of felt to the backs of the paper figures so they will hold to the flannel board. Place the figures on the flannel board as they are introduced in the story.

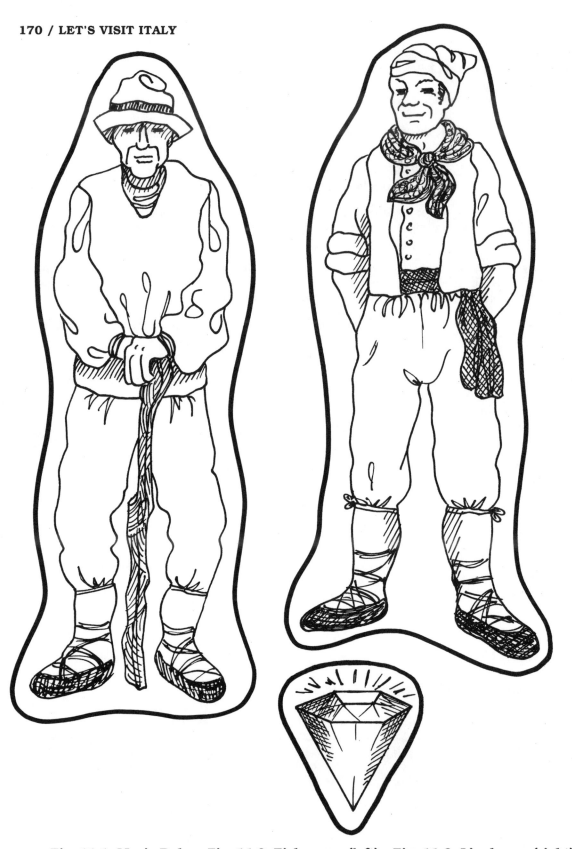

Fig. 11.1. Magic Ruby.   Fig. 11.2. Fisherman (left).   Fig. 11.3. Lionbruno (right).

From *Travel the Globe.* © 1998. Desiree Lorraine Webber, et al. Libraries Unlimited. (800) 237-6124.

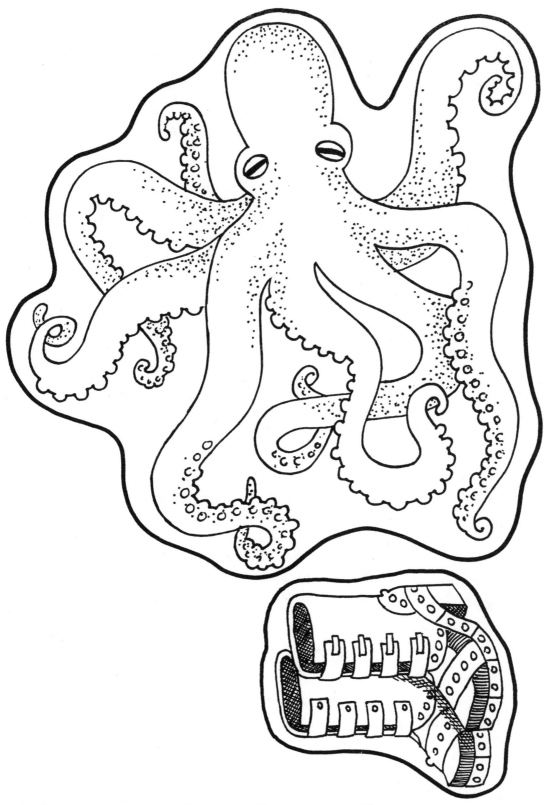

Fig. 11.4. Overgrown Octopus.   Fig. 11.5. Iron Shoes.

Fig. 11.6. Fairy Colina.

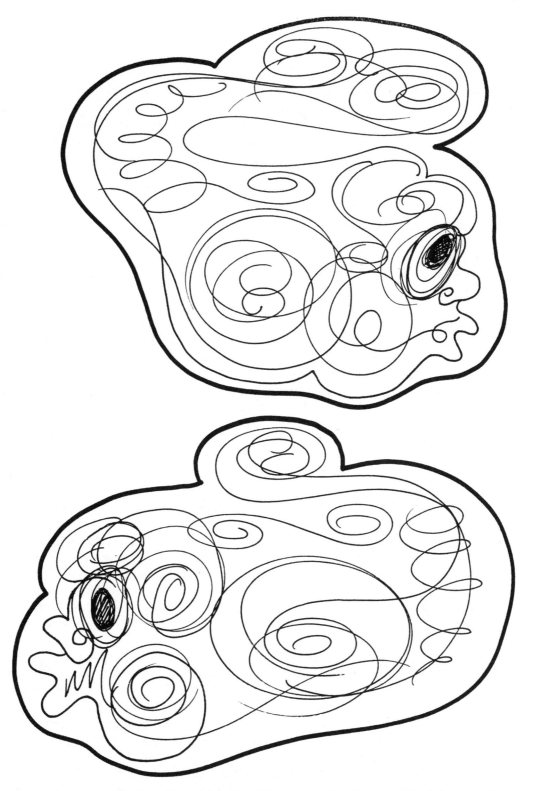

Fig. 11.7. Southwest Wind (top). Fig. 11.8. Northeast Wind (bottom).

Lionbruno
retold by Elaine Harrod

Once there was a fisherman who had lost his luck with catching fish. *(place the fisherman on the flannel board)* Every time he pulled in his nets, they were empty. One day, while out in his boat casting his nets, he looked up to see an odd, overgrown octopus. *(place the overgrown octopus on the flannel board)*

The octopus said, "I will help you catch fish once again, if you will do something for me." Of course, the fisherman was very interested. "I will make sure that your nets are full of fish every day for the rest of your life. In return, however, you must give me your unborn son. You must bring your son to me on his 13th birthday."

The fisherman did not like what the octopus said, but he didn't have this son yet, and perhaps he never would! He did, however, have a family to think about now, and he needed to feed them. So the fisherman agreed to the arrangement with the octopus. After the agreement was made, the odd, overgrown octopus disappeared into the sea. *(remove the overgrown octopus from the flannel board)*

The days that followed were very prosperous for the fisherman and his family. Soon, he and his wife were blessed with another child, a son. They named him Lionbruno. The fisherman privately hoped the odd, overgrown octopus would forget their agreement and not come for his son, for he loved the boy very much.

Years went by and the son grew. When his 13th birthday was near, the odd, overgrown octopus came to the fisherman during one of his fishing trips. *(place the overgrown octopus on the flannel board)* The octopus spoke the words the fisherman had dreaded hearing all these years: "Bring me the boy, tomorrow!" The fisherman was very sad.

The next day, he took his son to the beach and asked him to wait there. *(place Lionbruno on the flannel board and remove the fisherman)* Like a good son, Lionbruno sat on the beach waiting for his father. The odd, overgrown octopus swam close to the beach and tried to get the boy to come over to him. The boy kept his distance, for he did not have a good feeling about this sea creature. The odd, overgrown octopus came closer and closer until it grabbed the boy with one of its long tentacles. At that moment, a fairy swooped down from the sky and grabbed the boy away from the octopus. *(place Fairy Colina on the flannel board)* High into the sky the fairy flew with the boy clutched in her arms.

The boy and the fairy traveled a great distance before the fairy landed on the top of a mountain. When the boy looked up at her, he saw the most beautiful creature he had ever seen. She told Lionbruno that her name was Colina. Lionbruno thanked her for saving his life.

Lionbruno stayed on the mountain with Colina and the other fairies who lived there. Lionbruno and Colina became great friends. The fairies taught him how to joust and hunt, as well as many other skills that a man might need to know in the unpredictable world of the wilderness. The fairies trained Lionbruno to protect himself, for they knew they would not always be around to help him. As the years passed, Lionbruno and Colina grew closer, and, when they were grown, they were married.

After some time, Lionbruno began to think of his parents more and more often. He seemed to miss them more as every day went by. He spoke to Colina about visiting his parents. Colina understood, of course, but she said to Lionbruno, "Please take this magic ruby with you, *(place the magic ruby on the flannel board)* and if you need anything on your long journey, you can ask the ruby to grant your wish. I ask only one favor from you Lionbruno. Please do not tell anyone we are married. The people in your old world would not understand you being married to a fairy!" Lionbruno promised Colina he would not tell, said his goodbyes to all, and began his long journey to his parents' home.

When Lionbruno arrived in his old village, he was excited to see his parents after such a long time. But the grand house he remembered as a child was now old and run-down. His parents were so happy to see Lionbruno that they began to cry; they explained that their lives had had little meaning after they lost Lionbruno. Lionbruno used his magic ruby to make his parents' home grand once again. He promised to visit once a year from then on.

Lionbruno began his long journey home. Along the way, he came upon a castle. Inside the castle's walls was a jousting tournament. Lionbruno decided to use the skills the mountain fairies had taught him, and he entered the tournament. To his amazement, he won the tournament, but the prize was the king's daughter in marriage.

"I cannot marry the princess. I am already married, and my wife is 10 times more beautiful," boasted Lionbruno.

The king was insulted and demanded that Lionbruno produce his wife or be thrown in prison. Lionbruno took his magic ruby and called for Colina to appear. But because Colina did not want to reveal her identity, she never came. The crowd became angry and hissed and booed until Lionbruno ran out through the castle's gates.

When Lionbruno reached the road, Colina used her abilities as a fairy to appear before him. "Because you have broken your promise to me, I must leave," said Colina. "To find me, you must travel the world and wear out a pair of iron shoes." *(remove Fairy Colina from the flannel board)* Colina disappeared as quickly as she had appeared; in a cloud of fairy dust.

Lionbruno knew that he must find Colina, so he journeyed quickly to find a blacksmith to make him a pair of iron shoes. *(place the iron shoes on the flannel board)* Once Lionbruno had the shoes, he walked all over the world looking for his wife, asking everyone he met if they had seen her.

After many years, Lionbruno had almost worn out the iron shoes. Still, he had not found Colina, and he was very sad. In the distance, he saw a house upon a high hill. He decided to stop and ask for food and a place to sleep.

When he came to the house, he felt the strangest wind. It was warm, hot, cold, and cool, all at one time. He looked into the wind and saw two faces. *(place the southwest and the northeast wind on the flannel board)*

"Who are you?" asked Lionbruno.

"We are the southwest wind and the northeast wind," they answered. "We live here with our brothers and sisters, who are all the other winds."

Lionbruno told his story to the two brothers.

Puffing excitedly, the northeast wind said, "I know where Colina lives! I am the wind that blows through her castle every day. Hop on my back and I will take you to her."

When they arrived at the castle, Colina and Lionbruno hugged with joy. Lionbruno promised never to boast or to break his promises again, and Colina forgave his mistake.

The northeast wind took Colina and Lionbruno back to their mountain home, where they have lived happily to this day.

Flannel Board Presentation

Haskins, Jim. *Count Your Way Through Italy.* Illustrated by Beth Wright. Minneapolis, MN: Carolrhoda Books, 1990. (20 pages)
   The book introduces numbers 1–10 in Italian, alongside facts and historical information about Italy.

Using Haskins's book, create a flannel board presentation to teach children how to count to 10 in Italian. The part of the book that shows the number 6 (sei) in Italian also shows gondolas, Venetian boats. Make 10 gondolas out of construction paper; write the words one through ten in Italian on the gondolas. Next to the Italian words, write the numbers. Glue small pieces of felt to the backs of the figures so they will hold to the flannel board.

Source for Oral Stories

Vittorini, Domenico. *The Thread of Life: Twelve Old Italian Tales.* Illustrated by Mary GrandPré. New York: Crown, 1995. (80 pages)
   A collection of Italian folklore, including a story about a young man who gives the king the gift of a cat, and a story about an Italian cook who prepares a wonderful dish of one-legged crane.

Fingerplays, Songs, Action Rhymes, and Games

I'm a Venetian Gondolier
by Sandy Shropshire

A gondola is a long, narrow, flat-bottomed canalboat with high, pointed prow and stern, used on the canals of Venice. The gondola drivers (gondoliers) do not sit to paddle their boat; instead, they stand at the back, using long poles to push on the bottom of the shallow waterways. Have the children pretend to be Venetian gondoliers as they act out the following rhyme.

I'm a Venetian gondolier. *(Stand with hands on hips.)*
I paddle my gondola here and there. *(Pretend to paddle an oar on the left and right.)*
I transport children, ladies, and men, *(Wave like hailing a taxi cab.)*
Up the canals and back again. *(Paddle again.)*
I'm a Venetian gondolier. *(As above.)*
I paddle my gondola here and there. *(Pretend to paddle an oar on the left and right.)*
I work so hard; so I ask you now— *(Shake pointing finger.)*
"Please wave to me and call out ciao [CHOW]!" *(Wave and say CHOW.)*

Sources for Fingerplays, Songs, Action Rhymes, and Games

Beall, Pamela Conn, and Susan Hagen Nipp, with Nancy Spence Klein. "Mio Galletto" (My Little Rooster). In *Wee Sing Around the World.* Los Angeles: Price Stern Sloan, 1994. Book with audiocassette.
   This song is about a lost rooster.

Stewart, Georgiana. "Funiculi, Funicula." In *Children of the World: Multicultural Rhythmic Activities.* Long Branch, NJ: Kimbo Educational, 1991. Audiocassette.

"Funiculi, Funicula" is music to accompany the tarantella, the traditional dance of Italy. The tarantella is a rapid, whirling dance for couples. Play this music at the beginning of a story time, as you begin activities, or during a craft project.

———. "Tarantella." In *Multicultural Rhythm Stick Fun.* Long Branch, NJ: Kimbo Educational, 1991. Audiocassette.
The Tarantella dance music is played while children keep time by tapping rhythm sticks (or clapping).

Media Choices

Show a video or filmstrip as a transition between storytelling activities and crafts. This gives children an opportunity to rest quietly for a few minutes.

dePaola, Tomie. *The Clown of God.* 15 min. Weston, CT: Weston Woods, 1980. Filmstrip with audiocassette.
The life story of an Italian juggler whose last performance is special.

———. *Strega Nonna.* 8 min. Weston, CT: Children's Circle Studios, 1989. Videocassette.
Strega Nonna has a magic pasta pot. When she leaves Big Anthony alone with the pot, he fills the village with pasta.

Papa Piccolo. 18 min. Shawnee Mission, KS: Marshmedia, 1992. Videocassette.
Piccolo becomes a papa by surprise when two stray kittens enter his life.

Crafts and Other Activities

Choose a craft suited for the age level of the group and the time allotted for the story time.

"Pepitto" Marionette Puppet

In Italy, large, heavy marionettes were made and used by troops of puppeteers to tell heroic medieval tales. These troops traveled through Italy, and even to England, to tell stories using marionette puppets. This art form was first used to create characters for adult productions but later became a popular form used for children's storytelling. One famous Italian marionette puppet all children are familiar with is Pinnochio.

In this craft project have each child make their own marionette puppets. This project is best suited for second- and third-graders.

Supplies

Scissors
Yarn
Large paper clips (eight per puppet)
Clear tape
Hole punch
Thick photocopier paper or posterboard
Colored markers
Unsharpened pencils or straws

Fig. 11.9. Marionette Example.

Photocopy figures 11.10–11.18 for each child. School-age children can cut out all pattern pieces and trace on heavy photocopier paper or posterboard. If you are working with preschool children, the teacher or librarian may want to pre-cut the pieces. (This craft project is best suited for school-age children.) After the child traces the pattern onto the posterboard or photocopier paper, they need to cut out the pieces. Using markers, the child can then add details to the puppet pieces. The pattern will have details on it if they want to use it to give them some ideas for decorating their puppets. Using a hole punch, children punch holes on their puppet where marked on the pattern. (The hole for the hat will be punched after the hat is constructed.) The next step is for the children to roll and tape the arms, legs, hats, and nose pieces. (For arm and leg pieces, roll the paper to form thin, lengthwise tubes; the upper arm and leg tubes will have a hole at each end; the lower arm and leg tubes will have one hole.) With tape, attach the hands and feet to the long arm and leg tubes. Tape the head to the body, and tape the nose and hat to the face. Use large paper clips to connect the leg and arm pieces to each other and to the body. Tie a 30-inch piece of yarn to each end of an unsharpened pencil. With tape, attach the other ends of the yarn to the top, inside fronts of the long leg tubes. Tie a 19-inch piece of yarn to each end of another unsharpened pencil. With tape, attach the other ends of the yarn to the backs of the hands. Tie the 14-inch piece of yarn to the middle of this pencil, and tie the other end to the hole in the top of the hat.

Note: The pencil and strings that control the puppet's arm are held in front of the pencil and strings that control its body and legs.

Italian Mosaic Medallions

Mosaic designs are made using small pieces of a material such as stone, tile, or broken pottery. In Italy, this technique was used for decorative as well as practical purposes. Some mosaics were based on themes, such as hunting, an athletic contest, or the sea. This technique is still used in many places throughout the world.

In this craft project, children make a small mosaic medallion to wear as a necklace.

Supplies

Food coloring	Hole punch
White glue	Scissors
Rice	Posterboard
Mixing bowl and spoon	Cookie Sheets
Newspaper	Ribbon or yarn

Before children make the medallions, an adult should prepare the rice. It will take a day or so for the rice to dry. Mix an amount according to the number of children participating in the activity. For each child, use ¼ cup of rice; for every 2 cups of rice, use 5 drops of food coloring. Mix the rice and food coloring in a bowl; pour the mixture onto newspaper and let dry. Make several colors of rice(for preschool children, use two colors). After the rice is dry, place each color on a cookie sheet.

Photocopy figures 11.19 and 11.20 for each child. There are two designs to choose from: a butterfly and a flower. Have the child glue the medallion to a piece of posterboard. Cut out the medallion, along the circular edge. Punch a hole at the top of the medallion.

Give each child a bottle of glue. Explain that they should add one color of rice at a time. After they fill the desired spaces with glue, they add one color of rice by sprinkling it onto the medallion. Then repeat the process, filling other spaces with glue and adding another color of rice. Demonstrate this process for children.

After children have filled all the spaces with rice, let the medallions dry completely. Attach ribbon or yarn and the medallions are ready to wear.

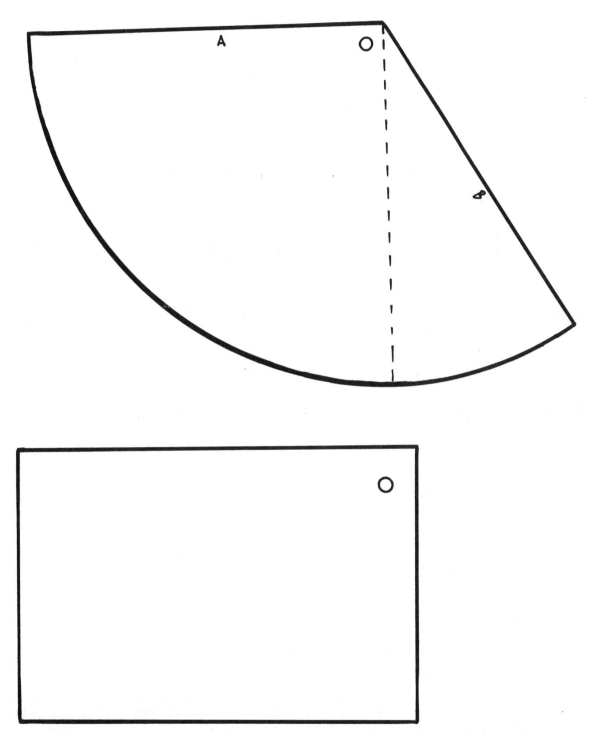

Fig. 11.10. Marionette Hat (top; cut 1) (roll to make a cone, overlapping edge A on edge B, and tape along dotted line). Fig. 11.11. Marionette Lower Arm and Lower Leg (bottom; cut 4).

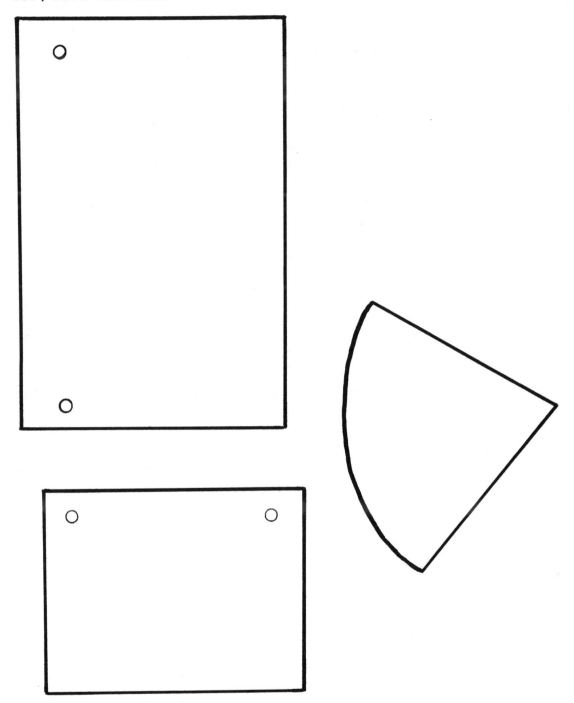

Fig. 11.12. Marionette Upper Leg (top left; cut 2). Fig. 11.13. Marionette Upper Arm (bottom left; cut 2). Fig. 11.14. Marionette Nose (right) (roll tightly and tape to form a cone with a sharp point).

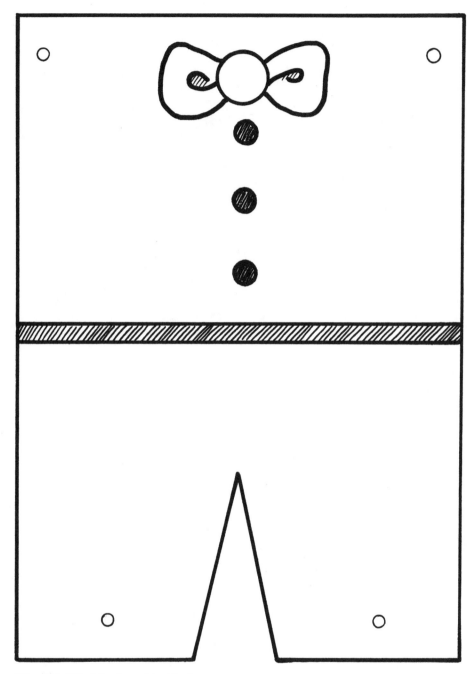

Fig. 11.15. Marionette Body.

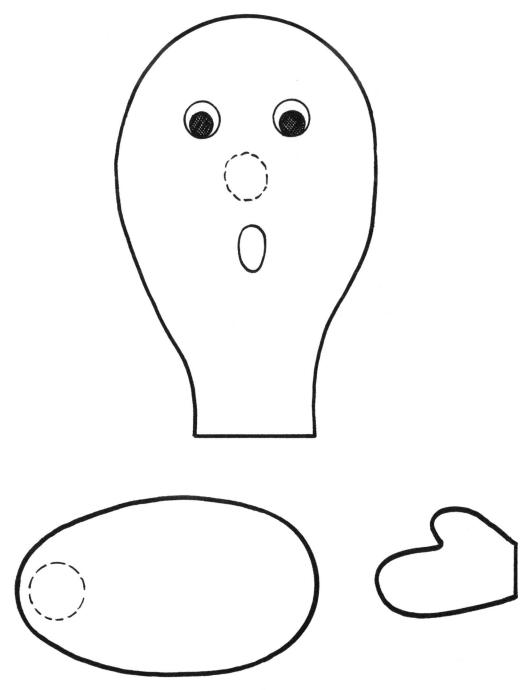

Fig. 11.16. Marionette Foot (bottom left; cut 2). Fig. 11.17. Marionette Hand (bottom right; cut 2). Fig. 11.18. Marionette Head.

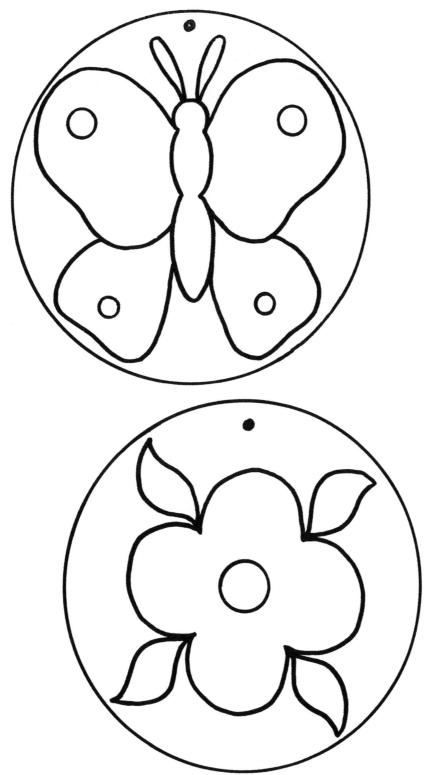

Fig. 11.19. Butterfly Mosaic Medallion. Fig. 11.20. Flower Mosaic Medallion.

Sources for Craft Ideas and Activities

Fiarotta, Phyllis, and Noel Fiarotta. *Confetti: The Kids' Make-It-Yourself, Do-It-Yourself Party Book.* New York: Workman, 1978. (pages 113–28)
Plan an Italian puppet party, including crafts, food, invitations, a centerpiece, and a puppet theater.

Press, Judy. *The Little Hands Big Fun Craft Book: Creative Fun for 2- to 6-Year-Olds.* Illustrated by Loretta Trezzo Braren. Little Hands series. Charlotte, VT: Williamson, 1996. (pages 98–99)
Some people in Italy celebrate a cricket festival. During this festival crickets are brought in the house and kept in small cages so everyone can enjoy the beautiful chirping. This book provides instructions for making a cricket basket.

Purdy, Susan. *Festivals for You to Celebrate.* New York: J. B. Lippincott, 1969. (pages 117–19)
Includes a pattern for making a Befana doll (Befana is a classic character in Italian folklore).

Let's Visit

Mexico

Sample Story Times

Story Time for Preschool

Song: "Hello Song"

Book: *In Rosa's Mexico* by Campbell Geeslin

Book: *Saturday Market* by Patricia Grossman

Book: *Uno, Dos, Tres: One, Two, Three* by Pat Mora

Fingerplay: "Five Little Elephants"

Video: *Borreguita and the Coyote* by Verna Aardema

Craft: "Banner Decorations"

Action Rhyme: "My Hands"

Story Time for Kindergarten Through Third Grade

Song: "Hello Song"

Book: *The Piñata Maker: El Piñatero* by George Ancona

Book: *The Little Red Ant and the Great Big Crumb: A Mexican Fable* by Shirley Climo

Action Rhyme: "Five Little Elephants"

Book: *The Iguana Brothers: A Tale of Two Lizards* by Tony Johnston

Puppet Presentation: "The Coyote Scolds His Tail" by Dan Storm

Video: *Hill of Fire* by Thomas P. Lewis

Craft: "Donkey Sack Piñata"

Book: *The Fabulous Firework Family* by James Flora

Action Rhyme: "My Hands"

___

Begin the story time with the "Hello Song." Then sing the song again, substituting the word *hello* with the Spanish greeting *hola* [OH-lah]. (Spanish is the primary language spoken in Mexico; see p. xxvii for "Hello Song" music.)

Hello Song

Hello ev'rybody,
And how are you? How are you?
Hello ev'rybody,
And how are you today?

OH-la ev'rybody,
And how are you? How are you?
OH-la ev'rybody,
And how are you today?

End the story time with the "My Hands" action rhyme, substituting the words *thank you* with the Mexican words *muchas gracias* [MOO-chahs GRAH-see-ahs], and *goodbye* with *adiós* [ah-DYOHS]. Have children stand up and follow the actions in the rhyme.

My Hands

My hands say MOO-chahs GRAH-see-ahs. *(hold up hands)*
With a clap, clap, clap. *(clap hands)*
My feet say MOO-chahs GRAH-see-ahs. *(point to feet)*
With a tap, tap, tap. *(stamp or tap feet)*
Clap! Clap! Clap! *(clap hands)*
Tap! Tap! Tap! *(stamp or tap feet)*
Turn myself around and bow. *(turn and bow)*
ah-DYOHS. *(wave goodbye)*

Books to Read Aloud

Ancona, George. *The Piñata Maker: El Piñatero*. San Diego, CA: Harcourt Brace, 1994. (40 pages)
The story of Tio Rico, who for 15 years has created beautiful piñatas, puppets, and masks for the children of his village.

Blanco, Alberto. *Angel's Kite (La Estrella de Angel)*. Illustrated by Rodolfo Morales. Emeryville, CA.: Children's Book Press, 1994. (32 pages)
Beautiful collage illustrations help tell the story of how Angel's wonderful kite somehow—mysteriously—brings home the town's mission bell, which had been lost for many years.

Climo, Shirley. *The Little Red Ant and the Great Big Crumb: A Mexican Fable*. Illustrated by Francisco X. Mora. New York: Clarion Books, 1995. (40 pages)
A fable about a persistent little red ant that finds a crumb in a Mexican corn field. Being so small, she goes for help, only to discover that help was not really necessary. (Moral: You can do it if you think you can.) Recommended for school-age children.

de Mariscal, Blanca López. *The Harvest Birds (Los Pájaros de la Cosecha)*. Illustrated by Enrique Flores. Emeryville, CA.: Children's Book Press, 1995. (31 pages)
A folktale from the old tradition of Oaxaca, Mexico. Juan Zantae wants to become a farmer, like his father and grandfather, but learns to determine his own destiny—with the help of his loyal friends, the harvest birds.

Flora, James. *The Fabulous Firework Family*. New York: Margaret K. McElderry Books, 1994. (32 pages)
Pepito; his sister, Amelia; and their parents are called the "Fabulous Firework Family" because they make the finest fireworks in their village. They are challenged to create the greatest castle (castillo) ever built to honor Santiago, the village's patron saint, for a big fiesta.

Geeslin, Campbell. *In Rosa's Mexico*. Illustrated by Andrea Arroyo. New York: Alfred A. Knopf, 1996. (32 pages)
Spanish words are introduced in each of these three stories about Rosa's adventures— one with a rooster, one with a burro, and one with a wolf.

Grossman, Patricia. *Saturday Market*. Illustrated by Enrique O. Sanchez. New York: Lothrop, Lee & Shepard, 1994. (30 pages)
People travel by moonlight to arrive at market by dawn. Each family has special items to sell, and a list of special things they want to buy.

Johnston, Tony. *The Iguana Brothers: A Tale of Two Lizards*. Illustrated by Mark Teague. New York: Blue Sky Press, 1995. (30 pages)
The story of two lizards known as the "iguana brothers," who discover that they are also best friends.

———. *The Magic Maguey*. Illustrated by Elisa Kleven. San Diego, CA: Harcourt Brace, 1996. (32 pages)
Miguel saves a large maguey from being cut down by decorating it for Christmas.

Mora, Pat. *Uno, Dos, Tres: One, Two, Three*. Illustrated by Barbara Lavallee. New York: Clarion Books, 1996. (34 pages)
A wonderful rhyming text tells the story of two young sisters going from shop to shop to buy presents for their mother's birthday.

Winter, Jeanette. *Josefina*. San Diego, CA: Harcourt Brace, 1996. (36 pages)
A counting book about Josefina, an artist who makes and paints clay figures.

Storytelling

Puppet Presentation

Storm, Dan. "The Coyote Scolds His Tail." In *Picture Tales from Mexico*. Illustrated by Mark Storm. Houston, TX: Gulf, 1995. (pages 65–71) Reprinted by permission of the illustrator Mark Storm.

"The Coyote Scolds His Tail." Coyote is a trickster figure from the old lore of many Indian tribes in North America. Don Coyote is a favorite trickster in Mexican tales. Coyote is known for his capacity to perform utterly silly acts, as children will see in this puppet presentation.

Use figures 12.1–12.5 to make the body parts for the Coyote hand puppet. Make a simple cloth or felt hand puppet for the body (see fig. 12.6). The puppet is introduced when Coyote enters the cave. Make the cave using a piece of black felt attached to round embroidery hoops; cut an X into the center of the felt to allow the puppet through (see fig. 12.7).

The body parts of Coyote—the feet, ears, eyes, and tail—are attached as they are introduced in the story. Sew or glue pieces of Velcro to the body parts and to the hand puppet in the proper places. Attach the nose before beginning the presentation.

The Coyote Scolds His Tail
by Dan Storm

Señor Coyote had escaped from many different kinds of animals so many times that he must have begun to think that nothing on two feet or wings could catch him. One day he was walking along the level valley between two mountains, when two large dogs that had been trying to catch him for a long time, sprang from behind a large stone and almost caught him before he could jump and run.

He tried to run to the woods, but the dogs had seen to it that he would have to take to the open country. As he ran around bushes and jumped over rocks and across dry arroyos, making the dust fly, he thought that he was gaining on the dogs behind. Their yelps of "YO! YO! YO!" were getting a little fainter he thought, as he gasped for his breath and began looking around for the best direction to go.

But while he was trying to make up his mind, two other large, red-and-white-spotted dogs rose up out of nowhere and made up his mind for him. He was forced to turn back more or less toward the direction he had come. The dogs had planned to take turns racing him back and forth across the desert till he was too tired to go any further. The new pair of dogs were cutting down the distance between themselves and the Coyote in a way that made the Coyote know he must think fast and act much faster.

Upon the side of the mountain he saw something dark and round that made him take heart. He wished that it were closer. It was a cave that he saw. And now the first pair of dogs had run over slowly and were coming up somewhat rested to join their comrades in the chase.

Fig. 12.1. Coyote Tail. Fig. 12.2. Coyote Nose. Fig. 12.3. Coyote Eyes. Fig. 12.4. Coyote Ears. Fig. 12.5. Coyote Feet. Fig. 12.6. Hand Puppet Example.

He made a sharp turn and raced for the foot of the mountain. Behind him now came all four dogs louder and closer as he reached the mountainside and bolted up toward the cave. The dogs were so close behind him that he could feel their breath upon him as they argued loudly as to which one of them was to get him. He saw the cave close in front of him and a new idea suddenly sent a chill of fear through his body. Was the cave big enough to allow the dogs to enter? Then what? While this cheerless thought haunted his mind, the dogs were now snapping hairs out of the end of the Coyote's tail, *clip-klop, snip-snap.* And with a flying dive, the Coyote sailed into the mouth of the cave. *(hold up "cave" with the left hand—have coyote on the right hand—have coyote puppet enter the cave)*

Fig. 12.7. Coyote Puppet in Embroidery-Hoop Cave Example.

It was lucky for him that the cave would not allow the dogs to enter. It was barely large enough to let him in. Inside the cave he ran as far back as he could. Outside, the dogs complained and whined and pawed around the cave a while and then he heard no more.

This was easily the worst fright the Coyote ever had; but once safe inside the cave, he began to feel brave again. He began to think he was quite a fellow to be able to get rid of the dogs. As his weary limbs became rested, a desire to boast and brag stole over him. There was no one in the cave to talk to, so he began chatting with the various parts of his body which had had some part in the race against the dogs. *(attach feet)*

"Patos," he said, looking at his four feet one at a time, "what did you do?"

"We carried you away," said the feet. "We kicked up dust to blind the bad dogs. We jumped the rocks, and bushes and brought you here."

"Bueno, bueno," said the Coyote, "good, fine. You feet did very well." Then he spoke to his ears. *(attach ears)*

"Ears, what did you do?"

"We listened to the right and to the left. We listened behind to see how far behind the dogs were, so that the Feet would know how fast to run." *(attach eyes)*

"Splendid!" said the Coyote. "And, Eyes, what did you do?"

"We pointed out the road through the rocks and brush and canyons. We were on the lookout for your safety. We saw this cave."

"Marvelous!" said the Coyote with a great laugh. "What a great fellow I am to have such fine eyes, feet, and ears." And so overcome was the Coyote with his own self and the great things he had done in his life that he reached over his shoulder to pat himself on the back. And it was then that he saw his tail back there. *(attach tail)*

"Aha, my tail," he said, "I had almost forgotten about you. Come, tell me what you did in this battle with the dogs."

The tail could tell by the tone of the Coyote's voice that he did not think too highly of him and so he did not answer.

"About all you did was add extra load," said the Coyote. "You held me back, more than anything else. Almost got me caught, too. You let the dogs grab the end of you. But let's hear from you. Speak up!"

"What did I do?" asked the tail. "I motioned to the dogs, like this, telling them to come and get you. While you were running I was back there urging the dogs to come on. Through the dust they could see my whiteness waving." The Coyote's scowl was becoming darker and darker.

"Silencio!" he shouted, stuttering and stammering with anger. "What do you mean?" and he reached back and gave a slap at his tail, and then reached around and bit at it.

"You do not belong here in this cave with the rest of us, you traitor." And the Coyote was backing his tail toward the door of the cave. "Out you go," he said. "Outside! There is no room in here for you. You belong outside. You are on the side of the dogs. You tried to help them catch me, and then you brag about it. Outside!"

And the Coyote pointed to his tail with one hand, and to the round piece of daylight which was the cave door, he pointed with the other hand. "Get Out!" *(back the coyote puppet out of the cave)*

And the Coyote backed his tail out the door into the open air. The dogs, who had been listening to the talk inside, were waiting hidden outside. When the Coyote's tail appeared outside the cave door, the dogs grabbed it. Of course the Coyote was jerked out of the cave with his tail. And what the dogs did to him is another story.

Sources for Flannel Board Presentations

Franco, Betsy. "The Three Brothers and the Singing Toad." In *Mexico: A Literature-Based Multicultural Unit.* Illustrated by Jo Supancich. Monterey, CA: Evan-Moor, 1993. (pages 16–23)
An old farmer is unhappy because a mysterious animal is eating his corn. He calls upon his three sons to help him solve the problem. He promises his cornfield and everything he owns to the one who brings back the mysterious animal, dead or alive.

Sierra, Judy, and Robert Kaminski. "La Hormiguita" (The Little Ant). In *Multicultural Folktales: Stories to Tell Young Children.* Phoenix, AZ: Oryx Press, 1991. (pages 49–55)
The little ant may not get justice in the end, but at least she does not get eaten.

Walters, Connie. "The Adventures of the Curious Animals." In *Multicultural Music: Lyrics to Familiar Melodies and Authentic Songs.* Minneapolis, MN: T. S. Denison, 1995. (pages 117–18)
A group of curious farm animals peer into the barn through the window but decide to leave and come back another day when El Toro, the bull, appears. Patterns are not included with this story, but the animals in this story are common and patterns can be found in other books with flannel board patterns (coloring books are also a good resource for patterns).

Sources for Oral Stories

Brusca, Maria Christina, and Tony Wilson. *Pedro Fools the Gringo, and Other Tales of a Latin American Trickster*. New York: Henry Holt, 1995. (54 pages)
Twelve short retellings of the adventures of Pedro, a Latin American trickster character.

Campbell, Camilla. "Mano Coyote." In *Star Mountain, and Other Legends of Mexico*. Illustrated by Ena McKinney. New York: Whittlesey House, 1946. (pages 72–75)
Mano Coyote is a shrewd creature, and not always too careful of his manners.

Edmonds, I. G. "Señor Coyote and the Tricked Trickster." In *Trickster Tales*. Illustrated by Sean Morrison. New York: J. B. Lippincott, 1966. (pages 77–85)
Mouse and Coyote have a quarrel and then refuse to speak to each other. When Mouse finds Coyote caught in a trap, he must decide whether or not to help.

Fingerplays, Songs, Action Rhymes, and Games

"Five Little Elephants." To make the finger puppets, photocopy figures 12.8 and 12.9 on white tagboard or construction paper. Use markers to color the elephants and their hats. Laminate and cut out the elephants and finger attachments. Tape together the three flaps of each finger attachment. This will fit over the tip of each finger like a thimble. Tape an elephant to each attachment. Place a puppet on your finger as each elephant is introduced in the rhyme. Substitute the Spanish numbers 1 through 5, and Spanish names for the elephants (Pancho, Pedro, Juan, Maria, and Lolita), when sharing the rhyme.

Optional: *Outline a web with glue in the palm of your hand and then sprinkle on silver glitter to make it sparkle (see fig. 12.10 for a pattern).*

1.	uno	[OO-noh]
2.	dos	[DOHS]
3.	tres	[TREHS]
4.	cuatro	[KWAH-tro]
5.	cinco	[SEEN-koh]

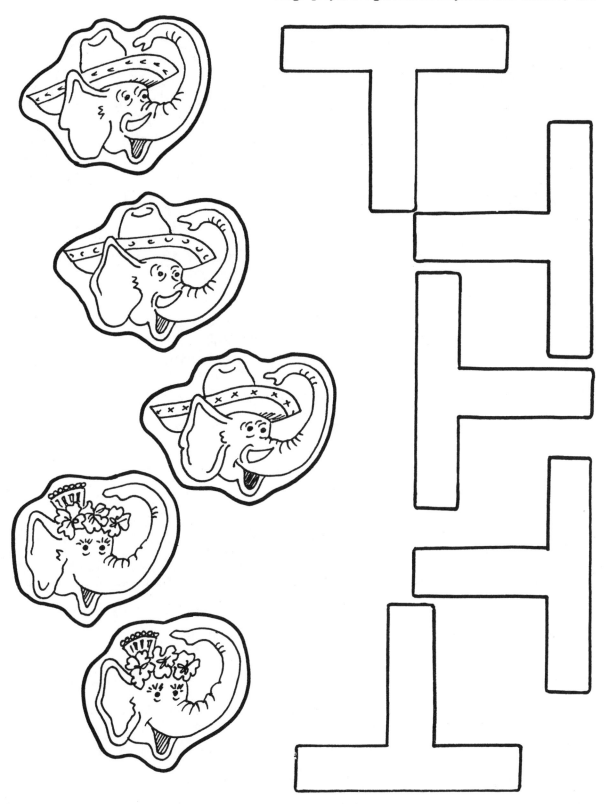

Fig. 12.8. Elephant Finger Puppets.   Fig. 12.9. Finger Puppet Attachments.

Five Little Elephants
by Donna Norvell

One (uno) little elephant (Pancho) went out to balance on a spider's web one day. *(show one puppet)*

The web seemed so strong, he called for his friend (Pedro) to come along and play.

Two (dos) little elephants (Pancho and Pedro) went out to balance on a spider's web one day. *(show two puppets)*

The web seemed so strong, they called for their friend (Juan) to come along and play.

Three (tres) little elephants (Pancho, Pedro, and Juan) went out to balance on a spider's web one day. *(show three puppets)*

Fig. 12.10. Spider Web Example.

The web seemed so strong, they called for their friend (Maria) to come along and play.

Four (cuatro) little elephants (Pancho, Pedro, Juan, and Maria) went out to balance on a spider's web one day. *(show four puppets)*

The web seemed so strong they called for their friend (Lolita) to come along and play. *(show five puppets)*

The spider web swings, and the spider web sways. Snap! went the spider web, and blew away. Five (cinco) little elephants can no longer play on the spider web today. *(remove puppets)*

Sources for Fingerplays, Songs, Action Rhymes, and Games

Bauer, Karen, and Rosa Drew. *Mexico: A Multicultural Study to Celebrate Our Diversity.* Edited by Bette McIntire. Illustrated by Catherine Yuh. World Neighbor series. Cypress, CA: Creative Teaching Press, 1994. (36 pages)
A sample study of Mexico with the use of literature, music, and hands-on activities, cooking, and crafts. Includes instructions for the game "Don Blanca: A Traditional Circle Game."

Franco, Betsy. *Mexico: A Literature-Based Multicultural Unit.* Illustrated by Jo Supancich. Monterey, CA: Evan-Moore, 1993.
Includes instructions for two games, "La Lotería" and "The Circle of San Miguel," a dancing game.

Ortega, José, and His Mariachi Ensemble. *The Music of Mexico.* Roswell, GA: Intersound, 1995. Compact disc.
Includes "The Mexican Hat Dance" (El Jarabe Tapatio), "Mexican Hand-Clap Song" (Las Chiapanecas), and "The Coyote" (El Coyote).

Rockwell, Anne, comp. *El Toro Pinto, and Other Songs in Spanish.* New York: Aladdin, 1995. (52 pages)
A collection of Spanish songs gathered from various Spanish-speaking countries.

Schon, Isabel, comp. and trans., with R. R. Chalquest. *Doña Blanca, and Other Hispanic Nursery Rhymes and Games.* Minneapolis, MN: T. S. Denison, 1983. (41 pages)
A variety of well-known nursery rhymes and games, presented in English and Spanish.

Stewart, Georgiana. "La Cucaracha." In *Multicultural Rhythm Stick Fun*. Long Branch, NJ: Kimbo Educational, 1992. Audiocassette.
>Children tap rhythm sticks (or clap) and sway side-to-side to the tune "La Cucaracha."

Walters, Connie. *Multicultural Music: Lyrics to Familiar Melodies and Native Songs*. Minneapolis, MN: T. S. Denison, 1995. (160 pages)
>Songs about the inhabitants of Mexico and their traditions, customs, and special events, including the songs "The Piñata" and "Mexican Hat Dance."

Weissman, Jackie. *Joining Hands with Other Lands: Multicultural Songs and Games*. Long Branch, NJ: Kimbo Educational, 1993. Audiocassette.
>A collection of activities, songs, and games, including "Mia Casa, My House," "Uno, Uno, Dos, Dos," and "Birthdays Around the World."

Media Choices

Show a video or filmstrip as a transition between storytelling activities and crafts. This gives children an opportunity to rest quietly for a few minutes.

Aardema, Verna. *Borreguita and the Coyote*. 30 min. Lincoln, NE: Reading Rainbow, 1994. Videocassette.
>A charming retelling of a Mexican folktale in which a little lamb uses her wits to gain the upper hand and outsmart a hungry coyote.

Lewis, Thomas P. *Hill of Fire*. 30 min. Lincoln, NE: Reading Rainbow, [n.d.] Videocassette.
>Based on the true story of the volcanic eruption of Paricutin in Mexico.

Crafts and Other Activities

Choose a craft suited for the age level of the group and the time allotted for the story time.

Fiestas

Fiestas (celebrations) are observed throughout Mexico daily. Individual towns and villages have fiestas to celebrate their patron saint, or to celebrate national and civic holidays. People dress in colorful, traditional costumes; dance; enjoy lively music; have parades; and enjoy lots of spicy food. Rodeos, bullfights, and fireworks are common events in most fiestas.

Donkey Sack Piñata

An important part of Mexican fiestas is the piñata, a decorated container traditionally filled with candy, gum, sweets, and small toys. Traditionally, the breaking of the piñata goes back almost 400 years, to the time when the Spaniards came to Mexico. The stick used to break the piñata is called "the stick of goodness." Symbolically, when the piñata is broken, the love of worldly goods is destroyed and blessings are showered upon the one who broke the piñata, and upon those who are celebrating.

In this craft project, children make their own piñatas. For more information about piñatas, share the book *The Piñata Maker: El Piñatero* by George Ancona (San Diego, CA: Harcourt Brace, 1994) (see "Books to Read Aloud").

Supplies

Lunch-size paper bags
Colored tissue paper
Wrapped pieces of candy (optional)
Brown tagboard
Twine, heavy yarn, or macramé cord
Glue sticks
Colored markers
Stapler
Hole punch
Scissors

Photocopy figures 12.13 and 12.14 on brown tagboard and cut out the patterns (pre-cut for younger children). Children can stuff a paper bag about two-thirds full of tissue paper and add candy. Fold the top of the bag two times and staple. Punch a hole in the center and tie a loop of twine or heavy yarn through the hole to make a hanger (see fig. 12.11). Cut some of the tissue paper into 1-inch strips and cut to make a fringe (cut every inch). Glue the strips of tissue paper around the bag, starting at the bottom and overlapping the fringe towards the top of the bag. (For younger children, pre-cut the fringed pieces of tissue paper.) Glue the head and legs to the bag and make a tail of yarn or macramé cord.

Fig. 12.11. Paper-Bag Donkey Piñata Example.

Banner Decorations

Banners are hung in the areas where a fiesta is to be held. In this craft project, children make simple banner decorations.

Supplies

Brightly colored pieces
    of 18-by-24-inch
    tissue paper
Scissors
Tape
Heavy yarn

Fold a piece of the tissue paper in half four or five times. (The pattern

Fig. 12.12. Fiesta Banners Example.

becomes more elaborate each time the paper is folded, but the paper is also more difficult for younger children to cut.) Cut out small pieces (designs) around the folded edges (see fig. 12.12). Carefully unfold the paper, tape it to heavy yarn, and hang it in the room.

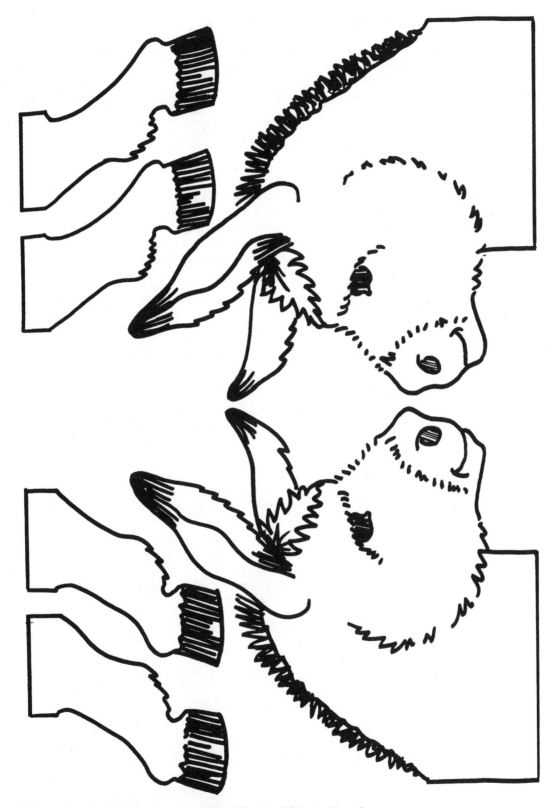

Fig. 12.13. Piñata Legs. Fig. 12.14. Piñata Head.

Mexican Hat Dance

Clear a space in the room and place a sombrero on the floor for children to dance around. Alternating feet, children jump, putting one heel forward and then the other. When the music changes, children join hands and move toward the sombrero with their hands raised, then lower their hands as they move back. Repeat until the music ends. Suggested music: "The Mexican Hat Dance," from the audiocassette *The Music of Mexico* by José Ortega and His Mariachi Ensemble (see "Sources for Fingerplays, Songs, Action Rhymes, and Games").

Sources for Craft Ideas and Activities

Bauer, Karen, and Rosa Drew. *Mexico: A Multicultural Study to Celebrate Our Diversity.* Edited by Bette McIntire. Illustrated by Catherine Yuh. World Neighbor series. Cypress, CA. Creative Teaching Press, 1994. (36 pages)
Art patterns and directions for piñatas, egg cup maracas, clay pinch pots, corn husk dolls, bark paper printing, yarn paintings (Ofrendas), and laquerware plates.

Franco, Betsy. *Mexico: A Literature-Based Multicultural Unit.* Illustrated by Jo Supancich. Monterey, CA. Evan-Moor, 1993. (48 pages)
Art activities, including masks, pottery toys, God's Eyes (ojo de dios), flags, flowers, and pinwheels.

Newbold, Patt, and Anne Diebel. *Paper Hat Tricks IV: A Big Book of Hat Patterns.* Northville, MI: Paper Hat Tricks, 1992. (40 pages)
Includes a pattern for a Mexican sombrero.

Ritter, Darlene. *Multicultural Art Activities: From the Cultures of Africa, Asia and North America.* Edited by Judy Urban. Illustrated by Diane Valko. Cypress, CA: Creative Teaching Press, 1993. (108 pages)
Instructions for making maracas, a paper "tree of life," paper flowers, and other crafts for decorating.

Let's Visit

Vietnam

Sample Story Times

Story Time for Preschool

Song: "Hello Song"

Book: *Angel Child, Dragon Child* by Michele Maria Surat

Fingerplay: "A Great Big Dragon" from *Small World Celebrations* by Jean Warren and Elizabeth McKinnon

Book: *Grandfather's Dream* by Holly Keller

Flannel Board Presentation: "How the Tiger Got His Stripes"

Fingerplay: "Five Golden Carp"

Flannel Board Presentation: "The Rabbit and the Tiger" from *Multicultural Folktales for the Feltboard and Readers' Theater* by Judy Sierra

Craft: "Carp Lantern"

Action Rhyme: "My Hands"

Story Time for Kindergarten Through Third Grade

Song: "Hello Song"

Book: *Why Ducks Sleep on One Leg* by Sherry Garland

Song: "Rice Harvesting Song" from *Songs That Children Sing* by Eleanor Chroman

Craft: "Tet Red Money Envelopes"

Flannel Board Presentation: "Under the Carambola Tree" from *Look What We've Brought You from Vietnam: Crafts, Games, Recipes, Stories and Other Cultural Activities from New Americans* by Phyllis Shalant.

Book: *Grandfather's Dream* by Holly Keller

Craft: "Dragon Mobile"

Action Rhyme: "My Hands"

Begin the story time with the "Hello Song." Then sing the song again, substituting the word *hello* with the Vietnamese greeting Ổng mạnh giỏi khổng [ong mang zoi khong]. (See p. xxvii for "Hello Song" music.)

Hello Song

Hello ev'rybody,
And how are you? How are you?
Hello ev'rybody,
And how are you today?

ong mang zoi khong ev'rybody,
And how are you? How are you?
ong mang zoi khong ev'rybody,

And how are you today?

End the story time with the "My Hands" action rhyme, substituting the words *thank you* with the Vietnamese words Cảm ổn nhiều [cam on new], and *goodbye* with Hẹn gặp lại [hen gap lay]. Have children stand up and follow the actions in the rhyme.

My Hands

My hands say cam on new. *(hold up hands)*
With a clap, clap, clap. *(clap hands)*
My feet say cam on new. *(point to feet)*
With a tap, tap, tap. *(stamp or tap feet)*
Clap! Clap! Clap! *(clap hands)*
Tap! Tap! Tap! *(stamp or tap feet)*
Turn myself around and bow. *(turn and bow)*
hen gap lay. *(wave goodbye)*

Books to Read Aloud

Garland, Sherry. *The Lotus Seed.* Illustrated by Tatsuro Kiuchi. New York: Harcourt Brace Jovanovich, 1993. (26 pages)
> A Vietnamese girl keeps a special seed for many years. When she becomes a grandmother, something special happens to the seed.

——. *Why Ducks Sleep on One Leg.* Illustrated by Jean Tseng and Mou-sien Tseng. New York: Scholastic, 1993. (30 pages)
> The Vietnamese folktale that explains why ducks sleep on one leg.

Keller, Holly. *Grandfather's Dream.* New York: Greenwillow Books, 1994. (28 pages)
> During the Vietnam War, the cranes of the Mekong Delta desert the area. This story is about a grandfather's faith that the cranes would return.

Lee, Jeanne M. *Toad Is the Uncle of Heaven: A Vietnamese Folk Tale.* New York: Holt, Rinehart and Winston, 1985. (30 pages)
> Toad and several animal friends travel to see the king of heaven to ask for rain.

Surat, Michele Maria. *Angel Child, Dragon Child.* Illustrated by Vo-Dinh Mai. Milwaukee, WI: Raintree, 1983. (30 pages)
> A young girl from Vietnam now lives in the United States. When she left Vietnam, her mother was unable to come with her and her father. Her classmates help her to reunite with her mother.

Tran, Kim-Lan. *Tet: The New Year.* Illustrated by Mai Vo-Dinh. Cleveland, OH: Modern Curriculum Press, 1992. (22 pages)
> A young boy celebrates Tet with his father and his schoolmates.

Storytelling

Flannel Board Presentation

"How the Tiger Got His Stripes." This Vietnamese legend is a common folktale of how a farmer uses his wisdom to outwit the tiger, and the tiger escapes with a new appearance. See figures 13.1–13.4 for patterns. Trace the patterns on felt, or photocopy and color them. If photocopying, glue small pieces of felt to the backs of the paper figures so they will hold to the flannel board.

Place the figures on the flannel board as they are introduced in the following story. When, in the story, the farmer uses a rope to tie up the tiger, wrap a piece of black yarn around the tiger (without stripes) at the appropriate time in the story. After the tiger is untied, place the tiger with stripes on the flannel board.

How the Tiger Got His Stripes
retold by Elaine Harrod

One day long ago in Vietnam, a water buffalo pulled a farmer's plow. *(place the water buffalo and the farmer on the flannel board)* The labor was hard and the weather was hot, but the farmer's buffalo always worked hard, and this day was no different than any other. The two strove very hard all morning. Lunch time finally came, and the man watered and fed his buffalo, then left to go to his hut to eat his noon meal. *(remove the farmer from the flannel board)*

After the man left, a tiger came out of the forest. *(place the tiger without stripes on the flannel board)* The buffalo felt nervous with the tiger so close, and just as he thought about running away, the tiger spoke to the buffalo.

"Please don't leave," the tiger said. "I am not here to hurt you. I only want to ask you a question."

Still not sure whether to trust the tiger, the buffalo asked, "What is your question?"

"When I was in the forest this morning," said the tiger, "I couldn't help but come closer and watch you work for the man. I wonder, why does a powerful beast such as yourself work for man? He is obviously weaker than you are."

The buffalo spoke to the tiger with much pride. "Yes, you are correct. I am a powerful beast and have much strength, but the man has a powerful mind. He has powerful wisdom. More wisdom than all the animals of the forest!"

The tiger flicked his tail with interest. He wished to have man's wisdom. *(place the farmer on the flannel board)*

As the man returned from his noon meal, he was very upset to see a tiger near his buffalo. As he approached, he picked up a large rock to use against the tiger. The tiger spoke to the man, repeating what he had said to the buffalo.

"Do not be afraid. I am not here to harm you or your water buffalo. I only wish to ask you a question."

"Yes?" the man said, still holding the rock and approaching very cautiously.

"My question is about your wisdom," said the tiger. "I can see you have power over creatures stronger than you. What is this wisdom the water buffalo speaks about?"

"Tiger, I don't carry my wisdom with me," the man answered. "It is back at my hut."

"Could I see your wisdom?" requested the tiger.

"I cannot just leave you here with my water buffalo while I am gone."

"I promise not to do anything to harm the water buffalo," said the tiger.

"I will go the hut and get my wisdom if you let me tie you to that tree stump." The tiger agreed to let the man tie him to the tree stump. *(wrap the black yarn around the tiger)* Then the man left for his hut.

When the tiger saw the man returning, he realized he was carrying something. That must be his wisdom that he is carrying, thought the tiger. As the man came closer, the tiger saw that it was not wisdom at all, but a bow and arrow. The tiger knew these weapons very well, for he had seen animals in the forest killed with them.

The tiger then realized that the man was going to kill him. He began to struggle to free himself from the ropes. He worked and pulled and tugged, but it seemed he would never be able to escape the tight knots of the rope. The tiger used strength he did not even know he possessed—and tigers are very strong, as you all know. Just as the man raised his bow and arrow to kill the tiger, the tiger broke free from the ropes and ran as fast as his legs could carry him, back into the forest, never to return! *(remove the tiger without stripes and place the tiger with stripes on the flannel board)*

When the tiger was a safe distance from the farm, he looked down at himself. He saw that he was changed: He was a new tiger, one with stripes! The ropes had cut through his fur and left black marks. To this day, the tiger still has stripes.

Fig. 13.1. Tiger Without Stripes. Fig. 13.2. Water Buffalo.

Fig. 13.3. Tiger with Stripes. Fig. 13.4. Farmer.

Sources for Flannel Board Presentations

Shalant, Phyllis. *Look What We've Brought You from Vietnam: Crafts, Games, Recipes, Stories, and Other Cultural Activities from New Americans.* Illustrated by Joanna Roy. New York: Julian Messner, 1988. (48 pages)

Includes recipes, stories, puppets shows, and facts about special holidays and festivals celebrated in Vietnam. In the story "The Carambola Tree," two brothers find that their futures lie in the branches of a carambola tree. The flannel board story, along with patterns for the characters, is included in this resource.

Sierra, Judy. *Multicultural Folktales for the Feltboard and Readers' Theater.* Phoenix, AZ: Oryx Press, 1996.

In the story "The Rabbit and the Tiger," the rabbit outwits the tiger. The flannel board story, along with the patterns for the characters, are included in this resource.

Fingerplays, Songs, Action Rhymes, and Games

"Five Golden Carp." For this fingerplay, begin with five carp puppets, one on each finger; bend down a finger each time a carp exits the poem. The storyteller will wear the finger puppets. The children will hold up five fingers and follow along. To make finger puppets, photocopy figures 13.5 and 13.6 on white tagboard or construction paper. Use markers to color the carp. Laminate and cut out the carp and finger attachments. Tape together the three flaps of each finger attachment. This will fit over the tip of each finger like a thimble. Tape a carp to each finger attachment.

Five Golden Carp
by Elaine Harrod

The pond was beautiful and had a bridge,
And one golden carp who lived past the ridge.

Two golden carp wanted to swim in the sea;
When those two carp turned around there were three.

Three golden carp who knew there could be more
Saw one under the bridge, and that made four.

Four golden carp learning how to dive,
Looked up and saw another; that made five.

Five golden carp eating bugs in the pond.
Spent many years together they had formed a bond.

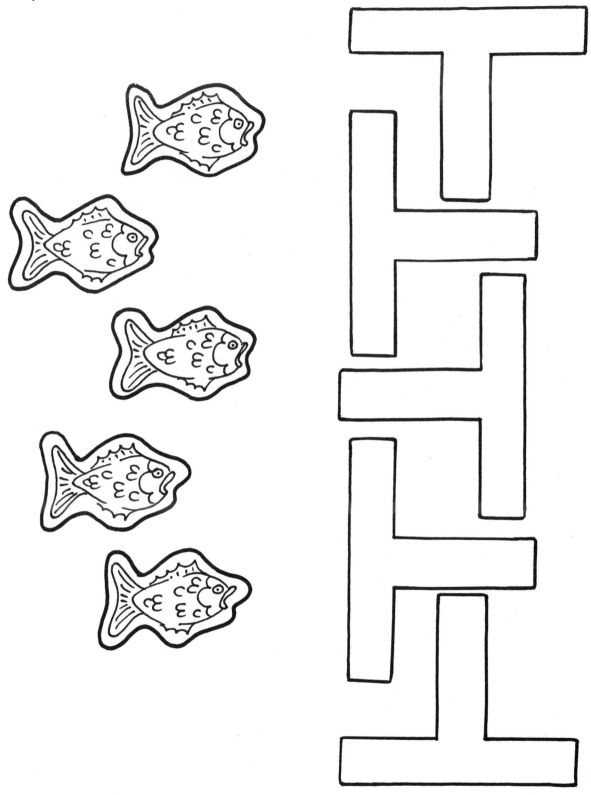

Fig. 13.5. Carp Finger Puppets.   Fig. 13.6. Finger Puppet Attachments.

From *Travel the Globe.* © 1998. Desiree Lorraine Webber, et al. Libraries Unlimited. (800) 237-6124.

"Chúc Mùng Nam Mói." [CHOOK MUNG NAHM MOY] This poem will help children imagine the Vietnamese New Year holiday, Tet. This poem might be shared before the craft project "Tet Red Money Envelopes" (see "Crafts and Other Activities").

Chúc Mùng Nam Mói (Happy New Year!)
by Elaine Harrod

In Vietnam the New Year holiday is Tet.
On New Year's Eve we dance the dragon dance.
Our parents make sweet cakes of rice for us to eat.
We make very loud sounds with our fire crackers.
One thing we like about Tet is the red envelopes.
Our parents put money in them for us.
They are red with the words *Chúc Mùng Nam Mói* written on them.
This means "Happy New Year!"

Sources for Fingerplays, Songs, Action Rhymes, and Games

Chroman, Eleanor. "Rice Harvesting Song" and "The Prince." In *Songs That Children Sing.* New York: Oak, 1970. (pages 93–94)
"Rice Harvesting Song" is sung by the people of Vietnam after the rice harvest, as they beat bags of rice against the ground. "The Prince" is a song about a Vietnamese legend. In this legend a prince is banished to live on the moon because of his bad deeds.

Stewart, Georgiana. "Chu Ech Con." In *Multicultural Rhythm Stick Fun.* Long Branch, NJ: Kimbo Educational, 1992. Audiocassette.
The music of the song Chu Ech Con is played while children keep time by tapping rhythm sticks (or clapping).

Warren, Jean, and Elizabeth McKinnon. "A Great Big Dragon" and "Full Moon." In *Small World Celebrations: Around the World Holidays to Celebrate with Young Children.* Illustrated by Marion Hopping Ekberg. Everett, WA: Warren, 1988. (page 94)
Two short songs sung to traditional children's tunes.

Crafts and Other Activities

Choose a craft suited for the age level of the group and the time allotted for the story time.

Tet Red Money Envelopes

To celebrate the Vietnamese New Year, Tet, children are given red envelopes with money inside. Even babies are given the envelopes. The envelope pattern provided in this book has the Vietnamese words *Chúc Mùng Nam Mói.* Before beginning this craft project, perhaps share with children the poem "Chúc Mùng Nam Mói" (see "Fingerplays, Songs, Action Rhymes, and Games").

Supplies

Red photocopier paper
Yellow yarn or ribbon
Gold star stickers
Scissors

On red photocopier paper, duplicate a copy of figure 13.8 for each child. Cut out the envelopes and have children fold them (see fig. 13.7). Use yellow yarn or ribbon to tie the envelopes and gold star stickers to decorate them.

Fig. 13.7. Money Envelope Example.

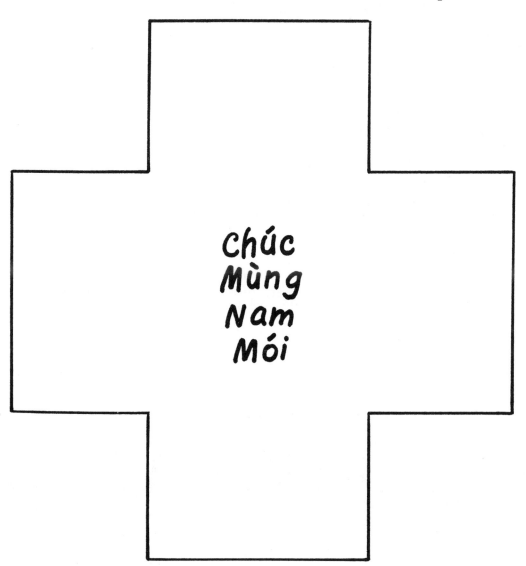

Fig. 13.8. Tet Red Money Envelope.

From *Travel the Globe.* © 1998. Desiree Lorraine Webber, et al. Libraries Unlimited. (800) 237-6124.

Carp Lantern

In Vietnam, children make lanterns for the mid-autumn festival Tet Trung-Thu, which is held in honor of the moon. The lanterns are constructed using rice paper and bamboo poles. When evening comes, children light a candle in their lantern and march in a parade. Not every child makes it to the end of the parade with their lantern: Sometimes the candle burns out or their lantern burns up! The children spend a lot of time creating the most attractive lantern they can. When they get home, they hang their lantern where everyone can see and admire it.

In this craft project, children make carp lanterns similar to those used in Tet Trung-Thu. After children have completed their lanterns, play music and have children participate in a lantern parade.

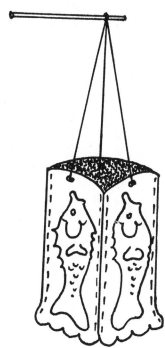

Supplies

Three sheets of orange or yellow paper (per lantern)
Colored markers
Hole punch
Three 12-inch lengths of yarn (per lantern)
Pencil or straw (one per lantern)

Photocopy figure 13.10 on yellow or orange paper (make three copies for each lantern). Have children cut out the carp and use markers to decorate them. Attach the first two sides together by placing them back-to-back and stapling one side. Add the third pattern by stapling its sides to the open sides of the other two patterns (the lantern will be three-sided; see fig. 13.9). Punch holes near the mouth of each fish, where indicated by the dots on the patterns. Tie a 12-inch piece of yarn to each hole, and tie all the yarn pieces together at the ends. Tie the yarn onto an unsharpened pencil or a straw.

Fig. 13.9. Carp Lantern Example.

Dragon Mobile

During Tet, the Vietnamese New Year holiday, many dragon dances are performed. The people of Vietnam gather in the streets to watch the dragon dances. The dragons are large puppets worn by many people together. The lead individual wears the large papier-mâché head; many others support the long body and tail. Music is played as the dragon makes his way down the streets.

In this craft project, children make their own dragon mobiles. They might hang the mobiles in their rooms at home and imagine that they are watching a dragon dance in Vietnam on Tet.

Fig. 13.10. Carp Lantern (cut 3 for each lantern).

Supplies

Yellow photocopier paper (or any bright color)
Hole punch
Metal hanger (one per mobile)
Seven 5-inch pieces of yarn
Four 3-inch pieces of yarn
White glue
Clear tape
Scissors
Dragon patterns

Fig. 13.11. Dragon Mobile Example.

Copy figures 13.12–13.16 onto yellow photocopier paper, one set for each child. Have children cut out their dragon mobile parts. Roll the head and tail parts into cone shapes and secure with tape. Punch holes in all parts of the dragon—the head, tail, and each of the sections. Each body section should have three holes punched in it. Glue the body sections together, matching up the holes. (These body sections will be two-sided after they are glued together.) Use the four 3-inch pieces of yarn to attach the head to the first circle, the first circle to the second, and so on. Use the 5-inch pieces of yarn to attach the dragon to the hanger (see fig. 13.11). Tape the fire and the tail spike to the dragon's mouth and tail. After the dragon is tied to the hanger, wind currents will make the dragon move like the dragons in the Tet dragon dance.

Sources for Craft Ideas and Activities

Press, Judy. *The Little Hands Big Fun Craft Book: Creative Fun for 2- to 6-Year-Olds.* Illustrated by Loretta Trezzo Braren. Little Hands series. Charlotte, VT: Williamson, 1996. (pages 92–93)
Includes instructions for making a lantern and a Vietnamese-style hat.

Ritter, Darlene. *Multicultural Art Activities: From the Cultures of Africa, Asia and North America.* Edited by Judy Urban. Illustrated by Diane Valko. Cypress, CA: Creative Teaching Press, 1993. (pages 28–31)
Includes instructions for making a lantern and a Vietnamese rice hat.

St. Tamara. *Asian Crafts.* New York: Lion Press, 1970. (pages 46–47 and 57)
Includes patterns for a rabbit balloon kite and a phoenix picture.

Warren, Jean, and Elizabeth McKinnon. *Small World Celebrations: Around the World Holidays to Celebrate with Young Children.* Illustrated by Marion Hopping Ekberg. Everett, WA: Warren, 1988. (pages 91–92)
Making lanterns, finger painting, and constructing a moon book are some of the Vietnamese crafts found in this resource.

Fig. 13.12. Dragon Body Circles.

From *Travel the Globe.* © 1998. Desiree Lorraine Webber, et al. Libraries Unlimited. (800) 237-6124.

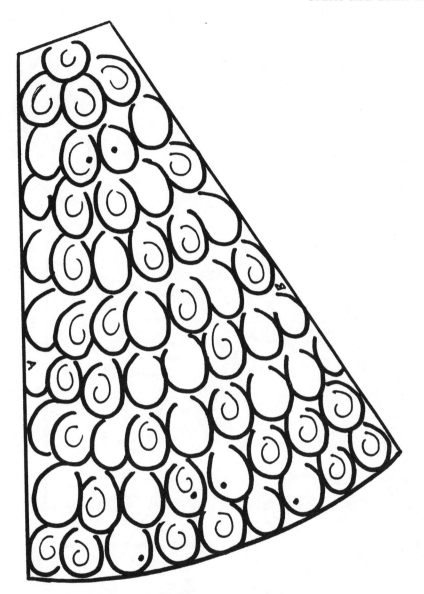

Fig. 13.13. Dragon Tail.

Fig. 13.14. Dragon Tail Spike (top left). Fig. 13.15. Dragon Mouth Fire (top right). Fig. 13.16. Dragon Head.

Let's Visit the United States— Native Americans

Sample Story Times

Story Time for Preschool

Song: "Hello Song"

Book: *Ten Little Rabbits* by Virginia Grossman

Poetry: Selections from *On the Road of Stars: Native American Night Poems and Sleep Charms* by John Bierhorst

Book: *Coyote: A Trickster Tale from the American Southwest* by Gerald McDermott

Song: "Firefly Song" In *Four Ancestors: Stories, Songs, and Poems from Native North America* by Joseph Bruchac

Flannel Board Presentation: "Baby Rattlesnake"

Puppet Presentation: "How the Chipmunk Got His Stripes" from *Crocodile! Crocodile! Stories Told Around the World* by Barbara Baumgartner

Video: *Hiawatha* by Henry Wadsworth Longfellow

Craft: "Baby Rattlesnake Hand Puppet"

Action Rhyme: "My Hands"

Story Time for Kindergarten Through Third Grade

Song: "Hello Song"

Book: *Amorak* by Tim Jessell

Book: *Red Bird* by Barbara Mitchell

Flannel Board Presentation: "Baby Rattlesnake"

Poetry: *Did You Hear Wind Sing Your Name? An Onieda Song of Spring* by Sandra De Coteau Orie

Oral Story: "Tricky Coyote" from *Meet Tricky Coyote!* by Gretchen Will Mayo

Video: *Knots on a Counting Rope* by Bill Martin Jr. and John Archambault

Craft: "Baby Rattlesnake Hand Puppet" or "Plains Indian Breastplate"

Action Rhyme: "My Hands"

Begin the story time with the "Hello Song." Then sing the song again, substituting the word *hello* with the Cherokee greeting ᎣᏏᏲ [O-see-YO]. (See p. xxvii for "Hello Song" music.)

Hello Song

Hello ev'rybody,
And how are you? How are you?
Hello ev'rybody,
And how are you today?

O-see-YO ev'rybody,
And how are you? How are you?
O-see-YO ev'rybody,
And how are you today?

End the story time with the "My Hands" action rhyme, substituting the words *thank you* with the Cherokee word ᎠᎥ [wa-DO], and *goodbye* with ᏙᏓᏓᎪᎲᎢ [DO-dada-GO-huh-E]. (This is how one says to goodbye to several others. When saying goodbye to one person, the word is ᏙᎾᏓᎪᎲᎢ [do-na-DA-go-huh-E].) Have children stand up and follow the actions in the rhyme.

My Hands

My hands say wa-DO. *(hold up hands)*
With a clap, clap, clap. *(clap hands)*
My feet say wa-DO. *(point to feet)*
With a tap, tap, tap. *(stamp or tap feet)*
Clap! Clap! Clap! *(clap hands)*
Tap! Tap! Tap! *(stamp or tap feet)*
Turn myself around and bow. *(turn and bow)*
DO-dada-GO-huh-E. *(wave goodbye)*

Books to Read Aloud

Bierhorst, John, comp. *On the Road of Stars: Native American Night Poems and Sleep Charms.* Illustrated by Judy Pedersen. New York: Macmillan, 1994. (32 pages)
Songs and poems collected from several Native American tribes.

Bruchac, Joseph. *A Boy Called Slow: The True Story of Sitting Bull.* Illustrated by Rocco Baviera. New York: Philomel Books, 1994. (32 pages)
A story about the young boy who would later become Sitting Bull, the great warrior and Holy Man of the Hunkpapa band of the Lakota Sioux. Recommended for school-age children.

——. *The First Strawberries: A Cherokee Tale.* Illustrated by Anna Vojtech. New York: Dial Books for Young Readers, 1993. (32 pages)
The Sun creates raspberries, blueberries, blackberries, and, finally, strawberries to heal an argument.

——. *Four Ancestors: Stories, Songs, and Poems from Native North America.* Illustrated by S. S. Burrus, et al. [N.p.]: BridgeWater Books, 1996. (96 pages)
A collection of songs and stories from many Native American tribes.

De Coteau Orie, Sandra. *Did You Hear Wind Sing Your Name? An Oneida Song of Spring.* Illustrated by Christopher Canyon. New York: Walker, 1995. (32 pages)
A story celebrating spring, told using elements of nature important to the Onieda tribe.

dePaola, Tomie. *The Legend of the Bluebonnet: An Old Tale of Texas.* New York: G. P. Putnam's Sons, 1983. (32 pages)
A small Comanche girl named She-Who-Is-Alone sacrifices her most valued possession to save her people. In return, the Great Spirits bring rain and the widely known flower, the bluebonnet. Recommended for school-age children.

Goble, Paul. *Iktomi and the Boulder: A Plains Indian Story.* New York: Orchard Books, 1988. (32 pages)
One of several stories about Iktomi, the Sioux trickster character. In this story, Iktomi gives a blanket to a boulder and then decides he wants it for himself. (Compare to Janet Steven's *Coyote Steals the Blanket: A Ute Tale,* below.) Recommended for school-age children.

Grossman, Virginia. *Ten Little Rabbits.* Illustrated by Sylvia Long. San Francisco: Chronicle Books, 1991. (28 pages)
A counting book with 10 Native American tribes represented. In the illustrations, the rabbits wear and use traditional items. Notes on each tribe are included.

Jessell, Tim. *Amorak.* Mankato, MN: Creative Education, 1994. (32 pages)
A beautifully illustrated Inuit tale of why Amorak, the wolf, came into the world. Recommended for preschoolers as well as school-age children.

McDermott, Gerald. *Coyote: A Trickster Tale from the American Southwest.* San Diego, CA: Harcourt Brace Jovanovich, 1994. (32 pages)
Coyote has a nose for trouble, and he finds trouble when he wants to dance and fly like a crow.

——. *Raven: A Trickster Tale from the Pacific Northwest.* San Diego, CA: Harcourt Brace Jovanovich, 1993. (32 pages)
Raven tricks the Sky Chief, takes the sun, and brings it into the sky for all people to enjoy.

Mitchell, Barbara. *Red Bird.* Illustrated by Todd L. W. Doney. New York: Lothrop, Lee & Shepard, 1996. (32 pages)
Katie and her family take part in the annual Nanticoke powwow.

Osofsky, Audrey. *Dreamcatcher*. Illustrated by Ed Young. New York: Orchard Books, 1992. (32 pages)
   Written in language that sings with music, this is the story of small woven nets used by the Ojibway to catch the bad dreams and let the good dreams slip through to the dreamer.

Pollock, Penny. *The Turkey Girl: A Zuni Cinderella Story*. Illustrated by Ed Young. Boston: Little, Brown, 1996. (32 pages)
   An orphan girl tends a flock of turkeys for her pueblo village. The turkeys help her attend the Dance of the Sacred Bird, but she must return to them before the sun sets. Recommended for school-age children.

Rodanas, Kristina. *Dance of the Sacred Circle: A Native American Tale*. Boston: Little, Brown, 1994. (32 pages)
   Based on a Sihasapa (Blackfoot) legend in which an orphan boy receives the gift of the horse from the Great Spirit from the Sky. This gift allows his people to hunt the buffalo. Recommended for school-age children.

Stevens, Janet. *Coyote Steals the Blanket: A Ute Tale*. New York: Holiday House, 1993. (32 pages)
   Trickster Coyote does not listen to Hummingbird's advice and reaps trouble when he steals a blanket covering a large rock.

Storytelling

Flannel Board Presentation

Te Ata. *Baby Rattlesnake*. Adapted by Lynn Moroney. Illustrated by Veg Reisberg. San Francisco: Children's Book Press, 1989. (30 pages) Reprinted by permission of the publisher.

"Baby Rattlesnake." The following story is a teaching tale from the book Baby Rattlesnake. *Te Ata was a Chickasaw storyteller who died October 26, 1995, at the age of 99. She was born in 1895 in what was then Oklahoma Territory. Her name means "Bearer of the Morning." Te Ata traveled the nation, sharing Native American stories, songs, and poetry; she performed several times for the Roosevelts at the White House. Lynn Moroney, an Oklahoma storyteller and author, received permission from Te Ata to retell "Baby Rattlesnake." Like Te Ata, Moroney travels the United States, telling this and other stories.*

See figures 14.1–14.8 for patterns. Trace the figures on felt, or photocopy and color them. If photocopying, glue small pieces of felt to the backs of the paper figures so they will hold to the flannel board. Place the figures on the flannel board as they are introduced in the story.

When Baby Rattlesnake receives his rattle, the storyteller should manipulate one of his arms like Baby Rattlesnake's tail: Bend the arm at the elbow with the palm of the hand facing the audience. Shake or quiver the hand while saying, "Ch-Ch-Ch! Ch-Ch-Ch!" An old 35mm film canister filled with a teaspoon of rice can add a lively sound effect.

Fig. 14.1. Baby Rattlesnake.   Fig. 14.2. Chief's Daughter.   Fig. 14.3. Rattle.

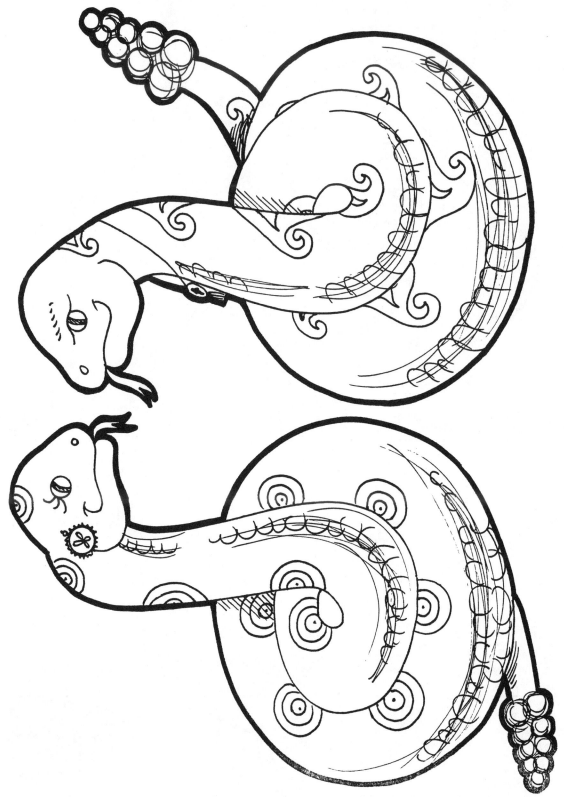

Fig. 14.4. Mother Rattlesnake (bottom). Fig. 14.5. Father Rattlesnake (top).

Fig. 14.6. Jack Rabbit.   Fig. 14.7. Old Man Turtle.   Fig. 14.8. Prairie Dog.

Baby Rattlesnake
by Te Ata; adapted by Lynn Moroney

Out in the place where the rattlesnakes lived, there was a little baby rattlesnake who cried all the time because he did not have a rattle. *(place Baby Rattlesnake on the flannel board)*

He said to his mother and father, "I don't know why I don't have a rattle. I'm made just like my brother and sister. How can I be a rattlesnake if I don't have a rattle?" *(place Mother and Father Rattlesnake on the flannel board)*

Mother and Father Rattlesnake said, "You are too young to have a rattle. When you get to be as old as your brother and sister, you will have a rattle, too."

But Baby Rattlesnake did not want to wait. So he just cried and cried. He shook his tail and when he couldn't hear a rattle sound, he cried even louder.

Mother and Father said, "Shhh! Shhh! Shhhhh!"

Brother and Sister said, "Shhh! Shhh! Shhhhh!"

But Baby Rattlesnake wouldn't stop crying. He kept the Rattlesnake People awake all night.

The next morning, the Rattlesnake People called a big council. *(remove Mother and Father Rattlesnake from the flannel board)* They talked and they talked just like people do, but they couldn't decide how to make that little baby rattlesnake happy. He didn't want anything else but a rattle.

At last one of the elders said, "Go ahead, give him a rattle. He's too young and he'll get into trouble. But let him learn a lesson. I just want to get some sleep."

So they gave Baby Rattlesnake a rattle. *(add the rattle to the end of Baby Rattlesnake's tail)*

Baby Rattlesnake loved his rattle. He shook his tail and for the first time he heard, "Ch-Ch-Ch! Ch-Ch-Ch!" He was so excited!

He sang a little rattle song, "Ch-Ch-Ch! Ch-Ch-Ch!"

He danced a rattle dance, "Ch-Ch-Ch! Ch-Ch-Ch!"

Soon Baby Rattlesnake learned to play tricks with his rattle. He hid in the rocks and when the small animals came by, he darted out rattling, "Ch-Ch-Ch! Ch-Ch-Ch!"

He made Jack Rabbit jump. *(place Jack Rabbit on the flannel board)*

He made Old Man Turtle jump. *(place Old Man Turtle on the flannel board)*

He made Prairie Dog jump. *(place Prairie Dog on the flannel board)*

Each time Baby Rattlesnake laughed and laughed. He thought it was fun to scare the animal people.

Mother and Father warned Baby Rattlesnake, "You must not use your rattle in such a way." *(place Mother and Father Rattlesnake on the flannel board)*

Big Brother and Big Sister said, "You are not being careful with your rattle."

The Rattlesnake People told Baby Rattlesnake to stop acting so foolish with his rattle.

Baby Rattlesnake did not listen.

One day, Baby Rattlesnake said to his mother and father, "How will I know a chief's daughter when I see her?"

"Well, she's usually very beautiful and walks with her head held high," said Father.

"And she's very neat in her dress," added Mother.

"Why do you want to know?" asked Father.

"Because I want to scare her!" said Baby Rattlesnake. And he started right off down the path before his mother and father could warn him never to do such a thing like that. *(remove all characters from the flannel board except Baby Rattlesnake)*

The little fellow reached the place where the Indians traveled. He curled himself up on a log and he started rattling. "Chh-Chh-Chh!" He was having a wonderful time.

All of a sudden he saw a beautiful maiden coming toward him from a long way off. She walked with her head held high, and she was very neat in her dress. *(place the chief's daughter on the flannel board)*

"Ah," thought Baby Rattlesnake. "She must be the chief's daughter."

Baby Rattlesnake hid in the rocks. He was excited. This was going to be his best trick.

He waited and waited. The chief's daughter came closer and closer. When she was in just the right spot, he darted out of the rocks.

"Ch-Ch-Ch-Ch-Ch!"

"Ho!" cried the chief's daughter. She whirled around, stepping on Baby Rattlesnake's rattle and crushing it to pieces. *(remove the rattle from Baby Rattlesnake's tail and remove the chief's daughter)*

Baby Rattlesnake looked at his beautiful rattle scattered all over the trail. He didn't know what to do.

He took off for home as fast as he could. *(place Mother and Father Rattlesnake on the flannel board)*

With great sobs, he told Mother and Father what had happened. They wiped his tears and gave him big rattlesnake hugs.

For the rest of that day, Baby Rattlesnake stayed safe and snug, close by his rattlesnake family.

Puppet Presentation

Baumgartner, Barbara. "How the Chipmunk Got His Stripes." In *Crocodile! Crocodile! Stories Told Around the World.* Illustrated by Judith Moffatt. New York: Dorling Kindersley, 1994. (pages 21–23)
    A Seneca story in which Nygyway, the bear, almost catches Jehookwiss, the chipmunk, scratching stripes down his back.

A storyteller can use stick puppets to tell this story. Make a bear's face using brown or black construction paper; glue a craft stick to the face. Create a double-sided chipmunk using brown construction paper; glue a craft stick between the sides. Draw stripes on one side of the chipmunk (the other side is plain brown).

Begin the story using the bear puppet and the plain-sided chipmunk. As the bear scratches the chipmunk's back, flip the chipmunk to the other side, showing his stripes.

Sources for Oral Stories

MacDonald, Margaret Read. "Coyote's Crying Song." In *Twenty Tellable Tales: Audience Participation for the Beginning Storyteller.* Illustrated by Roxane Murphy. Bronx: H. W. Wilson, 1986. (pages 10–19)
    Inspired by a Hopi tale in which Coyote insists that Dove is not crying but singing. A humorous story appropriate for audience participation.

Mayo, Gretchen Will. "Tricky Coyote." In *Meet Tricky Coyote!* New York: Walker, 1993. (pages 1–4)
Listeners will laugh as they come to the realization that Coyote is stealing Fancy Man's clothes and horse.

Fingerplays, Songs, Action Rhymes, and Games

The Comanches, Crow, Kiowas, and other Native Americans living on the plains, prior to the 1900s, hunted buffalo. The buffalo provided not only meat for food and hides for tipis and clothing, but other parts were also used to make tools, cooking utensils, and even baby powder. In this action rhyme, children go in search for buffalo and meet other animals who live on the plains.

Going on a Buffalo Hunt
by Desiree Webber and Sandy Shropshire

We're going on a buffalo hunt. *(walk in place)*
Ok? Are you ready?
Let's go!

Look high, look low, *(shade eyes with one hand)*
Look out for buffalo.

Oh, here's Grandfather Owl.
Grandfather Owl, have you seen any buffalo?

Whooo, Whooo, Whooo. *(hoot like an owl)*
Not here, not I,
May you find some,
Bye and bye.

Look high, look low, *(walk in place and shade eyes with one hand)*
Look out for buffalo.

Oh, here's Sister Snake.
Sister Snake, have you seen any buffalo?

Hisssss, Hisssss, Hisssss. *(hiss like a snake)*
Not here, not I,
May you find some,
Bye and bye.

Look high, look low, *(walk in place and shade eyes with one hand)*
Look out for buffalo.

Oh, here's Cousin Coyote.
Cousin Coyote, have you seen any buffalo?

Yip, Yip, Oooouuuuuu. *(yip and then howl like a coyote)*
Not here, not I,
May you find some,
Bye and bye.

Look high, look low, *(walk in place and shade eyes with one hand)*
Look out for buffalo.

Oh, here's Papa Prairie Dog.
Papa Prairie Dog, have you seen any buffalo?

Bark, bark, yip. *(make a short bark and yip)*
Not here, not I,
May you find some,
Bye and bye.

Wait . . . listen . . . *(pause between words)*
Shhhhh, a thunder low *(whisper)*
The ground is pounding *(stomp in place)*
Why, it's buffalo!
Bark, bark
Ooouuuuu
Hisssss, hisssss
Whoooo, whoooo.

Sources for Fingerplays, Songs, Action Rhymes, and Games

Frazier, Terry, and Shar Frazier. "Morning Star." In *Spirit Wings*. Norman, OK: Flutes by Frazier, 1991. Audiocassette.
In the background of "Morning Star" are the sounds of birds and coyotes as the flute calls forth the morning light of dawn. This song (and others) will set the mood for a story time; or, play this tape while children are making crafts. The flutes played by the Fraziers, such as the Lakota five-hole flute and the Sioux medicine flute, are handmade by the Fraziers. Write Flutes by Frazier, Rt. 2, Box 598A, Norman, OK 73071 or call (405) 360-1085 if this audiocassette is not available at local music stores.

Media Choices

Show a video or filmstrip as a transition between storytelling activities and crafts. This gives children an opportunity to rest quietly for a few minutes.

Bruchac, Joseph, and Jonathan London. *Thirteen Moons on a Turtle's Back*. Illustrated by Thomas Locker. 17 min. New Rochelle, NY: Spoken Arts, 1992. Videocassette.
Poetry by Bruchac and London honoring Native American legends related to the seasons and the moon.

Longfellow, Henry Wadsworth. *Hiawatha*. Illustrated by Susan Jeffers. 11 min. Weston, CT: Weston Woods, 1995. Videocassette.
This portion of Wadsworth's "The Song of Hiawatha" tells of Hiawatha's childhood and of his beloved grandmother, Nokomis. A short historical note as to why Wadsworth wrote this poem is also included at the beginning of the presentation.

Martin, Bill, Jr., and John Archambault. *Knots on a Counting Rope*. 13 min. New Rochelle, NY: Spoken Arts, 1989. Videocassette.
A grandfather teaches his grandson to retell a story using knots on a rope as a reminder.

Crafts and Other Activities

Choose a craft suited for the age level of the group and the time allotted for the story time.

Baby Rattlesnake Hand Puppet

This craft is an effective extending activity for children. Introduce the story "Baby Rattlesnake" (see *Baby Rattlesnake* by Te Ata, retold by Lynn Moroney, under "Flannel Board Presentations") and follow with this hand puppet activity. Encourage children to take their snake puppets home and retell "Baby Rattlesnake" to a friend or member of their family.

Supplies

Green, black, yellow, red, and orange
    construction paper
White glue
Rice
Scissors
Pencils
Stapler or clear tape

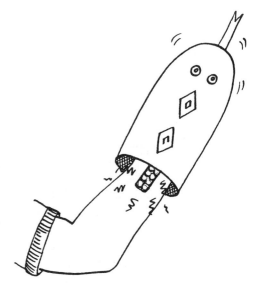

See figures 14.10–14.16 for patterns. The teacher or librarian should make the snake's rattle prior to beginning the craft project with children, to allow the glue to dry thoroughly. Using orange construction paper, trace and cut out the rattle pattern. Fold in half on the dashed line, and glue the bottom and side edges. Do not glue the top edge (the end with the dashed line). Allow the glue to dry.

After the glue has dried, pour approximately 2 teaspoons of rice through the opening at the top of the rattle. Glue the top edge. Allow the glue to dry completely.

Fig. 14.9. Rattlesnake Puppet Example.

For preschool children (or if time is limited) precut all the pieces. Using green construction paper, trace and cut out two hand puppet patterns. One pattern will be the bottom of the snake and the other pattern the top of the snake. Using red construction paper, trace and cut out the tongue. Glue the tongue to the inside of the bottom pattern piece, where the mouth would be located. Glue only about ½ inch of the tongue to the puppet, leaving the forked end sticking out. Next, glue the top pattern to the bottom pattern along the sides and head. Leave the bottom end open for the hand to enter. Tell children not to insert their hands until the glue has dried. (For quicker construction, staple or tape the two puppet pieces together instead of gluing.) Have the children decorate their snake. Using orange construction paper, trace and cut out two large diamonds (fig. 14.14); using yellow construction paper, trace and cut out two small diamonds (fig. 14.15). Glue these into place (see fig. 14.9). Using yellow construction paper, trace and cut out two eyes (fig. 14.12); using black construction paper, trace and cut out two pupils. Glue into place. The last step is to tape the end of the rattle, with the dashed line, to the inside of the top pattern piece of the puppet. Align the dashed line on the rattle with the bottom edge of the puppet piece. The rattle will hang down and rest on the top of the child's arm. As the child moves his hand up and down inside the puppet, the rattle will hit against the child's arm, making a rattling noise.

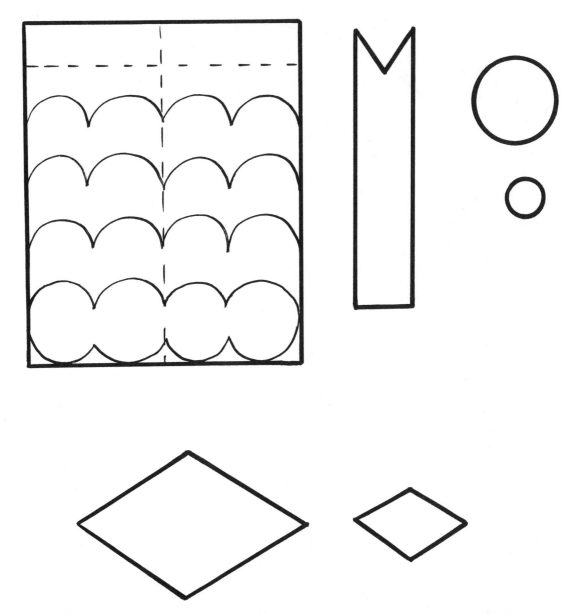

Fig. 14.10. Rattlesnake Rattle (cut 1 of orange). Fig. 14.11. Rattlesnake Tongue (cut 1 of red). Fig. 14.12. Rattlesnake Eye (cut 2 of yellow). Fig. 14.13. Rattlesnake Eye Pupil (cut 2 of black). Fig. 14.14. Rattlesnake Large Diamond (cut 2 of orange). Fig. 14.15. Rattlesnake Small Diamond (cut 2 of yellow).

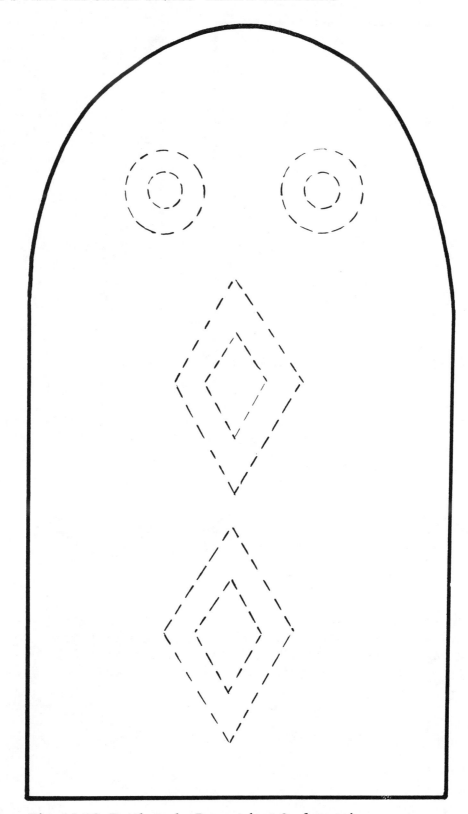

Fig. 14.16. Rattlesnake Puppet (cut 2 of green).

Plains Indian Breastplate

The breastplate was worn mainly for decoration. It was first used by American Indians living on the plains, although other tribes, such as the Utes, adopted this chest ornament. A breastplate typically included hair-pipes, which were long, thin bones held into place by leather strips. Seashells, beads, feathers, horsehair danglers, and colorful ribbons were sometimes used to decorate the front of the breastplate.

In this craft project, children make a breastplate using cardboard or posterboard, and straws, yarn, and pony beads. The straws represent hair pipes; the yarn represents the leather strips; and the pony beads can represent either seashells or beads.

Supplies

Cardboard or posterboard
Straws
Yarn
Pony beads
White glue
Hole punch
Scissors

Use figure 14.18 (half-pattern) to prepare a breast-plate for each child. An adult should pre-cut a breast-plate from cardboard or heavy ply posterboard. Using a single-hole punch, punch a hole near the top right and top left corners and three holes along each side of the breastplate.

Next, cut one piece of yarn 24-inches long and eight pieces of yarn 5-inches long for each child. Also cut several straws into 3-inch pieces. Each breastplate will need approximately 28 straw pieces, depending upon how close the children want to glue the straws next to each other.

Fig. 14.17. Breastplate Example.

The children can now decorate their breastplates. First, tie the 24-inch piece of yarn to the two holes punched at the top. There should be enough room for the child to slip the yarn over his or her head and allow the breastplate to lie flat on the chest.

The next step is to tie the eight 5-inch pieces of yarn to the holes punched along each side of the breastplate including the holes at the top. Thread one or several colorful pony beads onto each piece of yarn and knot each end. Finally, glue the straws into place horizontally as shown in figure 14.17.

Sources for Craft Ideas and Activities

Blood, Charles L. *American Indian Games and Crafts.* Illustrated by Lisa Campbell Ernst. New York: Franklin Watts, 1981. (32 pages)
　　The author, part Penobscot, provides instructions for simple crafts and games.

Hewitt, Sally. *The Plains People.* Footsteps in Time series. Danbury, CT: Children's Press, 1996. (24 pages)
　　Create inexpensive Native American crafts, such as a drum and drummer using cardboard, a paper grocery sack, and newspaper.

Newbold, Patt, and Anne Diebel. *Paper Hat Tricks IV: A Big Book of Hat Patterns.* Northville, MI: Paper Hat Tricks, 1992.
　　Includes instructions for making a totem hat and a medicine man hat.

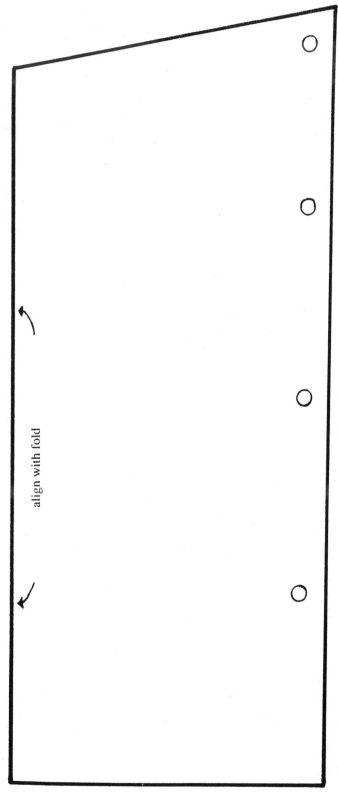

align with fold

Fig. 14.18. Breastplate.

Ritter, Darlene. *Multicultural Art Activities: From the Cultures of Africa, Asia and North America.* Edited by Judy Urban. Illustrated by Diane Valko. Cypress, CA: Creative Teaching Press, 1993. (pages 74–97)
   This resource includes unique Native American crafts, such as a paper plate shield, a decorated hide using a large paper bag, and a kachina headpiece.

Rudolph, Nancy Lyn. *Paper Animal Masks from Northwest Tribal Tales.* New York: Sterling, 1996. (79 pages)
   A unique book featuring animal tales from the northwest tribes of the United States and Canada, with instructions for creating animal masks from construction paper.

Terzian, Alexandra M. *The Kids' Multicultural Art Book: Art & Craft Experiences from Around the World.* Kids Can! series. Charlotte, VT: Williamson, 1993. (pages 12–45)
   Contains a section of simple, inexpensive crafts representing several Native American tribes of North America. Cultural notes are included.

Thomson, Ruth. *The Inuit.* Footsteps in Time series. Danbury, CT: Children's Press, 1996. (24 pages)
   Instructions for crafts and a simple game using handmade pieces fashioned from self-hardening or pottery clay.

Multicultural Series Bibliography

Ann Morris Series
New York: Lothrop, Lee & Shepard

Through simple text and sharp photography, these books give a snapshot look at people around the world. Photographs by Ken Heyman and others. Grades preschool–3. Ages 3–8.

Morris, Ann. *Bread, Bread, Bread.* 1989.
——. *Hats, Hats, Hats.* 1989.
——. *Houses and Homes.* 1992.
——. *Loving.* 1990.
——. *On the Go.* 1990.
——. *Shoes, Shoes, Shoes.* 1995.
——. *Tools.* 1992.
——. *Weddings.* 1995.

Around the World Series
Monterey, CA: Evan-Moor

This series is made for the classroom. Each book is a unit of study for a particular country and contains a retelling of a folktale plus activities for language arts, songs, cooking, craft ideas, and games. Grades 1–3. Ages 6–8.

Franco, Betsy. *Brazil: A Literature-Based Multicultural Unit.* Illustrated by Cheryl Kirk Noll. Vol. 10. 1995.
——. *China: A Literature-Based Multicultural Unit.* Illustrated by Jo Supanich. Vol. 5. 1993.
——. *India: A Literature-Based Multicultural Unit.* Illustrated by Jo Supanich. Vol. 6. 1993.
——. *Italy: A Literature-Based Multicultural Unit.* Illustrated by Susan O'Neill. Vol. 7. 1995.
——. *Japan: A Literature-Based Multicultural Unit.* Illustrated by Jo Supanich. Vol. 2. 1993.
——. *Mexico: A Literature-Based Multicultural Unit.* Illustrated by Jo Supanich. Vol. 1. 1993.
——. *Nigeria: A Literature-Based Multicultural Unit.* Illustrated by Jo Supanich. Vol. 4. 1993.
——. *Russia: A Literature-Based Multicultural Unit.* Illustrated by Jo Supanich. Vol. 3. 1993.
——. *South Korea: A Literature-Based Multicultural Unit.* Illustrated by Cheryl Kirk Noll. Vol. 8. 1995.
——. *Vietnam: A Literature-Based Multicultural Unit.* Illustrated by Cheryl Kirk Noll. Vol. 9. 1995.

Count Your Way Series
Minneapolis, MN: Carolrhoda Books

Provides the numbers 1 through 10 in the major language for each country, alongside historical and cultural information. (Note: The librarian or teacher can create flannel board counting pieces to adapt each book for younger children.) Grades 1–4. Ages 6–9.

Haskins, Jim. *Count Your Way Through Africa.* Illustrated by Barbara Knutson. 1989.
——. *Count Your Way Through Canada.* Illustrated by Steve Michaels. 1989.
——. *Count Your Way Through China.* Illustrated by Dennis Hockerman. 1987.
——. *Count Your Way Through Germany.* Illustrated by Helen Byers. 1990.
——. *Count Your Way Through India.* Illustrated by Liz Brenner Dodson. 1990.
——. *Count Your Way Through Israel.* Illustrated by Rick Hanson. 1990.
——. *Count Your Way Through Italy.* Illustrated by Beth Wright. 1990.
——. *Count Your Way Through Japan.* Illustrated by Martin Skoro. 1987.
——. *Count Your Way Through Korea.* Illustrated by Dennis Hockerman. 1989.
——. *Count Your Way Through Mexico.* Illustrated by Helen Byers. 1989.
——. *Count Your Way Through Russia.* Illustrated by Vera Medinkov. 1987.
——. *Count Your Way Through the Arab World.* Illustrated by Dana Gustafson. 1987.
Haskins, Jim, and Kathleen Benson. *Count Your Way Through Brazil.* Illustrated by Liz Brenner Dodson. 1996.
——. *Count Your Way Through France.* Illustrated by Andrea Shine. 1996.
——. *Count Your Way Through Greece.* Illustrated by Janice Lee Porter. 1996.
——. *Count Your Way Through Ireland.* Illustrated by Beth Wright. 1996.

Discovery Flap Series
Chicago: Child's Play (International)

This series has flaps for the reader to lift as they discover what children in other countries eat, what games they play, and what their homes are like. Illustrated by Annie Kubler and Caroline Formby. Grades preschool–2. Ages 3–7.

Come and Eat with Us! 1995.

Come and Play with Us! 1995.
Come and Ride with Us! 1995.
Come Home with Us! 1995.

Food Around the World Series
New York: Thompson Learning

Each title gives a brief history of the country plus information on celebrations, foods, and recipes. Grades 3–5. Ages 8–10.

Denny, Roz. *A Taste of Britain.* 1994.
Denny, Roz. *A Taste of China.* 1994.
Denny, Roz. *A Taste of France.* 1994.
Denny, Roz. *A Taste of India.* 1994.
Goodwin, Bob, and Candi Perez. *A Taste of Spain.* 1995.
Harris, Colin. *A Taste of West Africa.* 1995.
Illsley, Linda. *A Taste of Mexico.* 1995.
McKenley, Yvonne. *A Taste of the Caribbean.* 1995.
Ridgwell, Jenny. *A Taste of Italy.* 1994.
Ridgwell, Jenny. *A Taste of Japan.* 1994.

Footsteps in Time Series
Danbury, CT: Children's Press/Chicago: Childrens Press

Books in this series contain instructions for making simple crafts, supplemented by some background information. Occasionally, instructions for games are also included. Illustrated by Cilla Eurich and Ruth Levy. Photographs by Peter Millard. Grades 2–3. Ages 6–7.

Hewitt, Sally. *The Aztecs.* Danbury, CT: Children's Press, 1996.
———. *The Greeks.* Chicago: Childrens Press, 1995.
———. *The Plains People.* Danbury, CT: Children's Press, 1996.
———. *The Romans.* Chicago: Childrens Press, 1995.
Thomson, Ruth. *The Egyptians.* Chicago: Childrens Press, 1995.
———. *The Inuit.* Danbury, CT: Children's Press, 1996.
———. *The Rainforest Indians.* Danbury, CT: Children's Press, 1996.
———. *The Vikings.* Chicago: Childrens Press, 1995.

The World's Children Series
Minneapolis, MN: Carolrhoda Books

An engaging series for children, particularly suited to a story time setting because of color photographs. Titles show how children in various countries around the world live, dress, go to school, play, and so on. Grades 3–6. Ages 8–11.

Bierne, Barbara. *Children of the Ecuadorean Highlands.* Photographs by author. 1996.
Goodsmith, Lauren. *The Children of Mauritania: Days in the Desert and by the River Shore.* Photographs by author. 1993.
Hermes, Jules. *The Children of Bolivia.* Photographs by author. 1996.
———. *The Children of Guatemala.* Photographs by author. 1997.
———. *The Children of India.* Photographs by author. 1993.

——. *The Children of Micronesia.* Photographs by author. 1994.

——. *The Children of Morocco.* Photographs by author. 1995.

Härkönen, Reijo, trans. *The Children of Egypt.* Photographs by Matti A. Pitkänen. 1991.

——. *The Children of Nepal.* Photographs by Matti A. Pitkänen. 1990.

——. *The Children of China.* Photographs by Matti A. Pitkänen. 1990.

Kinkade, Sheila. *The Children of Philippines.* Photographs by Elaine Little. 1996.

Lorbiecki, Marybeth. *The Children of Vietnam.* Photographs by Paul P. Rome. 1997.

Staub, Frank. *Children of Belize.* Photographs by author. 1997.

——. *The Children of Cuba.* Photographs by author. 1996.

——. *The Children of Sierra Madre.* Photographs by author. 1996.

——. *The Children of Yucatan.* Photographs by author. 1996.

AUTHOR/TITLE INDEX

ACTIVITY INDEX

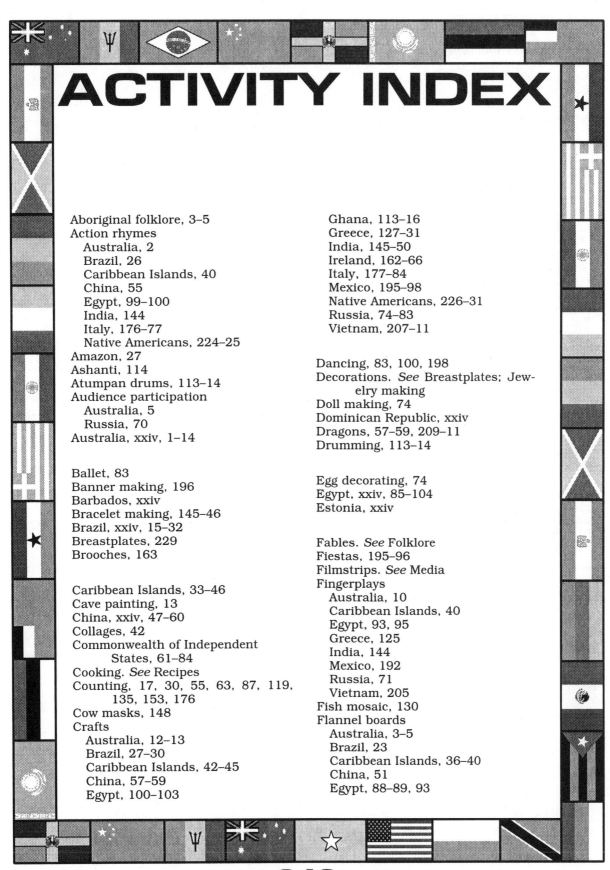